Developing Feeds with RSS and Atom

Other resources from O'Reilly

Related titles

XML Hacks™
XML in a Nutshell
Learning XML
Google Hacks™
We the Media
Essential Blogging
Running Weblogs with Slash
Practical RDF

oreilly.com

oreilly.com is more than a complete catalog of O'Reilly books. You'll also find links to news, events, articles, weblogs, sample chapters, and code examples.

oreillynet.com is the essential portal for developers interested in open and emerging technologies, including new platforms, programming languages, and operating systems.

Conferences

O'Reilly brings diverse innovators together to nurture the ideas that spark revolutionary industries. We specialize in documenting the latest tools and systems, translating the innovator's knowledge into useful skills for those in the trenches. Visit *conferences.oreilly.com* for our upcoming events.

Safari Bookshelf (*safari.oreilly.com*) is the premier online reference library for programmers and IT professionals. Conduct searches across more than 1,000 books. Subscribers can zero in on answers to time-critical questions in a matter of seconds. Read the books on your Bookshelf from cover to cover or simply flip to the page you need. Try it today with a free trial.

Developing Feeds with RSS and Atom

Ben Hammersley

O'REILLY®

Beijing • Cambridge • Farnham • Köln • Paris • Sebastopol • Taipei • Tokyo

Developing Feeds with RSS and Atom
by Ben Hammersley

Published by O'Reilly Media, Inc., 1005 Gravenstein Highway North, Sebastopol, CA 95472.

O'Reilly books may be purchased for educational, business, or sales promotional use. Online editions are also available for most titles (*safari.oreilly.com*). For more information, contact our corporate/institutional sales department: (800) 998-9938 or *corporate@oreilly.com*.

Editor: Simon St.Laurent

Production Editor: Mary Anne Weeks Mayo

Cover Designer: Ellie Volckhausen

Interior Designer: David Futato

Printing History:

April 2005: First Edition, with content from *Content Syndication with RSS*.

This book uses RepKover™, a durable and flexible lay-flat binding.

ISBN: 0-596-00881-3
[M]

Table of Contents

Preface

This book is about RSS and Atom, the two most popular content-syndication technologies. From distributing the latest web site content to your desktop and powering loosely coupled applications on the Internet, to providing the building blocks of the Semantic Web, these two technologies are among the Internet's fastest growing.

There are millions of RSS and Atom feeds available across the Web today; this book shows you how to read them, how to create your own, and how to build applications that use them. It covers:

- RSS 2.0 and its predecessors
- RSS 1.0 and the Semantic Web
- Atom and the latest generation of feed technology
- How to create and parse feeds
- Extending RSS and Atom through modules
- Using RSS and Atom on the desktop, on the Web, and in the enterprise
- Building RSS- and Atom-based applications

Audience

This book was written with two somewhat interrelated groups in mind:

Web developers and web site authors
: This book should be read by all web developers who want to share their site with others by offering feeds of their content. This group includes everyone from webloggers and amateur journalists to those running large-budget, multiuser sites. Whether you're working on projects for multinational news organizations or neighborhood sports groups, with RSS and Atom, you can extend the reach, power, and utility of your product, and make your life easier and your work more productive. This book shows you how.

Developers

This book is also for developers who want to use the content other people are syndicating and build applications that produce feeds as their output. This group includes everyone from fan-site developers wanting the latest gaming news and intranet builders needing up-to-date financial information on the corporate Web, to developers looking to incorporate news feeds into artificially intelligent systems or build data-sharing applications across platforms. For you, this book delves into the interpretation of metadata, different forms of content syndication, and the increasing use of web services technology in this field. We'll also look at how you can extend the different flavors of RSS and Atom to fit your needs.

Depending on your interests, you may find some chapters more necessary than others. Don't be afraid to skip around or look through the index. There are all kinds of ways to use RSS and Atom.

Assumptions This Book Makes

The technology used in this book is not all that hard to understand, and the concepts specific to RSS and Atom are fully explained. The book assumes some familiarity with HTML and, specifically, XML and its processing techniques, although you will be reminded of important technical points and given places to look for further information. (Appendix A provides a brief introduction to XML if you need one.)

Most of the code in this book is written in Perl, but the examples are commented sufficiently to make things clear and easily portable. There are also some examples in PHP and Ruby. However, users of any language will get a lot from this book: the explanations of the standards and the uses of RSS and Atom are language-agnostic.

How This Book Is Organized

Because RSS and now Atom come in a number of flavors, and there are lots of ways to use them, this book has a lot of parts.

Chapter 1 explains where these things came from and why there is so much diversity in what seems on the surface to be a relatively simple field. Chapter 2 and 3 look at what you can do with RSS and Atom without writing code or getting close to the data. Chapter 2 looks at these technologies from the ordinary user's perspective, showing how to read feeds with a number of tools. Chapter 3 digs deeper into the challenge of creating RSS and Atom feeds, but does so using tools that don't require any programming.

The next four chapters look at the most common varieties of syndication feeds and how to create them. Chapter 4 examines RSS 2.0, inheritor of the 0.91 line of RSS. Chapter 5 looks at RSS 1.0, and its rather different philosophy. Chapter 6 explores the many modules available to extend RSS 1.0. Chapter 7 looks at a third alternative: the recently emerging Atom specification.

Chapters 8 through 11 focus on issues that developers building and consuming feeds will need to address. Chapter 8 looks at the complex world of parsing these many flavors of feeds, and the challenges of parsing feeds that aren't always quite right. Chapter 9 looks at ways to integrate feeds with publishing models, particularly publish-and-subscribe. Chapter 10 demonstrates a number of applications for feeds that aren't the usual blog entries or news information, and Chapter 11 describes how to extend RSS 2.0 or RSS 1.0 with new modules in case the existing feed structures don't do everything you need.

Finally, there are two appendixes. Appendix A provides a quick tutorial to XML that should give you the foundation you need to work with feeds, while Appendix B provides a list of sites and software you can explore while figuring out how best to apply these technologies to your projects.

Conventions Used in This Book

The following font conventions are used in this book:

Italic is used for:

- Unix pathnames, filenames, and program names
- Internet addresses, such as domain names and URLs
- New terms where they are defined

`Constant width` is used for:

- Command lines and options that should be typed verbatim
- Names and keywords in programs, including method names, variable names, and class names
- XML element tags and URIs

`Constant width italic` is used for:

- Replaceable items, such as variables or optional elements, within syntax lines or code

This icon signifies a tip, suggestion, or general note.

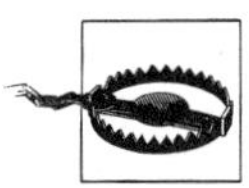

This icon indicates a warning or caution.

Using Code Examples

The examples from this book are freely downloadable from the book's web site at *http://www.oreilly.com/catalog/deveoprssatom*.

This book is here to help you get your job done. In general, you may use the code in this book in your programs and documentation. You do not need to contact us for permission unless you're reproducing a significant portion of the code. For example, writing a program that uses several chunks of code from this book does not require permission. Selling or distributing a CD-ROM of examples from O'Reilly books *does* require permission. Answering a question by citing this book and quoting example code does not require permission. Incorporating a significant amount of example code from this book into your product's documentation *does* require permission.

We appreciate, but don't require, attribution. An attribution usually includes the title, author, publisher, and ISBN. For example: "*Developing Feeds with RSS and Atom*, by Ben Hammersley. Copyright 2005 O'Reilly Media, Inc., 0-596-00881-3."

If you feel your use of code examples falls outside fair use or the permission given above, feel free to contact us at *permissions@oreilly.com*.

Safari Enabled

When you see a Safari® Enabled icon on the cover of your favorite technology book, it means the book is available online through the O'Reilly Network Safari Bookshelf.

Safari offers a solution that's better than e-books. It's a virtual library that lets you easily search thousands of top tech books, cut and paste code samples, download chapters, and find quick answers when you need the most accurate, current information. Try it for free at *http://safari.oreilly.com*.

Comments and Questions

Please address comments and questions concerning this book to the publisher:

O'Reilly Media, Inc.
1005 Gravenstein Highway North
Sebastopol, CA 95472
(800) 998-9938 (in the United States or Canada)
(707) 829-0515 (international or local)
(707) 829-0104 (fax)

We have a web page for this book, where we list errata, examples, and any additional information. You can access this page at:

http://www.oreilly.com/catalog/deveoprssatom

To comment or ask technical questions about this book, send email to:

bookquestions@oreilly.com

For more information about our books, conferences, Resource Centers, and the O'Reilly Network, see our web site at:

http://www.oreilly.com

Acknowledgments

Thanks, as ever, go to my editor Simon St.Laurent and my technical reviewers Roy Owens, Tony Hammond, Timo Hannay, and Ben Lund. Thanks also to Mark Pilgrim, Jonas Galvez, Jorge Velázquez for their lovely code. Bill Kearney, Kevin Hemenway, and Micah Dubinko earned many thanks for their technical-reviewing genius on the first edition. Not to forget Dave Winer, Jeff Barr, James Linden, DJ Adams, Rael Dornfest, Brent Simmons, Chris Croome, Kevin Burton, and Dan Brickley. Cheers to Erhan Erdem, Dan Libby, David Kandasamy, and Castedo Ellerman for their memories of the early days of CDF and RSS and to Yo-Yo Ma for his recording of Bach's Cello Suite No.1, to which much of this book was written.

But most of all, of course, to Anna.

CHAPTER 1

Introduction

"Data! Data! Data!" he cried impatiently.
—Sir Arthur Conan Doyle, *The Adventure of the Copper Beeches*

In this chapter, I'll first talk about what RSS and Atom are for and then take a look at a little of their history. We then move on to the business cases for syndicating your own content and a discussion of the philosophy behind content syndication. The chapter finishes with a brief discussion of the legal issues surrounding the provision and use of syndication feeds.

What Are RSS and Atom for?

The original, and still the most common, use for RSS and Atom is to provide a *content syndication feed*: a consistent, machine-readable file that allows web sites to share their content with other applications in a standard way. Originally, as shown in the next section, this was used to share data among web sites, but now it's most commonly used between a site and a desktop application called a *reader*.

Feeds can be anything from just headlines and links to stories to the entire content of the site, stripped of its layout and with metadata liberally applied. Content syndication allows users to experience a site on multiple devices and be notified of updates over a variety of services. It can range from a simple list of links sent from site to site to the beginnings of the Semantic Web.

However, feeds are starting to be used as content in their own right: people are building services that only output to a feed and don't actually have a "real" site at all. In later chapters of this book, we'll look at the cool things you can do with this, and build some of our own.

A Short History of RSS and Atom

In the Developer's Bars of the world—those dark, sordid places filled with grizzled coders and their clans—a special corner is always reserved for the developers of content-syndication standards. There, weeping into their beer, you'll find the veterans of a long and difficult process. Most likely, they will have the Thousand Yard Stare of those who have seen more than they should. The standards you will read about in this book were not born fresh and innocent, of a streamlined process overseen by the Wise and Good. Rather, the following chapters have been dragged into the world and tempered through brawls, knife fights, and the occasional riot. What has survived, it is hoped, is hardy enough to prosper for the foreseeable future.

To fully understand these wayward children, and to get the most out of them, it is necessary to understand the motivations behind the different standards and how they evolved into what they are today.

HotSauce: MCF and RDF

The deepest, darkest origins of the current versions of RSS began in 1995 with the work of Ramanathan V. Guha. Known to most simply by his surname, Guha developed a system called the Meta Content Framework (MCF). Rooted in the work of knowledge-representation systems such as CycL, KRL, and KIF, MCF's aim was to describe objects, their attributes, and the relationships between them.

MCF was an experimental research project funded by Apple, so it was pleasing for management that a great application came out of it: ProjectX, later renamed HotSauce. By late 1996, a few hundred sites were creating MCF files that described themselves, and Apple HotSauce allowed users to browse around these MCF representations in 3D. Documentation still exists on the Web for MCF and HotSauce. See *http://www.eclectica-systems.co.uk/complex/hotsauce.php* and Example 1-1 for more.

Example 1-1. An example of MCF

```
begin-headers:
MCFVersion: 0.95
name: "Eclectica"
end-headers:

unit: "tagging.mco"
name: "Tagging and Acrobat Integration"
default_genl_x: -109
default_genl_y: -65
typeOf: #"SubjectCategory"

unit: "http://www.nplum.demon.co.uk/temptin/temptin.htm"
name: "TemptIn Information Management Template"
genls_pos: ["tagging.mco" -85 -137]
```

Example 1-1. An example of MCF (continued)

```
unit: "http://www.nplum.demon.co.uk/temptin/tryout.htm"
name: "Download Try-out Version"
genls_pos: ["tagging.mco" -235 120]
```

It was popular, but experimental, and when Steve Jobs's return to Apple's management in 1997 heralded the end of much of Apple's research activity, Guha left for Netscape.

There, he met with Tim Bray, one of the original XML pioneers, and started moving MCF over to an XML-based format. (XML itself was new at that time.) This project later became the Resource Description Framework (RDF). RDF is, as the World Wide Web Consortium (W3C) RDF Primer says, "a general-purpose language for representing information in the World Wide Web." It is specifically designed for the representation of metadata and the relationships between things. In its fullest form, it is the basis for the concept known as the *Semantic Web*—the W3C's vision wherein computers can understand the meaning of, and the relationships between, documents and other data. You can read *http://en.wikipedia.org/wiki/Semantic_Web* for more details.

Channel Definition Format

In 1997, XML was still in its infancy, and much of the Internet's attention was focused on the increasingly frantic war between Microsoft and Netscape.

Microsoft had been watching the HotSauce experience, and early that year the Internet Explorer development team, along with some others, principally a company called Pointcast, created a system called the Channel Definition Format (CDF).

Released on March 8, 1997, and submitted as a standard to the W3C the very next day, CDF was XML-based and described both the content and a site's particular ratings, scheduling, logos, and metadata. It was introduced in Microsoft's Internet Explorer 4.0 and later into the Windows desktop itself, where it provided the backbone for what was then called Active Desktop. The CDF specification document is still online at *http://www.w3.org/TR/NOTE-CDFsubmit.html,* and Example 1-2 shows a sample.

Example 1-2. An example CDF document

```
<!DOCTYPE Channel SYSTEM "http://www.w3c.org/Channel.dtd" >
<Channel HREF="http://www.foosports.com/foosports.cdf" IsClonable=YES >

<IntroUrl
VALUE="http://www.foosports.com/channel-setup.html" />
<LastMod VALUE="1994.11.05T08:15-0500" />
<Title VALUE="FooSports" />
<Abstract VALUE="The latest in sports and atheletics from FooSports" />
<Author VALUE="FooSports" />
```

Example 1-2. An example CDF document (continued)

```
<Schedule>
<EndDate VALUE="1994.11.05T08:15-0500" />
<IntervalTime DAY=1 />
<EarliestTime HOUR=12 />
<LatestTime HOUR=18 />
</Schedule>

<Logo HREF="http://www.foosports.com/images/logo.gif" Type="REGULAR" />

<Item HREF="http://www.foosports.com/articles/a1.html">
<LastMod VALUE="1994.11.05T08:15-0500" />
<Title VALUE="How to get the most out of your mountain bike" />
<Abstract VALUE="20 tips on how to work your mountain-bike
to the bone and come out on top." />
<Author VALUE="FooSports" />
</Item>

<Channel IsClonable=NO >
<LastMod VALUE="1994.11.05T08:15-0500" />
<Title VALUE="FooSports News" />
<Abstract VALUE="Up-to-date daily sports news from FooSports" />
<Author VALUE="FooSports" />

<Logo HREF="http://www.foosports.com/images/newslogo.gif" Type="REGULAR" />
<Logo HREF="http://www.foosports.com/images/newslogowide.gif" Type="WIDE" />

<Item HREF="http://www.foosports.com/articles/news1.html" >
<LastMod VALUE="1994.11.05T08:15-0500" />
<Title VALUE="Michael Jordan does it again!"/>
<Abstract VALUE="Led by Michael Jordan in scoring, the Chicago Bulls make it to the
playoffs again!"/>
<Author VALUE="FooSports" />
</Item>

<Item HREF="http://www.foosports.com/articles/news2.html" />
<LastMod VALUE="1994.11.05T08:15-0500" />
<Title VALUE="Islanders winning streak ends"/>
<Abstract VALUE="The New York islanders' 10-game winning streak ended with a disappointing
loss to the Rangers" />
<Author VALUE="FooSports" />
</Item>

</Channel>

<Item HREF="http://www.foosports.com/animations/scrnsvr.html" />
<Usage VALUE="ScreenSaver"></Usage>
</Item>

<Item HREF="http://www.foosports.com/ticker.html" />
<Title VALUE="FooSports News Ticker" />
<Abstract VALUE="The latest sports headlines from FooSports" />
```

Example 1-2. An example CDF document (continued)

```
<Author VALUE="FooSports" />
<LastMod VALUE="1994.11.05T08:15-0500" />

<Schedule>
<StartDate VALUE="1994.11.05T08:15-0500" />
<EndDate VALUE="1994.11.05T08:15-0500" />
<IntervalTime DAY=1 />
<EarliestTime HOUR=12 />
<LatestTime HOUR=18 />
</Schedule>
</Item>

</Channel>
```

Very soon after its release, the potential of a standard, XML-based syndication format became apparent. By April 14, 1997, just over a month since Microsoft gave the standard its first public viewing, Dave Winer's UserLand Software released support for the format into its Frontier product. Written by Wes Felter, and built upon by Dave Winer, it would be the company's first foray into XML-based syndication, but by no means its last. UserLand was to become a major character in our story.

CDF was an exciting technology. It had arrived just as XML was being lauded as the Next Big Thing, and that combination—of a useful technology with a whole new thing to play with—made it rather irresistible for the nascent weblogging community. CDF, however, was really designed for the bigger publishers. A lot of the elements were overkill for the smaller content providers (who, at any rate, didn't consider themselves *content providers* at all), and so a lot of webloggers started to look into creating a simpler specification.

Weblogging?

RSS 1.0, RSS 2.0, and Atom are all deeply entrenched within the weblogging community, and I refer to weblogging, webloggers, and weblogs themselves frequently within this book. If you've never heard of the activity, it is easily explained. A *weblog* is, at heart, a personal web site, consisting of diary-like entries displayed in reverse chronological order. *Weblogging*, or blogging for short, is the activity of writing a weblog, or blog, upon which a weblogger, or blogger, spends his time. Weblogging is extremely popular: at time of writing, in late 2004, there are an estimated four million weblogs being written worldwide. The vast majority of these produce a syndication feed.

For good examples of weblogs, visit *http://www.weblogs.com* for a list of recently updated sites. My own weblog is found at *http://www.benhammersley.com/weblog/index.html*.

O'Reilly has also published a book on weblogging, *Essential Blogging*.

On December 27, 1997, Dave Winer started to publish his own weblog, Scripting News (*http://www.scripting.com)* in his own scriptingNews format, in addition to the CDF feed he had been providing since the spring. This, it was soon to be apparent, was a major step toward the RSS we have today. By early 1998, other formats were appearing, notably the Wilma Project, but all things considered, none were proving particularly popular. Mostly, it has to be said, because at this point, the weblogging world was very small.

RSS First Appears

By 1998, Netscape's share of the browser market was in trouble. Microsoft's release of Internet Explorer 4.0 the previous year was eating into Netscape's position at the top of the market. Something had to be done, and so, in May 1998, Netscape formed a development team to work on the internally code-named "Project 60."

When it launched on July 28, 1998, Project 60 was the My Netscape portal. It was a personalized front page that—in the traditional dot-com era business model—would capture eyeballs and provide sticky content. To this end, Netscape signed content-sharing deals with publishers like CNET to display its content within the portal.

Internally, this was done with an ever developing set of tools that were forever being renamed. Starting out as Site Preview Format (SPF) and then called Open-SPF, the format was developed by Dan Libby and based on the work Guha was doing with RDF. Netscape, at that time, was building an RDF parser into the Netscape 5 browser; Libby ripped that out and built a feed parsing system to drive the Netscape pages on its server. Content providers gave Netscape feeds, and Netscape incorporated those feeds into its site.

My Netscape benefited from this in many ways: it suddenly had a massive amount of content given to it for free. Of course, Netscape had no control over it or any real way to make money from it directly, but the additional usefulness of Netscape's site made people stick around longer. In the heat of the dot-com boom, allowing people to put their own content on a Netscape page, alongside advertising sold by Netscape, was a very good idea: the portal could both save money on content and make more on ad sales. The user also benefited: having favorite sites summarized on one page meant one-stop shopping for a day's browsing—a feature many found extremely useful. The feed provider didn't lose out either, gaining both additional traffic and wider exposure.

The technology didn't stop moving. The Open-SPF format was released as an Engineering Vision Statement on February 1, 1999, and a week later, Dave Winer picked up on it and suggested out loud that an XML format for webloggers might be useful (*http://static.UserLand.com/UserLandDiscussArchive/msg002809.html*):

> I get frequent requests to channel Scripting News content thru my.netscape.com. I don't have time to learn how it works. However, we have an always-current XML version of the last day of Scripting News, and would be happy to support Netscape and others in writing syndicators of that content flow. No royalty necessary. It would be

> easy to have a search engine feed off this flow of links and comments. There are starting to be a bunch of weblogs, wouldn't it be interesting if we could agree on an XML format between us?

Then everything sped up. On February 11, Bill Humphries documented the XML format he was using for his Whump weblog, calling it "More Like This." On February 22, Scripting News was publishing in Open-SPF and was available on the Netscape site. On March 1, 1999, after yet another name change, Dan Libby released the specification document for RDF-SPF 0.9. One final name change later, it became RSS 0.9, and RSS was here.

The first desktop aggregator, Carmen's Headline Viewer, was released on April 25, 1999. UserLand followed Netscape with the second web-based aggregator, my.UserLand.com, on June 10. On July 2, the Syndication mailing list was started, and later Winer spoke on the telephone with the Netscape team to suggest some changes. After a short rest, the standard was off again.

The Standards Evolve

The first draft of the RSS format, as designed by Dan Libby, was a fully RDF-based data model that people inside Netscape felt was too complicated for end users. The resultant compromise—RSS 0.9—was not truly useful RDF nor was it as simple as it could be.

Some felt that using RDF improperly was worse than not using it at all, so when RSS 0.91 arrived, the RDF nature of the format was dropped. As Dan Libby explained to the rss-dev email list (*http://groups.yahoo.com/group/rss-dev/message/239*):

> At the time, the primary users of RSS (Dave Winer the most vocal among them) were asking why it needed to be so complex and why it didn't have support for various features, e.g. update frequencies. We really had no good answer, given that we weren't using RDF for any useful purpose. Further, because RDF can be expressed in XML in multiple ways, I was uncomfortable publishing a DTD for RSS 0.9, since the DTD would claim that technically valid RDF/RSS data conforming to the RDF graph model was not valid RSS. Anyway, it didn't feel "clean". The compromise was to produce RSS 0.91, which could be validated with any validating XML parser, and which incorporated much of UserLand's vocabulary, thus removing most (I think) of Dave's major objections. I felt slightly bad about this, but given actual usage at the time, I felt it better suited the needs of its users: simplicity, correctness, and a larger vocabulary, without RDF baggage.

On July 10, 1999, three days after the fateful phone call, RSS 0.91 was released. It incorporated new features from UserLand Software's scriptingNews format and was completely RDF-free. So, as would become a habit whenever a new version of RSS was released, the meaning of the RSS acronym was changed. While before it stood for "RDF Site Summary" in the RSS 0.91 specification, Dave Winer explained:

> There is no consensus on what RSS stands for, so it's not an acronym, it's a name. Later versions of this spec may say it's an acronym, and hopefully this won't break too many applications.

A great deal of research into RDF continued, however. Indeed, Netscape's RSS development team was always keen to use it. Their original specification (the one that was watered down to produce RSS 0.9) was published on the insistence of Dan Libby, and, although it has long since gone from the Netscape servers, you can find it in the Internet Archive (*http://web.archive.org/web/20001204123600/http://my.netscape.com/publish/help/futures.html*).

Netscape, however, was never to release any new versions: the RSS team was disbanded as the My Netscape Network was closed. So, when work began on a new version of RSS, it was left to the development community in general to sort out. The first pressing need involved including categories in the feed. By September 9, for example, Jon Udell was suggesting the use of a `category` element. It was the urge to add this and other new features that broke the development community in two.

The first camp, led by O'Reilly's Rael Dornfest, wanted to introduce some form of extensibility to the standard. The ability to add new features, perhaps through modularization, necessitated such complexities as XML namespaces and the reintroduction of RDF, as envisioned by the Netscape team.

However, the second camp, led by Dave Winer, feared that this would add a level of complexity unwelcome to users. They wanted to keep RSS as simple as possible. The thinking at the time was that RSS, like HTML, would be learned by users viewing source and experimenting. An RDF-based specification would look extremely daunting.

The First Fork

The debate raged for nearly a year. August 14, 2000 saw the start of the RSS 1.0 mailing list and increasing polarization between the simple and RDF camps. On December 6, 2000, after a great deal of heated discussion, RSS 1.0 was released. It embraced the use of modules, XML namespaces, and a return to a full RDF data model. Two weeks later, on Christmas Day 2000, Dave Winer released RSS 0.92 as a rebuttal of the RDF alternative. The standard had forked.

It remained like this for four months: Netscape published the RSS 0.91 specification; UserLand published the 0.92 specification, which was upward-compatible with 0.91; and the RSS 1.0 Working Group published a 1.0 specification, which was not. Then, in early April 2001, My Netscape closed. A few weeks later, in mid-April, the RSS 0.91 DTD document Netscape had been hosting was pulled offline. Immediately, every parser that had been verifying feeds against it stopped working. This was early on in the XML world, and people didn't know that this sort of architecture was a bad idea. (That DTD, incidentally, was written by Lars Marius Garshol, who wasn't working at Netscape at all. He'd created the DTD by reverse engineering the specification, and had then given it to Dan Libby.)

UserLand came to the rescue. On April 27, Winer published a copy of the Netscape DTD on his own server. It's still there: *http://www.scripting.com/dtd/rss-0_91.dtd*. Through this act, more than any other, UserLand claimed the right to be seen as the guardian of the 0.9x side of the argument.

Version 0.92, therefore, superseded 0.91, and that was how it remained for two years: two standards—RSS 0.92 as the simple, entry-level specification and RSS 1.0 as the more complex, but ultimately more feature-packed specification. And, of course, some people didn't use the additional features of 0.91 and so were de facto RSS 0.91 users as well.

For the users of RSS feeds, this fork was not a major worry because the two standards remained compatible in practice. Even parsers specifically built to parse only RSS, rather than XML in general, can usually read simple examples of either version with equal ease, although the RDF implications go straight over the head of all but specifically designed RDF parsers.

All this, however, was changing.

The Second Fork

In late summer 2002, the RSS community forked again, perhaps irreversibly. Ironically enough, the fork came from an effort to merge the 0.9x and 1.0 strands from the previous fork and create an RSS 2.0 that would satisfy both camps.

Once again, the argument quickly settled into two sides. On one side, Dave Winer and a few others continued to believe in the importance of simplicity above all else, and regarded RDF as a technology that had yet to show any value within RSS. Winer also, for his own reasons, didn't want the discussion over RSS 2.0 to take place on the traditional email lists. Rather, he wanted people to express their points of view in their weblogs, to which he would link his own at *http://www.scripting.com*.

On the other side, the members of the rss-dev mailing list, from which RSS 1.0 was born and nurtured to maturity, still wanted to include RDF within the specification—albeit in various simplified forms—and wished to hold the discussion on a publicly archived, centralized mailing list not subject to anyone's filtering.

In many ways, both things happened. After a great deal of acrimony, UserLand released a specification they it RSS 2.0 and declared RSS frozen. That this was done without acknowledging, much less taking into account, the increasing concerns—both technical and social—of the rss-dev and RDF communities at large, caused much unhappiness.

After RSS 2.0's release on September 16, 2002, the members of the rss-dev list started discussions on a possible name change to their own new, RSS 1.0–based specification. This would go hand in hand with a complete retooling of the specification, based on a totally open discussion and a rethink of the use of RDF. This ended up being, as you'll see, a far more radical effort than it started out to be.

Pie, Echo, Necho, Atom

By June 2003, it was obvious that the continual in-fighting was going to go nowhere. The RSS specification process had reached an impasse, and was socially, if not technically, dead. From this wreckage, Sam Ruby, a programmer at IBM, started to discuss, quietly, the philosophical basis of what a syndication feed should be. He based his thinking not on the business needs of Microsoft or Netscape, nor on the long and bitter history of the RSS community but, instead, decided to start afresh. The idea was to build a conceptual model of a weblog entry, then design both a syndication format and a posting and editing API around the model. It was to be new and vendor-neutral, and the specification was to be very detailed indeed, which addressed a common criticism of both RSS 2.0 and 1.0.

It would also be developed in a rather unusual way. Instead of the bickering mailing lists, or the deeply biased weblog discussions, the new format would be developed on a wiki. The standard would be continually refactored by all comers until something good was revealed, and then further polished by many hands.

Meanwhile, Dave Winer had moved from UserLand Software to take up a one-year fellowship at the Berkman Center for Internet and Society at Harvard Law School. On July 15, 2003, UserLand gave the copyright of the RSS 2.0 specification to Harvard, who then published it under the Creative Commons Attribution/Share Alike license. In addition to this, Harvard created a three-man Advisory Board to aid RSS 2.0's evolution. It consisted of Dave Winer, Jon Udell, and Brent Simmons (the author of NetNewsWire, a very popular RSS reader application).

Now the syndication world had three different groups: the RSS 2.0 Advisory Board; the RSS 1.0 working group, which was now almost completely dormant, having long considered the specification finished; and the ad hoc community surrounding the new effort.

The ad hoc group needed to decide on a name for its project. Initially nicknamed Pie, it went through Echo and Necho before going into a long process that whittled down over 260 different suggestions. In the end, as the title of this book suggests, the group voted to call it Atom.

Today's Scene

Atom's development continues: this book is based on Atom 0.5. Things may have changed by this book's publication, but in general, the furor seems to have settled down. RDF isn't included within Atom, but each individual element is very finely specified. This, as you'll see in later chapters, makes a good deal of difference.

Just over a year after he formed it, on July 1, 2004, Dave Winer resigned from the RSS 2.0 Advisory Board. The other two members did likewise, and have been replaced by Rogers Cadenhead, Adam Curry, and Steve Zellers, who remain to this day. The RSS 2.0 specification has not changed at all since then.

Although the core specification has remained the same for a couple of years, RSS 1.0 is still in heavy development, although in areas far from those Atom is concerned with. When RSS 1.0 was first developed, its novelty was matched by that of the RDF standard itself. Now that RDF has matured, RSS 1.0 is there with it, and being used very heavily, albeit in entirely different fields from RSS 2.0 or Atom. You'll see how in later chapters.

As it stands, therefore, the versioning-number system of RSS is misleading. Taken chronologically, 0.9 was based on RDF, 0.91 was not; 1.0 was, 0.92 was not; and now 2.0 is not. Version 1.0 is, and Atom currently isn't. It should be noted that there is an RSS 3.0, proposed by Aaron Swartz as part of long rss-dev in-joke. (The joke culminated with a proposal to have RSS 4.0 expressed entirely through the medium of interpretive dance.) Search engine results finding these specifications are therefore wrong, though dryly funny.

In this book, therefore, I will concentrate on three flavors of syndication feeds: RSS 2.0, RSS 1.0, and Atom 0.5. For feed publishers, the three strands each have their own advantages and disadvantages, and their own specific uses. I'll cover these in each of the relevant chapters.

Why Syndicate Your Content?

The advantages of using other people's feeds are obvious, but what about supplying your own? There are at least nine reasons to do so:

- It increases traffic to your site.
- It builds brand awareness for your site.
- It can help with search engine rankings.
- It helps cement relationships within a community of sites.
- It improves the site/user relationship.
- With additional technologies, it allows others to give additional features to your service—update-notification via instant messaging, for example.
- It makes the Internet an altogether richer place, pushing semantic technology along and encouraging reuse. Good things happen when you share your data.
- It gives you a good excuse to play with some cool stuff.
- By reducing the amount of screen-scraping of your site, it saves wasted bandwidth.

There you are: social, spiritual, and mercenary reasons to provide a feed for your site.

Legal Implications

The copyright implications for RSS feeds are quite simple. There are two choices for feed publishers, and these reflect on the user.

First, the publisher can decide that the feed must be licensed in some way. In this case, only authorized users can use the feed. It is good manners on the part of the publisher to make it as obvious as possible that this is the case—by providing a copyright notice in an XML comment, at least, and preferably by making it difficult for unauthorized users to get to the feed. Password protection is a reasonable minimum. Registering a pay-only feed with aggregators or allowing Google to see the feed is asking for trouble.

Second, and most commonly, the publisher can decide that the RSS feed is entirely free to use. In this case, it is only polite for the publishers of public RSS feeds to consider the feed entirely in the public domain—free to be used by anyone, for anything. This might sound a little radical to the average company vice president, but remember: there is nothing in the RSS feed that didn't, in some way, in the actual source information in the first place. It is rather futile to get upset that someone might not be using your headlines in the company-approved font, or committing a similar infraction; it's somewhat against the spirit of the exercise.

Screen-scraping a site to create a feed, by writing a script to read the site-specific layout, is a different matter. It has already been legally found, in U.S. courts at least (in the Ticketmaster versus Tickets.com case of October 1999 to March 2000), that linking to a page didn't in itself a breach of copyright. And you can argue, perhaps less convincingly, that reproducing headlines and excerpts from a site comes under fair-use guidelines for review purposes. However, it is extremely bad form to continue scraping a site if the site owner asks you to stop. Instead, try to evangelize RSS to the site owner and get him to start a proper feed.

Nevertheless, for private use, screen-scraping is a useful technique. In later chapters you'll see how running screen-scraping scripts on your local machine can produce extremely useful feed-based applications. Because these are entirely self-contained, there's no legal issue at all.

If You Are Scraped

If you are being scraped heavily and want it stopped, there are four ways to do so. First, scrapers should obey the *robots.txt* directive; setting a *robots.txt* file in the root directory of your site sends a definite signal most will follow. Second, you can contact the scraper and ask her to stop; if she is professional, she will do so immediately. Third, you can block the IP address of the scraper, although this is sometimes rather like herding cats; scrapers can move around.

The fourth and best way is to make a feed of your own. I'll show how to do so in the following chapters.

CHAPTER 2
Using Feeds

I took a speed-reading course and read War and Peace *in twenty minutes. It involves Russia.*
—Woody Allen

Before we get into the tricky business of producing, parsing, scripting, and extending our own RSS and Atom feeds, it makes sense to look at how they are consumed. In this chapter, therefore, we shall look at the various reader applications currently available for your pleasure.*

Web-Based Applications

The earliest, and still perhaps the most common, method of reading syndication feeds, the web-based application is a convenient way to stay up to date whereever you find yourself. It's especially good if you use more than one computer. In this section, when I talk about web-based applications, I mean applications hosted elsewhere, by other people. Applications that use your browser as the interface and sit on your local machine are in the next section.

Bloglines

Bloglines (*http://www.bloglines.com*) may not have been the first web-based aggregator, but it is certainly the most popular today (see Figure 2-1). It's free to use and very slick, offering email subscriptions, services for webloggers, and an interesting Application Programming Interface.

* I have not attempted to give a complete overview of all available RSS applications: many applications have been omitted for no reason other than space or my own oversight. Nor do I have an opinion about which is best for the job.

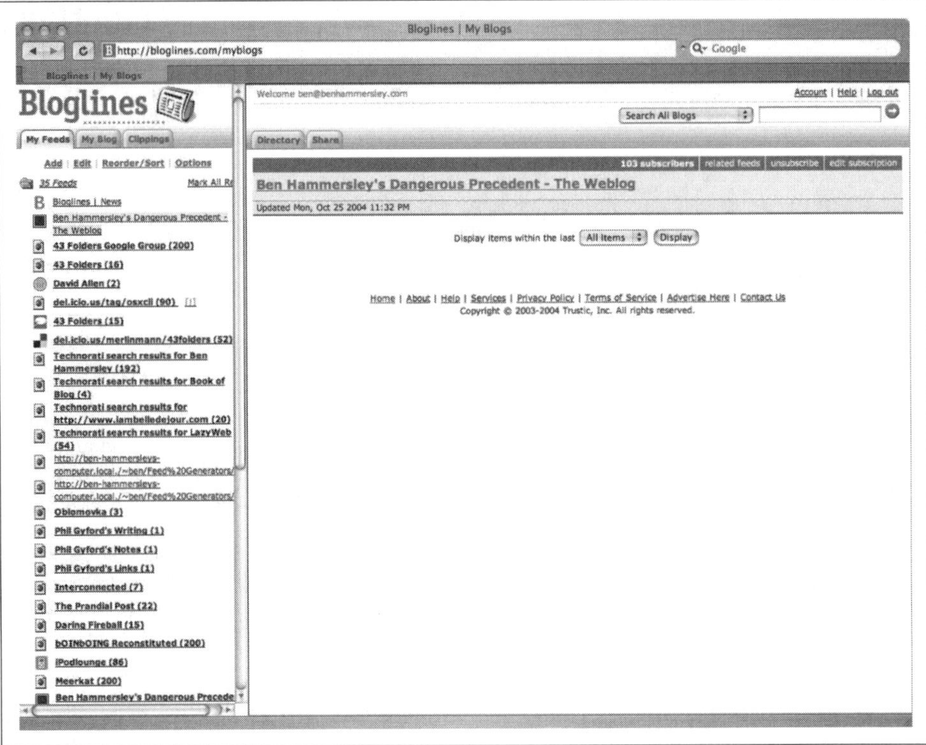

Figure 2-1. Bloglines.com

Kinja

Kinja (*http://www.kinja.com*; see Figure 2-2) is slightly different from most RSS and Atom applications in that it doesn't mention either standard anywhere. It is specifically designed to require no knowledge of the rest of this book, and it's free and tremendously easy to use. It's also, in my opinion, marvelously good looking. It has fewer features than Bloglines, however, especially for bloggers.

Rocketinfo RSS Reader

Another competitor in this space, Rocketinfo's RSS Reader (see Figure 2-3) is a free advertorial application for the Rocketinfo range of enterprise titles. It's also not as fully featured as Bloglines, but it does have a three-pane interface many people prefer.

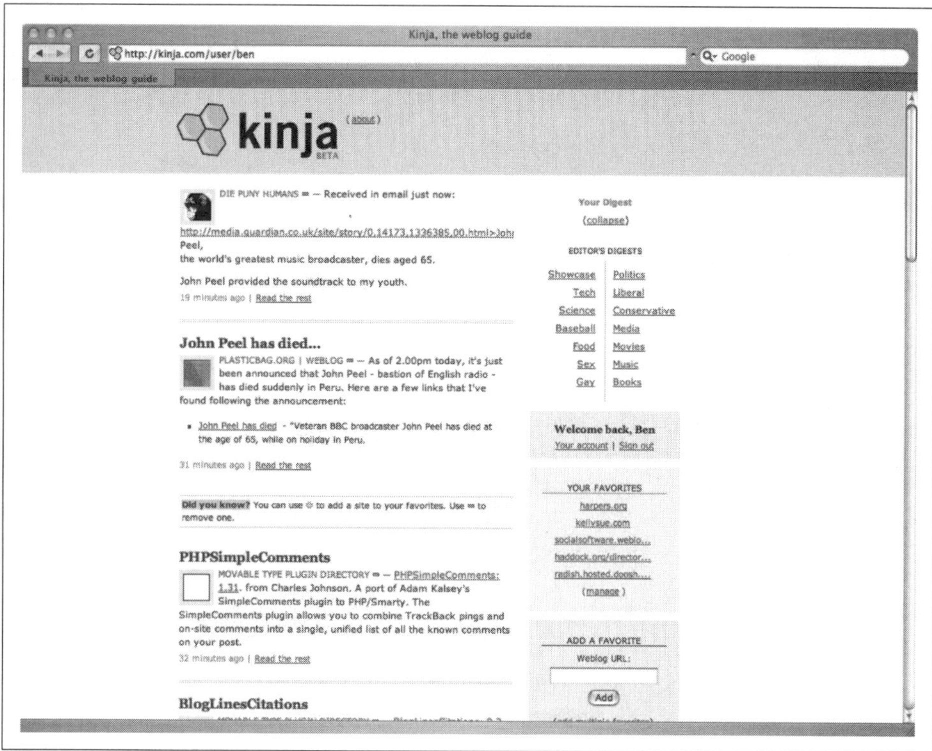

Figure 2-2. Kinja.com

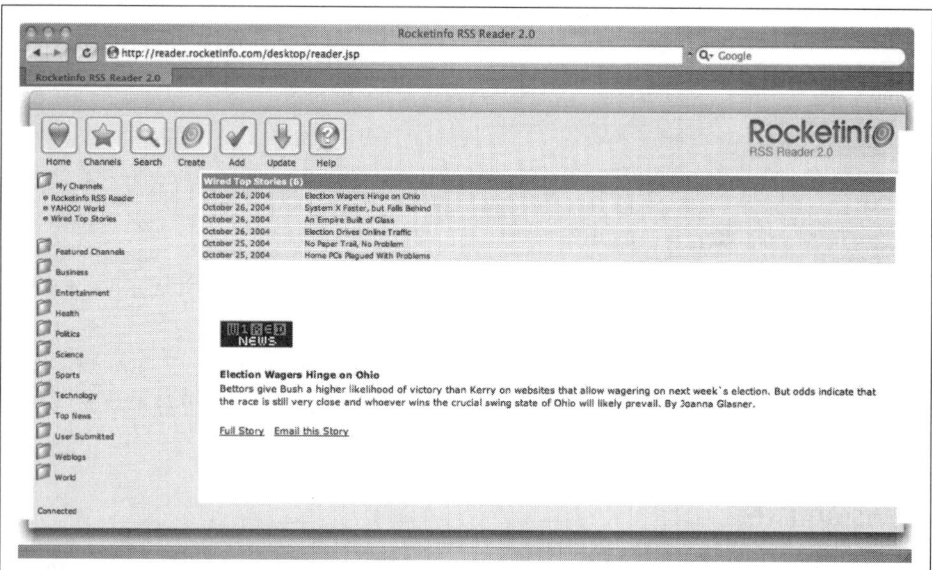

Figure 2-3. reader.rocketinfo.com

Desktop Applications

If you prefer to run a dedicated application to read your RSS, you have lots of options.

NetNewsWire

Because of its beauty and utility, the leading feed-reading application on Apple OS X, NetNewsWire (*http://ranchero.com/netnewswire/*; see Figure 2-4) caused a stir when it was first released. Version 2 is even better and is my personal favorite. It's not free, but you can try out a 30-day demo.

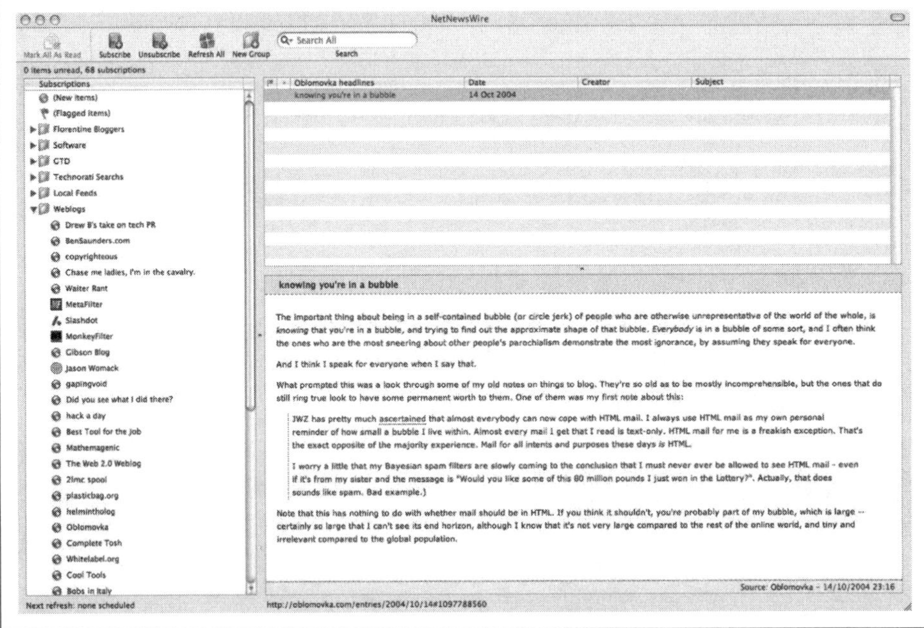

Figure 2-4. NetNewsWire in action

FeedDemon

The most popular feed application on Windows, FeedDemon (see Figure 2-5) is an accomplished three-pane display newsreader. It's not free, but there is a trial version. It even has a built-in web browser.

NewsMonster

Never has an application been so fittingly named. NewsMonster (*http://www.newsmonster.org/*) is an enormous application. It's cross-platform and runs on

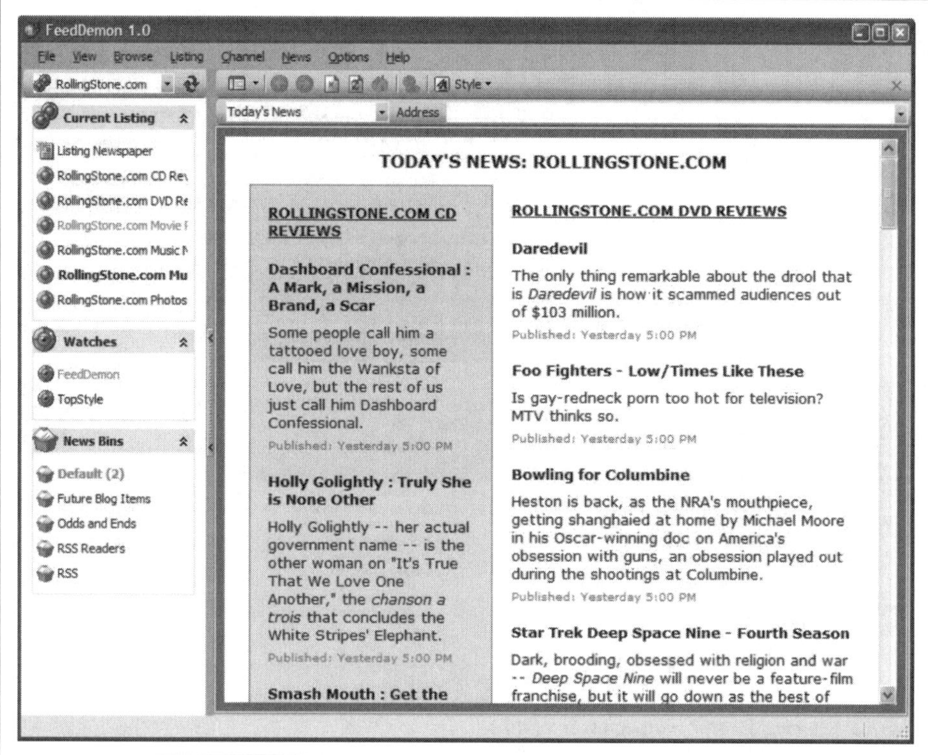

Figure 2-5. FeedDemon in action

Windows, Mac OS X, and Linux, off the back of Mozilla 1.0 or better. It's a truly ambitious piece of work with a lot of features you won't find anywhere else—for example, reputation networks, where users can recommend feeds to each other, and so on. It's well worth a look (see Figure 2-6).

Other Cunning Techniques

The PC isn't the only way to access a feed. Due to the lightweight XML nature of RSS and Atom, many other devices and conduits can use the formats to deliver information.

Mobile Devices

PDAs, mobile phones, and the incessant merging of the two can't escape the power of RSS and Atom:

- PocketPC (*http://www.happyjackroad.com/AtomicDB/pocketpc/pocketRSS/pocketRSS.asp*)

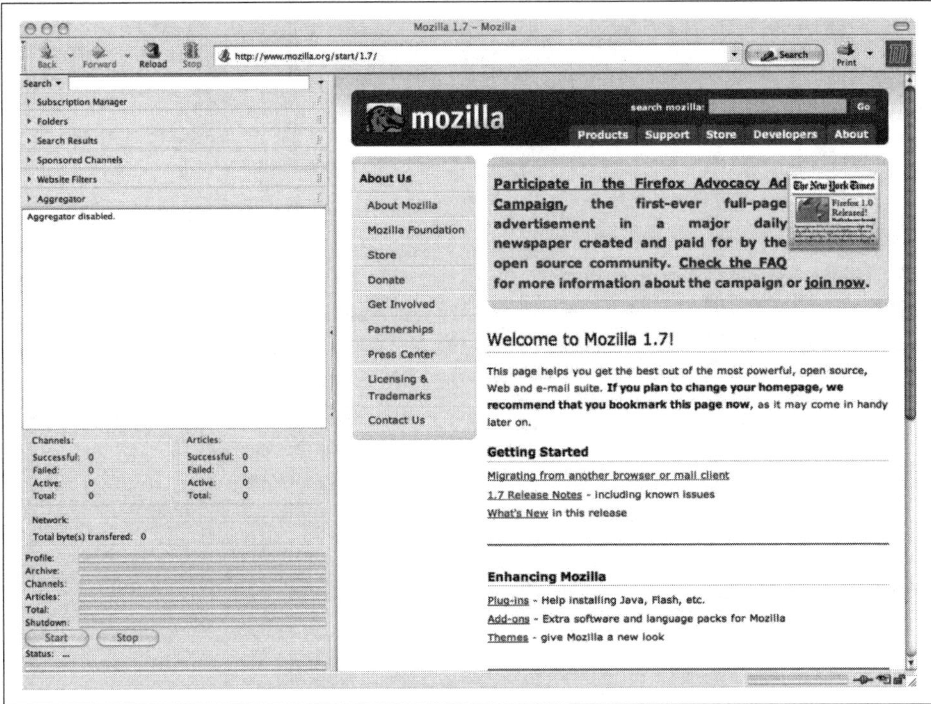

Figure 2-6. NewsMonster in action inside Mozilla 1.7 on OS X

- Hand/RSS (*http://standalone.com/palmos/hand_rss/*) is a nice, nonfree but with a 30-day trial, RSS feed for Palm devices.
- mobilerss (*http://www.mobilerss.net*) isn't an application per se but a service for turning RSS feeds into HTML simple enough to read on any mobile device's browser. It's built on the MagpieRSS parser shown in Chapter 8.
- The FeedBurner Mobile Feed Reader (*http://www.feedburner.com/fb/a/mfr*) comes from the same people who provide the FeedBurner service detailed in Chapter 9. It should run on any of the latest mobile devices compatible with the J2ME MIDP 2.0/CLDC1.0 platform.

Email Clients

If you'd rather get your RSS through your already convenient email software, you're not alone. A number of tools will make this easy:

- IzyNews (*http://izynews.com/de/default.aspx?*) sets up RSS feeds as unread messages in an IMAP directory. It requires some server-side setup, but it's perfect for a corporate environment with locked-down desktop machines.

- NewsGator Outlook Edition (*http://www.newsgator.com/outlook.aspx*) is an RSS reader extension for Microsoft Outlook. Many people swear by it, and it features synchronization with an online version for when you're away from your main machine.

Feed-Based Search Engines

For anyone wanting to start a search engine, RSS and Atom are godsent. It's no surprise that a handful of search engines have started up fed solely by syndication feeds. They're usually based around weblogs and the news sites that publish feeds, and can be extraordinarily up to date.

- Feedster (*http://www.feedster.com/*) is the original, and perhaps the best. It claims to index close to one million feeds.
- Medlogs (*http://www.medlogs.com/*) is a good example of feeds powering a specialist search engine. This one aggregates medical news.
- Bulkfeeds (*http://bulkfeeds.net/*) is much like a smaller Feedster, only based in Japan and concentrating on Japanese feeds. It's a fine example of the internationalization of feed technology.

Finding Feeds to Read

Identifying sites that make feeds available can be tricky. There is no standard place to publish a feed, nor is there any particular filename or path to look for one. Of course, there are various methods for sites to identify their feeds, but none are universal. Nevertheless, if you can't see an explicit link to a feed, here's a few things you can try:

- Look for the traditional feed icon, the white writing on an orange background, usually reading "XML" (see Figure 2-7). There are variants on this theme, but they're all recognizable.

XML

Figure 2-7. The garden variety eggplant

- View Source on the site's main page. If you see a line within the `head` section of the code that reads:

  ```
  <link rel="alternate" type="application/rss+xml" title="RSS" href= "http://www.
  example.org/rss.xml"/>
  ```

  the `href` part is the URL you want. This is a called an Auto-Discovery link and is discussed in Chapter 9.

- You can try the most common URLs. Look for `index.xml`, `index.rdf`, `rss.xml`, `rss.php`, `index.rss`, or `index.atom`; usually, one of these will work.
- Look up the site in Syndic8 (*http://www.syndic8.com*). This directory, also covered in Chapter 9, has over 200,000 feeds listed.

If the site you're most keen on doesn't have a feed available, it helps to ask it for one. A lot of site authors just don't know how welcome it would be. Ask!

CHAPTER 3

Feeds Without Programming

I do not take a single newspaper, nor read one a month, and I feel myself infinitely the happier for it.

—Thomas Jefferson

Now that you're set up with your own aggregator or reader application, and before we get into the horrible business of the standards themselves, it's a good idea to start creating your own personal feeds. Feeds are much more than just the latest news and articles from regular web sites. As you will see in Chapter 10, you can push all sorts of data through them. Chapter 10, however, contains a lot of code you will need to run yourself. In this chapter, we'll use other people's services to produce some interesting and useful feeds.

From Email

You can use a feed to display all your announcement-only mailing lists; you can also use it as a disposable email address when you register with web sites and the like. This frees your inbox and protects your real email address from being sold to spammers.

There are two services that do this, and both are very reliable: MailBucket (*http://www.mailbucket.org/*) and Dodgeit (*http://www.dodgeit.com/*).

Both operate in the same way. You send mail to `xxx@mailbucket.org` or `xxx@dodgeit.com`, where xxx is your own chosen identity. There's no sign up, so you need to check that your chosen identity isn't already taken. This highlights one issue: your mail isn't private, so don't use it for things you don't want others to see. (You could use an incredibly unguessable identity to make such risks very unlikely.)

Once the mail starts to arrive into your inbox, it will look like Figure 3-1.

You can then subscribe to the feed at either *http://www.mailbucket.org/xxx.xml* or *http://www.dodgeit.com/run/rss?mailbox=xxx*. You will then see something like Figure 3-2 in your reader application.

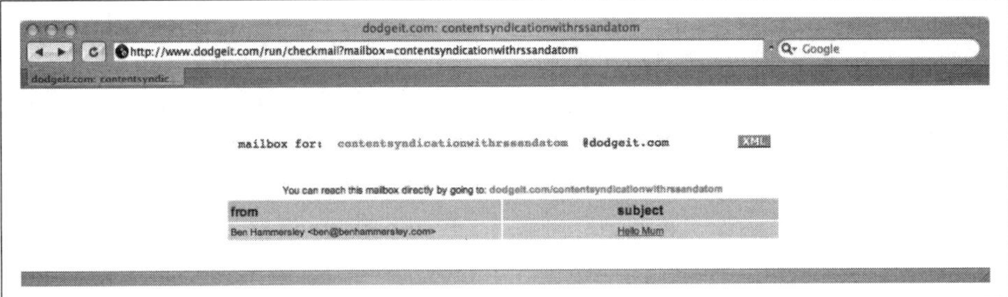

Figure 3-1. The Dodgeit.com inbox on the Web

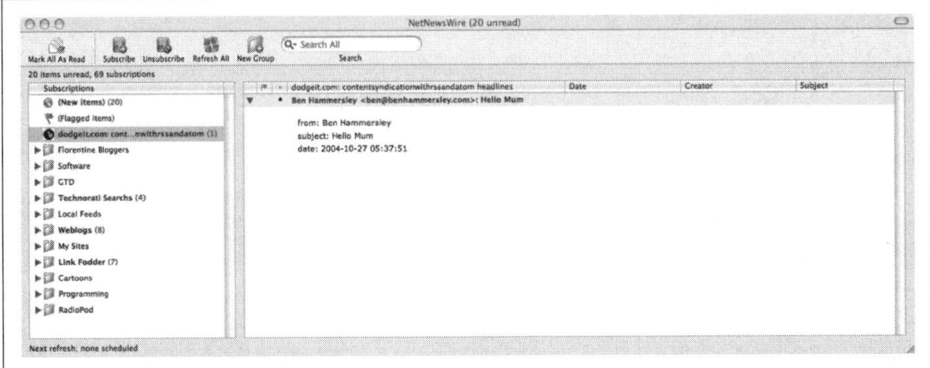

Figure 3-2. The Dodgeit.com inbox inside NetNewsWire

Personally speaking, I think these services are the cat's pajamas. There are many mailing lists that don't require the ability to reply, or to which you might not actually want to contribute, or whose traffic is so great, you might not want your email application to keep firing off new mail alerts. These services are perfect for that.

Gmail, Google's beta email product, also produces a feed of your inbox, but because it's in beta, it's hard to say if the feed will still be there by the time you read this.

From a Search Engine

The current popular search engines have many great features, but they don't usually provide any form of feed for search results. Such a feed is extremely useful for people trying to keep track of specific search topics (for example, their name).

Google

I personally host a Google-to-RSS service, which you are free to use. It's at *http://www.benhammersley.com/tools/google_to_rss.html*. To use it, simply add your search request to the end of the URL *http://www.benhammersley.com/tools/googlerss.cgi?q=*. For example:

```
http://www.benhammersley.com/tools/googlerss.cgi?q=ben%20hammersley
```

Now, subscribe to that URL in your newsreader.

Note that I'm running this service from my own Google API key, which has a limit of 1,000 queries a day. If you'd like to help out, you can get your own key from *http://www.google.com/apis/* and use it with your own queries. Add it to the URL with a `&k=123456789` attribute, like this:

```
http://www.benhammersley.com/tools/googlerss.cgi?q=ben%20hammersley&k=123456789
```

The source code for this service is discussed in Chapter 10.

Google News

Google News searches can also be turned into feeds via a service hosted by Julian Bond, found at *http://www.voidstar.com/gnews2rss.php*.

That page has a form to help generate the feed's URL, or you can make it up yourself with this pattern:

```
http://www.voidstar.com/gnews2rss.php?num=number_of_items&q=your_query
```

Note that this Google News service is for personal aggregators only and not for redisplay on another web site. The source code for this service is in Chapter 10.

Yahoo!

Despite its tiresomely exclaiming name, Yahoo! goes one better than Google in that it provides feeds of its News Search results as standard. For example, go to *http://search.news.yahoo.com/search/news/?c=&p=Conkers* for news of the greatest autumnal sport, and look for the standard orange XML logo. It's impossible for me to give you a shortcut URL structure, however, because Yahoo! employs redirects.

The standard Yahoo! search does not provide results in feeds, and no one has, as yet, produced a service to do so. Now's your chance.

One service that is being provided is the My Yahoo! to RSS facility run by Mikel Maron. The site (*http://brainoff.com/myy2rss/*) takes your My Yahoo! username and password and returns an RSS feed of any personalized Stock Quotes, Weather, Movie Listings, and Yahoo! Mail alerts you may have set up on your My Yahoo! page.

As with the Yahoo! News Search service, the URL pattern is too obscure to print here, so you have to go through the service's main page.

From Online Stores

E-commerce sites can make very good use of feeds. Customers wanting to subscribe to, say, an individual artist's discography can be alerted the instant that a new title is available. More of this sort of thing is dealt with in Chapter 10, but in the meantime, the following sites are available now:

Amazon.com
: The Internet's biggest retailer has started to publish feeds itself, but they're not as configurable as those produced by the Lockergnome Amazon RSS Feed Generator, *http://channels.lockergnome.com/rss/resources/amazon.phtml*. It's a simple checkbox and submit page, and worth playing with, although it only supports searching Amazon.com at the moment.

  There is also an Amazon.co.jp-to-RSS service at *http://723.to/azrssmake.php*.

iTunes Music Store
: Apple's iTunes Music Store is extremely well-enabled for feeds. You can subscribe to feeds of new releases, top songs and albums, featured tracks, and so on for any combination of musical genres. Do this by visiting its RSS Generator at the marvellously memorable *http://phobos.apple.com/WebObjects/MZSearch.woa/wa/MRSS/rssGenerator* (see Figure 3-3).

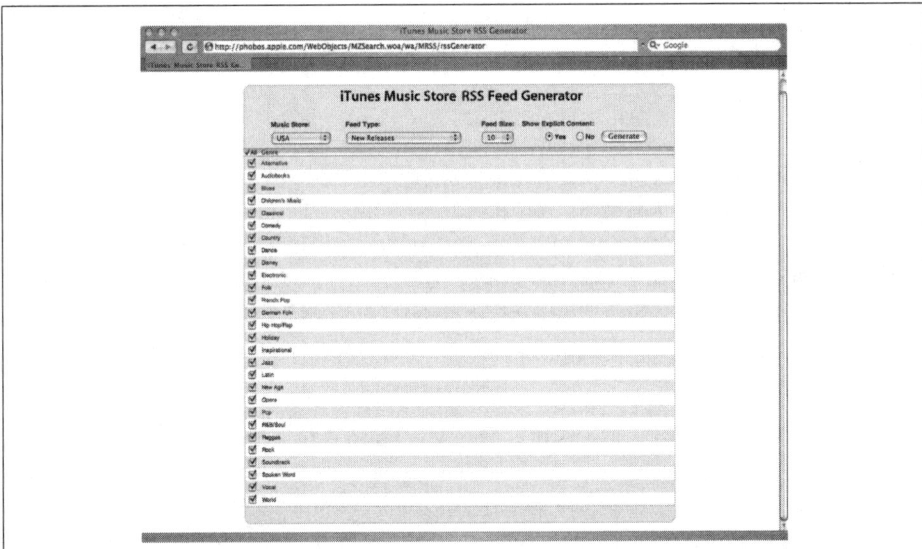

Figure 3-3. The iTunes Music Store RSS Generator

CHAPTER 4

RSS 2.0

A facility for quotation covers the absence of original thought.

—Dorothy L. Sayers, Lord Peter Wimsey in *Gaudy Night*

This chapter describes the RSS 2.0 specification in detail, how it works, and how it is created. It also explores RSS 2.0 predecessors—the largely compatible 0.91 and 0.92 specifications—and how they relate and can be converted to the latest standard.

Bringing Things Up to Date

RSS 2.0 has a long history. As was shown in Chapter 1, it's based on a succession of specifications: RSS 0.91, 0.92, 0.93, and 0.94. Because of this history and because of a lack of any adequate documentation for many of these standards, there is a massive gulf between the quality of the document you can produce and the quality of what you might have to parse. In other words, many people are doing it wrong.

This confusion forces this chapter to address two different issues. The first is how to create a perfectly specification-compliant feed, and the second is how to deal with feeds produced by those with less exacting standards.

This decision brings us to another one: what to do about the older versions that led to 2.0? The answer is this: although many people are still learning to produce 0.91, 0.91, et al, we will not. You'll learn how to parse them, but from now on, as far as the simple strain of syndication feeds goes, we'll be creating only 2.0 feeds.

With that decided, steel yourself, visit the official specification document for RSS 2.0 at *http://blogs.law.harvard.edu/tech/rss*, and let's get on with it.

The Basic Structure

The top level of an RSS 2.0 document is the `rss version="2.0"` element. This is followed by a single `channel` element. The `channel` element contains the entire feed contents and all associated metadata.

Required Channel Subelements

There are 3 required and 16 optional subelements of `channel` within RSS 2.0. Here are the required subelements:

`title`
: The name of the feed. In most cases, this is the same name as the associated web site or service.

```
<title>RSS and Atom</title>
```

`link`
: A URL pointing to the associated resource, usually a web site. The link must be an IANA-registered URI scheme, such as http://, https://, news://, or ftp://, though it isn't necessary for a application developer to support all these by default. The most common by a large margin is http://. For example:

```
<link>http://www.benhammersley.com</link>
```

`description`
: Some words to describe your channel.

```
<description>This is a nice RSS 2.0 feed of an even nicer weblog</description>
```

Although it isn't explicitly stated in the specification, it is highly recommended that you *do not* put anything other than plain text in the `channel/title` or `channel/description` elements. There are some existing feeds with HTML within those elements, but these cause a considerable amount of wailing, and at least a small amount of gnashing of teeth. *Do not do it*. Use plain text only in these elements. The following sidebar, "Including HTML Within title or description," gives a fuller account of this, but in my opinion it's a bad idea.

Optional Channel Subelements

There are 16 optional `channel` subelements of RSS 2.0. Technically speaking, you can leave these out altogether. However, I encourage you to add as many as you can. Much of this stuff is static; the content of the element never changes. Placing it into your RSS template or adding another line to a script is little work for the additional value of your feed's metadata. This is especially true for the first three subelements listed here:

Including HTML Within title or description

Since the early days of RSS 0.91, there's been an ongoing debate about whether the item/title or item/description elements may, or should, contain HTML. In my opinion, they should not, for both practical and philosophical reasons. Practically speaking, including HTML markup requires the client software to be able to parse or filter it. While this is fine with many desktop agents, it restricts developers looking for other uses of the data. This brings us to the philosophical aspect. RSS's second use, after providing headlines and content to desktop readers and sites, is to provide indexable metadata. By combining presentation and content (i.e., by including HTML markup within the description element), you could disable this feature.

However, my opinion lost out on this one. RSS 2.0 now allows for entity-encoded HTML within the item/description tag. It doesn't mention anything, in either direction, regarding item/title, and people are basically making it up as they go along. With that in mind, I still state that item/title at least should be considered plain text.

If you want to put HTML within the item/description element, you can do it in two ways:

Entity encoding
: With entity encoding, the angle brackets of HTML tags are converted to their respective HTML entities, < and >. If you need to show angle brackets as literal characters, the ampersand character itself should be encoded as well:

```
This is a &lt;em&gt;lovely left angle bracket:&lt;/em&gt; &amp;lt;
```

Within a CDATA block
: The alternative is to enclose the HTML within a CDATA block. This removes one level of entity encoding, as in:

```
<![CDATA[This is a <em>lovely left angle bracket:</em> &lt;]]>
```

Either approach is acceptable according to the specification, and there is no way for a program to tell the difference between the two, or to tell if the description is actually just plain text that *resembles* encoded HTML. This is a major problem with the RSS 2.0 specification, as you'll see when we talk about parsing feeds. Atom and RSS 1.0 both have their own ways around this issue.

language
: The language the feed is written in. This allows aggregators to index feeds by language and should contain the standard Internet language codes as per RFC 1766.

```
<language>en-US</language>
```

copyright
: A copyright notice for the content in the feed:

```
<copyright>Copyright 2004 Ben Hammersley</copyright>
```

`managingEditor`
: The email address of the person to contact for editorial enquiries. It should be in the format: *`name @example.com`* (*`FirstName LastName`*).

```
<managingEditor>ben@benhammersley.com (Ben Hammersley)</managingEditor>
```

`webMaster`
: The email address of the person responsible for technical issues with the feed:

```
<webMaster>techsupport@benhammersley.com (Geek McNerdy)</webMaster>
```

`pubDate`
: The publication date of the content within the feed. For example, a daily morning newspaper publishes at a certain time early every morning. Technically, any information in the feed should not be displayed until after the publication date, so you can set `pubDate` to a time in the future and expect that the feed won't be displayed until after that time. Few existing RSS readers take any notice of this element in this way, however. Nevertheless, it should be in the format outlined in RFC 822:

```
<pubDate>Sun, 12 Sep 2004 19:00:40 GMT</pubDate>
```

`lastBuildDate`
: The date and time, RFC 822–style, when the feed last changed. Note the difference between this and `channel/pubDate`. `lastBuildDate` must be in the past. It is this element that feed applications should take as the "last time updated" value and not `channel/pubDate`.

```
<pubDate>Sun, 12 Sep 2004 19:01:55 GMT</pubDate>
```

`category`
: Identical in syntax to the `item/category` element you'll see later. This takes one optional attribute, `domain`. The value of `category` should be a forward-slash-separated string that identifies a hierarchical location in a taxonomy represented by the `domain` attribute. Sadly, there is no consensus either within the specification or in the real world as to any standard format for the `domain` attribute. It would seem most sensible to restrict it to a URL; however, it needn't necessarily be so.

```
<category domain="Syndic8">1765</category>
```

`generator`
: This should contain a string indicating which program created the RSS file:

```
<generator>Movable Type v3.1b3</generator>
```

`docs`
: A URL that points to an explanation of the standard for future reference. This should point to *http://blogs.law.harvard.edu/tech/rss:*

```
<docs>http://blogs.law.harvard.edu/tech/rss</docs>
```

`cloud`

The `<cloud/>` element enables a rarely used feature known as "Publish and Subscribe," which we shall investigate fully in Chapter 9. It takes no value itself, but it has five mandatory attributes, themselves also explained in Chapter 9: `domain`, `path`, `port`, `registerProcedure`, and `protocol`.

```
<cloud domain="rpc.sys.com" port="80" path="/RPC2" registerProcedure= "pingMe"
protocol="soap"/>
```

`ttl`

`ttl`, short for Time-to-Live, should contain a number, which is the minimum number of minutes the reader should wait before refreshing the feed from its source. Feed authors should adjust this figure to reflect the time between updates and the number of times they wish their feed to be requested, versus how up to date they need their consumers to be.

```
<ttl>60</ttl>
```

`image`

This describes a feed's accompanying image. It's optional, but many aggregators look prettier if you include one. It has three required and two optional subelements of its own:

`url`

The URL of a GIF, JPG, or PNG image that corresponds to the feed. It is, quite obviously, required.

`title`

A description of the image, normally used within the ALT attribute of HTML's `<img>` tag. It is required.

`link`

The URL to which the image should be linked. This is usually the same as the `channel/link`.

`width` *and* `height`

The width and height of the icon, in pixels. The icons should be a maximum of 144 pixels wide by 400 pixels high. The emergent standard is 88 pixels wide by 31 pixels high. Both elements are optional.

```
<image> <title>RSS2.0 Example</title> <url>http://www.exampleurl.com/example/
images/logo.gif</url> <link>http://www.exampleurl.com/example/index.html</link>
<width>88</width> <height>31</height> <description>The World's Leading Technical
Publisher</description> </image>
```

`rating`

The PICS rating for the feed; it helps parents and teachers control what children access on the Internet. More information on PICS can be found at *http://www.w3.org/PICS/*. This labeling scheme is little used at present, but an example of a PICS rating would be:

```
<rating>(PICS-1.1 "http://www.gcf.org/v2.5" labels on "1994.11.05T08:15-0500"
until "1995.12.31T23:59-0000" for "http://w3.org/PICS/Overview.html" ratings
(suds 0.5 density 0 color/hue 1))</rating>
```

`textInput`
: An element that lets RSS feeds display a small text box and Submit button, and associates them with a CGI application. Many RSS parsers support this feature, and many sites use it to offer archive searching or email newsletter sign-ups, for example. `textInput` has four required subelements:

  `title`
  : The label for the Submit button. It can have a maximum of 100 characters.

  `description`
  : Text to explain what the `textInput` actually does. It can have a maximum of 500 characters.

  `name`
  : The name of the text object that is passed to the CGI script. It can have a maximum of 20 characters.

  `link`
  : The URL of the CGI script.

```
<textInput> <title>Search</title> <description>Search the Archives</
description> <name>query</name> <link>http://www.exampleurl.com/example/
search.cgi</link> </textInput>
```

`skipDays` *and* `skipHours`
: A set of elements that can control when a feed user reads the feed. `skipDays` can contain up to seven `day` subelements: Monday, Tuesday, Wednesday, Thursday, Friday, Saturday, or Sunday. `skipHours` contains up to 24 `hour` subelements, the numbers 1–24, representing the time in Greenwich Mean Time (GMT). The client should not retrieve the feed during any day or hour listed within these two elements. The elements are ORed not ANDed: in the example here, the application is instructed not to request the feed during 8 p.m. on any day, and never on a Monday:

```
<skipDays><day>Monday</day></skipDays> <skipHours><hour>20</hour></skipHours>
```

item Elements

RSS 2.0 can have any number of `item` elements. The `item` element is at the heart of RSS; it contains the primary content of the feed. Technically, `item` elements are optional, but a syndication feed with no `items` is just a glorified link. Not having any `items` doesn't mean the feed is invalid, just extremely boring.

All `item` subelements are optional, with the proviso that at least one of `item/title` or `item/description` is present. You can use this feature to build lists (more on that later).

With `item`, there are the 10 standard `item` subelements available:

`title`
: Usually, this is the title of the story linked to by the `item`, but it can also be seen as a one-line list item. There is controversy over whether HTML is allowed within this element; for more information, see the sidebar "Including HTML Within title or description."

`link`
: The URL of the story the item is describing.

`description`
: A synopsis of the story. The `description` can contain entity-encoded HTML. Again, as with `item/title`, see the pertinent sidebar "Including HTML Within title or description."

`author`
: This should contain the email address of the resource's author referred to within the `item`. The specification's example is in the format `user@example.com (firstname lastname)` but isn't explained further:

```
<author>ben@benhammersley.com (Ben Hammersley)</author>
```

`category`
: Exactly the same as `channel/category`, but it pertains to the individual `item` only:

```
<category domain="the twisted passages of my mind">up/to_the_left/there</category>
```

`comments`
: This should contain the URL of any comments page for the item; it's primarily used with weblogs:

```
http://www.example.com/comments.cgi?post=12345
```

`enclosure`
: This describes a file associated with an `item`. It has no content, but it takes three attributes: `url` is the URL of the enclosure, `length` is its size in bytes, and `type` is the standard MIME type for the enclosure. Some feed applications can download these files automatically. The original idea was for configuring a feed aggregator to automatically download large media files overnight, thereby deferring the extra bandwidth required. This is an underused feature of RSS 2.0 because most aggregators don't support it, but in 2004, it became the focus of a lot of development around the idea of podcasting. See the sidebar "Including HTML Within title or description" for details.

```
<enclosure url="http://www.example.com/hotxxxpron.mpg" length= "34657834"
type="video/mpeg"/>
```

`guid`
: Standing for Globally Unique Identifier, this element should contain a string that uniquely identifies the item. It must never change, and it must be unique to the object it is describing. If that content changes in any way, it must gain a new `guid`. This element also has the optional attribute `isPermalink`, which, if `true`, denotes that the value of the element can be taken as a URL to the object

referred to by the item. Therefore, if no `item/link` element is present, but the `isPermalink` attribute is set to `true`, the application can take the value of `guid` in its place. The specification doesn't say what to do if both are present and aren't the same, but it seems sensible to give preference within any application to the `item/link` element.

```
<guid isPermalink="true">http://www.example.com/example.html</guid>
```

`pubDate`

The publication date of the `item`. Again, as with `channel/pubDate`, any information in the `item` shouldn't be displayed until after the publication date, but few existing RSS readers take any notice of this element in this way. The date is in RFC 822 format.

```
<pubDate>Mon, 13 Sep 2004 00:23:05 GMT</pubDate>
```

`source`

This should contain the name of the feed of the site from which the `item` was derived, and the attribute url should be the URL of that other site's feed:

```
<source url="http://www.metafilter.com/rss.xml">Metafilter</source>
```

Example 4-1 shows these parts assembled into an RSS 2.0 XML document.

Example 4-1. An example RSS 2.0 feed

```
<?xml version="1.0"?>
<rss version="2.0">
<channel>
  <title>RSS2.0Example</title>
  <link>http://www.exampleurl.com/example/index.html</link>
  <description>This is an example RSS 2.0 feed</description>
  <language>en-gb</language>
  <copyright>Copyright 2002, Oreilly and Associates.</copyright>
  <managingEditor>example@exampleurl.com</managingEditor>
  <webMaster>webmaster@exampleurl.com</webMaster>
  <rating> </rating>
  <pubDate>03 Apr 02 1500 GMT</pubDate>
  <lastBuildDate>03 Apr 02 1500 GMT</lastBuildDate>
  <docs>http://blogs.law.harvard.edu/tech/rss</docs>
  <skipDays><day>Monday</day></skipDays>
  <skipHours><hour>20</hour></skipHours>
  <category  domain="http://www.dmoz.org">Business/Industries/Publishing/Publishers/
Nonfiction/Business/O'Reilly_and_Associates/</category>
  <generator>NewsAggregator'o'Matic</generator>
  <ttl>30<ttl>
  <cloud domain="http://www.exampleurl.com" port="80" path="/RPC2"
registerProcedure="pleaseNotify" protocol="XML-RPC" />

  <image>
    <title>RSS2.0 Example</title>
    <url>http://www.exampleurl.com/example/images/logo.gif</url>
    <link>http://www.exampleurl.com/example/index.html</link>
    <width>88</width>
```

Example 4-1. An example RSS 2.0 feed (continued)

```
      <height>31</height>
      <description>The World's Leading Technical Publisher</description>
    </image>

    <textInput>
      <title>Search</title>
      <description>Search the Archives</description>
      <name>query</name>
      <link>http://www.exampleurl.com/example/search.cgi</link>
    </textInput>

    <item>
      <title>The First Item</title>
      <link>http://www.exampleurl.com/example/001.html</link>
      <description>This is the first item.</description>
      <source url="http://www.anothersite.com/index.xml">Another Site</source>
      <enclosure url="http://www.exampleurl.com/example/001.mp3" length="543210"
                     type"audio/mpeg"/>
      <category domain="http://www.dmoz.org">Business/Industries/Publishing/Publishers/
Nonfiction/Business/O'Reilly_and_Associates/</category>
      <comments>http://www.exampleurl.com/comments/001.html</comments>
      <author>Ben Hammersley</author>
      <pubDate>Sat, 01 Jan 2002 0:00:01 GMT</pubDate>
      <guid isPermaLink="true">http://www.exampleurl.com/example/001.html</guid>
    </item>

    <item>
      <title>The Second Item</title>
      <link>http://www.exampleurl.com/example/002.html</link>
      <description>This is the second item.</description>
      <source url="http://www.anothersite.com/index.xml">Another Site</source>
      <enclosure url="http://www.exampleurl.com/example/002.mp3" length="543210"
                          type"audio/mpeg"/>
      <category domain="http://www.dmoz.org">Business/Industries/Publishing/Publishers/
Nonfiction/Business/O'Reilly_and_Associates/</category>
      <comments>http://www.exampleurl.com/comments/002.html</comments>
      <author>Ben Hammersley</author>
      <pubDate>Sun, 02 Jan 2002 0:00:01 GMT</pubDate>
      <guid isPermaLink="true">http://www.exampleurl.com/example/002.html</guid>
    </item>

    <item>
      <title>The Third Item</title>
      <link>http://www.exampleurl.com/example/003.html</link>
      <description>This is the third item.</description>
      <source url="http://www.anothersite.com/index.xml">Another Site</source>
      <enclosure url="http://www.exampleurl.com/example/003.mp3" length="543210"
                      type"audio/mpeg"/>
      <category domain="http://www.dmoz.org">Business/Industries/Publishing/Publishers/
Nonfiction/Business/O'Reilly_and_Associates/</category>
      <comments>http://www.exampleurl.com/comments/003.html</comments>
      <author>Ben Hammersley</author>
```

Example 4-1. An example RSS 2.0 feed (continued)

```
    <pubDate>Mon, 03 Jan 2002 0:00:01 GMT</pubDate>
    <guid isPermaLink="true">http://www.exampleurl.com/example/003.html</guid>
  </item>
</channel>
</rss>
```

The Simplest Possible RSS 2.0 Feed

This, really, is the key to the success of RSS 2.0. The simplest thing you need to do to make the feed validate is very uncomplicated indeed (see Example 4-2). While this isn't any help when you are trying to convey complex information, as with RSS 1.0, or if you're trying to build a complete document-centric system, as with Atom, it is very useful for many other applications.

Example 4-2. The simplest possible RSS 2.0 feed

```
<?xml version="1.0" encoding="utf-8"?>
<rss version="2.0">

<channel>
<title>The Simplest Feed</title>
<link>http://example.org/index.html</link>
<description>The Simplest Possible RSS 2.0 Feed</description>

<item>
<description>Simple Simple Simple</description>
</item>
</channel>
</rss>
```

Chapter 10 describes many useful applications that take this a minimalist approach to using RSS 2.0–compliant feeds.

Producing RSS 2.0 with Blogging Tools

The vast majority of RSS 2.0 feeds are produced by weblogging tools that use templates. The most popular of these is Movable Type, written by Ben and Mena Trott, which is freely available for personal use at *http://www.movabletype.org*. In order to discuss a few important implementation points, Example 4-3 shows a template for Movable Type that produces an RSS 2.0 feed.

Example 4-3. A Movable Type template for producing RSS 2.0

```
<?xml version="1.0"?>
<rss version="2.0">
<channel>
<title><$MTBlogName$></title>
<link><$MTBlogURL$></link>
```

Example 4-3. A Movable Type template for producing RSS 2.0 (continued)

```
<description><$MTBlogDescription$></description>
<language>en-gb</language>
<copyright>All content Public Domain</copyright>
<managingEditor>ben@benhammersley.com</managingEditor>
<webMaster>ben@benhammersley.com</webMaster>
<docs>http://blogs.law.harvard.edu/tech/rss</docs>
<category  domain="http://www.dmoz.org">Reference/Libraries/Library_and_Information_
Science/Technical_Services/Cataloguing/Metadata/RDF/Applications/RSS/</category>
<generator>Movable Type/2.5</generator>
<lastBuildDate><$MTDate format="%a, %d %b %Y %I:%M:00 GMT"$></lastBuildDate>
<ttl>60</ttl>

<MTEntries lastn="15">
<item>
<title><$MTEntryTitle encode_html="1"$></title>
<description><$MTEntryExcerpt encode_html="1"$></description>
<link><$MTEntryLink$></link>
<comments><$MTEntryLink$></comments>
<author><$MTEntryAuthorEmail$></author>
<pubDate><$MTEntryDate format="%a, %d %b %Y %I:%M:00 GMT"$></pubDate>
<guid isPermaLink="false">GUID:<$MTEntryLink$></g<$MTEntryDate format=
"%a%d%b%Y%I:%M"$></guid>
</item>
</MTEntries>
</channel>
</rss>
```

The vast majority of this template is standard Movable Type fare. Taken from one of my own blogs, it uses the `<$MT$>` tags to insert information directly from the Movable Type database into the feed. So far, so simple.

Two things are worth close examination. First, the date format:

```
<pubDate><$MTEntryDate format="%a, %d %b %Y %I:%M:00 GMT"$></pubDate>
```

Care must be taken to ensure that the format of the contents of the date fields are correctly formed. RSS 2.0 feeds require their dates to be written to comply with RFC 822—for example: `Mon, 03 Jan 2002 0:00:01 GMT`.

Common errors found in RSS 2.0 feeds include missing commas, seconds values, and time zones. You must ensure these are all present because some desktop readers and aggregators aren't as forgiving as others, and many are getting less so as they develop.

Implementation of the `guid` element is equally important. The RSS 2.0 standard doesn't discuss the form of the guid; it only asks the author to ensure that it is globally unique. There is no scope for the OSF GUID standard to be used within most blogging tools, so you have to formulate your own system. (I'll touch upon this again when we talk about Atom in Chapter 7.)

For the template shown earlier, I considered various things. First, the guid's purpose is to tell applications if the entry is new or if it has changed. Second, within my own blogs I allow people to add comments to the entries. I consider this a change to the entry, so my guid must reflect this. Because this change isn't reflected in the link to the entry, the link alone isn't a good guid. So, by combining the link with the last-updated-date value, I can make a guid that is globally unique and changes when it needs to. For added measure, I add the string GUID to the front of it to prevent it from looking too much like a retrievable URL—which, of course, it isn't. Hence:

```
<guid isPermaLink="false">GUID:<$MTEntryLink$></g<$MTEntryDate format=
"%a%d%b%Y%I:%M"$></guid>
```

This works well as an RSS 2.0 guid, but it has one feature that might annoy: because weblog comments cause the guid to change, it also causes the item to be marked as unread in many feed aggregators. This might not be desirable behavior for you.

Introducing Modules

Modules are additional sets of elements, giving the feed a greater range of expression: they allow the specification to be extended without actually being changed, which is a very clever trick. You can make your own module match any data you might wish to syndicate. Admittedly, most aggregators will ignore it, but your own applications can take advantage of it. And, happily, the most popular modules are increasingly being supported by the latest aggregators as a matter of course.

Modules in RSS, both Versions 2.0 and 1.0, are created with a system known as XML Namespaces. Namespaces are the XML solution to the classic language problem of one word meaning two things in different contexts. Take "Windows," for example. In the context of houses, "windows" are holes in the wall through which we can look. In the context of computers, "Windows" is a trademark of the Microsoft Corporation and refers to its range of operating systems. The context within which the name has a particular meaning is called its namespace.

In XML, you can distinguish between the two meanings by assigning a namespace and placing the namespace's name in front of the element name, separated by a colon, like this:

```
<computing:windows>This is an operating system</computing:windows>

<building:windows>This is a hole in a wall</building:windows>
```

Namespaces solve two problems. First, they allow you to distinguish between different meanings for words that are spelled the same way, which means you can use words more than once for different meanings. Second, they allow you to group together words that are related to each other; for example, using a computer to look through an XML document for all elements with a certain namespace is easy.

Both RSS 1.0 and 2.0 use namespaces to allow for *modularization*. This modularization means that developers can add new features to RSS documents without changing the core specification.

Modularization has great advantages over the older RSS 0.9x's method for including new elements. For starters, anyone can create a module: there are no standards issues or any need for approval, aside from making sure that the namespace URI you use has not been used before. And, it means both RSS 1.0 and 2.0 are potentially far more powerful than RSS 0.9x ever was.

A module works in the actual RSS document by declaring a namespace within the root element of the feed and by prefixing the element's names with that namespace prefix, like so:

```
<?xml version="1.0"?>
<rss version="2.0" xmlns:blogChannel="http://backend.userland.com/blogChannelModule">
...

  <blogChannel:blink>http://www.benhammersley.com</blogChannel:blink>
...
```

You should note that the URI the namespace declaration points to is the unique identifier of the namespace and not the namespace prefix. In other words, from the perspective of a program processing XML, this:

```
<?xml version="1.0"?>
<rss version="2.0" xmlns:blogChannel="http://backend.userland.com/blogChannelModule">
...

  <blogChannel:blink>http://www.benhammersley.com</blogChannel:blink>
...
```

is absolutely identical to this:

```
<?xml version="1.0"?>
<rss version="2.0" xmlns:bingbangbong="http://backend.userland.com/
blogChannelModule">
...

  <bingbandbong:blink>http://www.benhammersley.com</bingbangbong:blink>...
```

This will become clear as we study some common modules. It is customary, and also very good manners, to have documentation for the module to be found at the namespace's URI, but this isn't technically necessary. As discussed in Chapter 11, the different feed standards have different scopes for the form this documentation can take. The presence of anything at all at the namespace URI is entirely optional, both in terms of RSS and within the scope of the broader XML specification itself.

blogChannel Module

Designed by Dave Winer only a week after he formalized RSS 2.0, the `blogChannel` module allows the inclusion of data used by weblogging applications and, specifically, the newer generation of aggregating and filtering systems.

It consists of three optional elements, all of which are subelements of `channel` and have the following namespace declaration:

```
xmlns:blogChannel="http://backend.userland.com/blogChannelModule"
```

The elements are:

`blogChannel:blogRoll`
: Contains a literal string that is the URL of an OPML file containing the blogroll for the site. A *blogroll* is the list of blogs the blog author habitually reads.

`blogChannel:blink`
: Contains a literal string that is the URL of a site the blog author recommends the reader visits.

`blogChannel:mySubscriptions`
: Contains a literal string that is the URL of the OPML file containing the URLs of the RSS feeds to which the blog author is subscribed in her desktop reader.

Example 4-4 shows the beginning of an RSS 2.0 feed using the `blogChannel` module.

Example 4-4. An RSS 2.0 feed with the blogChannel module

```
<?xml version="1.0"?>
<rss version="2.0" xmlns:blogChannel="http://backend.userland.com/blogChannelModule">
<channel>
  <title>RSS2.0Example</title>
  <link>http://www.exampleurl.com/example/index.html</link>
  <description>This is an example RSS 2.0 feed</description>
  <blogChannel:blogRoll>http://www.exampleurl.com/blogroll.opml</blogChannel:blogRoll>
<blogChannel:blink>http://www.benhammersley.com</blogChannel:blink>
<blogChannel:mySubscriptions>http://www.exampleurl.com/mySubscriptions.opml
</blogChannel:mySubscriptions>
...
```

Creative Commons Module

Also designed by Dave Winer, the Creative Commons module allows RSS 2.0 feeds to specify which Creative Commons license applies to them. The Creative Commons organization, *http://creativecommons.org/*, offers a variety of content licenses that allow feed publishers to release content under more flexible copyright restrictions than previously available. Feed consumers can consult the license to see how they can reuse the content for their own work.

The element can apply to either the complete `channel` or the individual `item`.

It consists of only one element, `creativeCommons:license`, which contains the URL of the Creative Commons license on the Creative Commons site. It has the following namespace declaration:

```
xmlns:creativeCommons="
http://backend.userland.com/creativeCommonsRssModule"
```

In action, it looks like Example 4-5.

Example 4-5. Part of an RSS 2.0 feed with the Creative Commons module

```
<rss version="2.0" xmlns:creativeCommons="http://backend.userland.com/
   creativeCommonsRssModule">

<channel>
<title>Creative Commons Example</title>
<link>http://www.example.com/</link>
<creativeCommons:license>http://www.creativecommons.org/licenses/by-nd/1.0
</creativeCommons:license>
...
<item>
<description>blah blah blah</description>
<creativeCommons:license>http://www.creativecommons.org/licenses/by-nc/1.0
 </creativeCommons:license>
</item>
...
```

Note that a `creativeCommons:license` element on an `item` overrides the same on the `channel` for that `item`.

More details can be found at:

http://backend.userland.com/creativeCommonsRssModule

Simple Semantic Resolution Module

One of the never-ending arguments within the RSS world is that between the pro- and anti-RDF camps. The fork between RSS 0.91 and 1.0 was almost entirely caused by this disagreement. The pro-RDF camp stated, quite rightly, that RDF data has a great deal more meaningful utility than plain XML, whilst the anti-RDF camp stated, also quite rightly, that the RDF syntax was horrible, and that no one can understand it without reading the documentation and having a nice lie down.

That may be—we'll find out your own feelings on this in the next chapters—but in the meantime, the Simple Semantic Resolution module was one idea put forward to bridge the divide between the two cultures.

Written by Danny Ayers, its presence in an RSS 2.0 feed simply means "this data should be considered RDF, and to use it with an RDF-compatible application you should apply this transformation to it first." Whereupon, it points you to a nice

XSLT stylesheet. That stylesheet consists of one single element, a subelement of `channel`, and has the following namespace declaration:

```
xmlns:ssr="http://purl.org/stuff/ssr"
```

The element is:

`ssr:rdf`
: It's empty, but contains a single attribute, `transform`, which is equal to the URL of the necessary stylesheet:

```
<ssr:rdf transform="http://w3future.com/weblog/gems/rss2rdf.xsl" />
```

Example 4-6 shows the SSR module in use.

Example 4-6. Part of an RSS 2.0 feed with the SSR module

```
<?xml version="1.0"?>
<rss version="2.0" xmlns:ssr="http://purl.org/stuff/ssr">
<ssr:rdf transform="http://w3future.com/weblog/gems/rss2rdf.xsl" />
...
```

More details can be found at *http://ideagraph.net/xmlns/ssr/*.

Trackback Module

The trackback system for weblog content management systems (see *http://www.movabletype.org/docs/mttrackback.html* for the technical details) has grown up in the same neighborhood as RSS, so it's only fair that the one should be represented in the other.

This module, also available in tasty RSS 1.0, comes from Justin Klubnik and allows RSS 2.0 feeds to display both the URL that people should trackback to, but also the URL that the `item` has trackbacked itself. The idea is that aggregators can send pings and also follow links to find related pages, because `items` might ping places they don't explicitly link to.

This module is made up of two elements, subelements of `item`, and has the following namespace declaration:

```
xmlns:trackback="http://madskills.com/public/xml/rss/module/trackback/"
```

Here are the elements:

`trackback:ping`
: This contains the `item`'s trackback URL:

```
<trackback:ping>http://foo.com/trackback/tb.cgi?tb_id=20020923</trackback:ping>
```

`trackback:about`
: This contains any trackback URL that was pinged in reference to the `item`:

```
<trackback:about>http://foo.com/trackback/tb.cgi?tb_id=20020923</trackback:about>
```

More details can be found at *http://madskills.com/public/xml/rss/module/trackback/*.

ICBM Module

This module, written by Matt Croydon and Kenneth Hunt, allows RSS feeds to state the geographical location of the origin of the feed or an individual `item` within it.

It's alleged that ICBM does actually stand for intercontinental ballistic missile, and certainly a half-arsed attempt at Googling for it produces only the explanation that describing one's position as an ICBM address is so that, should anyone wish, your data will allow the baddies to target you directly, presumably for being far too clever with your syndication feeds.

Either way, the namespace declaration is thus:

```
xmlns:icbm="http://postneo.com/icbm"
```

It contains two elements, usable in either the `channel` or the `item` context. The `item` context overrides the former, as you might expect.

`icbm:latitude`
: This contains the latitude value as per the geographic standard WGS84:

```
<icbm:latitude>43.7628</icbm:latitude>
```

`icbm:longitude`
: This contains the longitude value as per the geographic standard WGS84.

```
<icbm:longitude>11.2442</icbm:longitude>
```

That's my house, actually.

Go to *http://www.postneo.com/icbm/* for more verbose details on the thinking behind the specification.

Yahoo!'s Media RSS Module

In December 2004, Yahoo! launched a beta video search engine at *http://video.search.yahoo.com/*. The original system spidered the Web looking for video files and indexed them with the implied information found in the filename and link text. To make it easier for video content producers to have Yahoo! index their sites, and to give the search engine much better data to play with, Yahoo! is now offering to regularly spider RSS feeds containing details of media files. This additional data is encoded in its new Media RSS Module.

That module consists of one element, `<media:content>`, with a namespace declaration of:

```
xmlns:media="http://tools.search.yahoo.com/mrss/"
```

and four optional subelements. `<media:content>` is a subelement of `item` and consists of ten optional attributes.

`url`
: `url` specifies the direct URL to the media object. It is an optional attribute. If a URL isn't included, a `playerURL` must be specified.

`fileSize`
: The size, in bytes, of the media object. It is an optional attribute.

`type`
: The standard MIME type of the object. It is an optional attribute.

`playerURL`
: `playerURL` is the URL of the media player console. It is an optional attribute.

`playerHeight`
: `playerHeight` is the height of the window the `playerURL` should be opened in. It is an optional attribute.

`playerWidth`
: `playerWidth` is the width of the window the `playerURL` should be opened in. It is an optional attribute.

`isDefault`
: `isDefault` determines if this is the default object that should be used for this element. It can be `true` or `false`. So, if an `item` contains more than one `media:content` element, setting this to `true` makes it the default. It's an optional attribute but can be used only once within each `item`.

`expression`
: `expression` determines if the object is a sample or the full version of the object. It can be either `sample` or `full`. It is an optional attribute.

`bitrate`
: The bit rate of the file, in kilobits per second. It is an optional attribute.

`duration`
: The number of seconds the media plays, for audio and video. It is an optional attribute.

There are also four optional subelements to `<media:content>`, which can be also used as subelements to `item`:

`<media:thumbnail>`
: Allows a particular image to be used as the representative image for the media object:

```
<media:thumbnail height="50" width="50">
        http://www.foo.com/keyframe.jpg</media:thumbnail>
```

It takes two optional attributes. `height` specifies the height of the thumbnail. `width` specifies the width of the thumbnail.

<media:category>

Allows a taxonomy to be set that gives an indication of the type of media content and its particular contents:

```
<media:category>music/artist name/album/song</media:category>
<media:category>television/series/episode/episode number</media:category>
```

<media:people>

Lists the notable individuals or businesses and their contribution to the creation of the media object.

```
<media:people role="editor">Simon St Laurent</media:people>
```

`role` specifies the role individuals played. Examples include: `producer`, `artist`, `news anchor`, `cast member`, etc. It is an optional attribute.

<media:text>

Allows the inclusion of a text transcript, closed captioning, or lyrics of the media content:

```
<media:text>Oh, say, can you see, by the dawn's early light,</media:text>
```

Once your site has a feed working with the Media RSS Module, like that shown in Example 4-7, you can submit it to Yahoo! at *http://tools.search.yahoo.com/mrss/submit.html*.

Example 4-7. media:content in action

```
<media:content url="http://www.example.com/movie.mov" fileSize="12345678" type-
            "video/quicktime"
    playerUrl="http://http://www.example.com/player?id=1" playerHeight="200"
            playerWidth="400"
    isDefault="true" expression="full" bitrate="128" duration="185">
    <media:thumbnail height="50" width="50">http://www.example.com/thumbnail.jpg
            thumbnail></media:

    <media:category>comedy/slapstick/custard</media:category>
    <media:people role="stuntman">Ben Hammersley</media:people>
    <media:text>Take that! And that! And that!</media:text>
</media:content>
```

The development of your own modules is covered in Chapter 11.

Creating RSS 2.0 Feeds

RSS 0.91 and 0.92 feeds are created in the same way; the additional elements found in 0.92 are well-handled by the existing RSS tools.

Of course, you can always hand-code your RSS feed. Doing so certainly gets you on top of the standard, but it's neither convenient, quick, nor recommended. Ordinarily, feeds are created by a small program in one of the scripting languages: Perl, PHP, Python, etc. Many CMSs already create RSS feeds automatically, but you may want to create a feed in another context. Hey, you might even write your own CMS!

There are various ways to create a feed, all of which are used in real life:

XML transformation
: Running a transformation on an XML master document converts the relevant parts into RSS. This technique is used in Apache Axkit–based systems, for example.

Templates
: You can substitute values within a RSS feed template. This technique is used within most weblogging platforms, for example.

An RSS-specific module or class within a scripting language
: This method is used within hundreds of little ad hoc scripts across the Net, for example.

We'll look at all three methods, but let's start with the third, using an RSS-specific module. In this case, it's Perl's `XML::RSS`.

Creating RSS with Perl Using XML::RSS

The `XML::RSS` module is one of the key tools in the Perl RSS world. It is built on top of `XML::Parser`—the basis for many Perl XML modules—and is object-oriented. Actually, `XML::RSS` also supports the creation of the older versions of RSS, plus RSS 1.0, and it can parse existing feeds, but in this section we will deal only with its 2.0 creation capabilities.

Incidentally, `XML::RSS` is an open source project. You can lend a hand, and grab the latest version, at *http://sourceforge.net/projects/perl-rss*.

Examples 4-8 and 4-9 show a simple Perl script and the feed it creates.

Example 4-8. A sample XML::RSS script

```
#!/usr/bin/perl

use Warnings;
use Strict;
use XML::RSS;

my $rss = new XML::RSS( version => '2.0' );

$rss->channel(
    title         => 'The Title of the Feed',
    link          => 'http://www.oreilly.com/example/',
    language      => 'en',
    description   => 'An example feed created by XML::RSS',
    lastBuildDate => 'Tue, 14 Sep 2004 14:30:58 GMT',
    docs          => 'http://blogs.law.harvard.edu/tech/rss',
);

$rss->image(
    title       => 'Oreilly',
    url         => 'http://meerkat.oreillynet.com/icons/meerkat-powered.jpg',
```

Example 4-8. A sample XML::RSS script (continued)

```
    link        => 'http://www.oreilly.com/example/',
    width       => 88,
    height      => 31,
    description => 'A nice logo for the feed'
);

$rss->textinput(
    title       => "Search",
    description => "Search the site",
    name        => "query",
    link        => "http://www.oreilly.com/example/search.cgi"
);

$rss->add_item(
    title       => "Example Entry 1",
    link        => "http://www.oreilly.com/example/entry1",
    description => 'blah blah',
);

$rss->add_item(
    title       => "Example Entry 2",
    link        => "http://www.oreilly.com/example/entry2",
    description => 'blah blah'
);

$rss->add_item(
    title       => "Example Entry 3",
    link        => "http://www.oreilly.com/example/entry3",
    description => 'blah blah'
);

print $rss->as_string;
```

Example 4-9. The resultant RSS 2.0 feed

```
<?xml version="1.0" encoding="UTF-8"?>

<rss version="2.0" xmlns:blogChannel="http://backend.userland.com/blogChannelModule">

<channel>
<title>The Title of the Feed</title>
<link>http://www.oreilly.com/example/</link>
<description>An example feed created by XML::RSS</description>
<language>en</language>
<lastBuildDate>Tue, 14 Sep 2004 14:30:58 GMT</lastBuildDate>
<docs>http://blogs.law.harvard.edu/tech/rss</docs>

<image>
<title>Oreilly</title>
<url>http://meerkat.oreillynet.com/icons/meerkat-powered.jpg</url>
<link>http://www.oreilly.com/example/</link>
<width>88</width>
```

Example 4-9. The resultant RSS 2.0 feed (continued)

```
<height>31</height>
<description>A nice logo for the feed</description>
</image>

<item>
<title>Example Entry 1</title>
<link>http://www.oreilly.com/example/entry1</link>
<description>blah blah</description>
</item>

<item>
<title>Example Entry 2</title>
<link>http://www.oreilly.com/example/entry2</link>
<description>blah blah</description>
</item>

<item>
<title>Example Entry 3</title>
<link>http://www.oreilly.com/example/entry3</link>
<description>blah blah</description>
</item>

<textInput>
<title>Search</title>
<description>Search the site</description>
<name>query</name>
<link>http://www.oreilly.com/example/search.cgi</link>
</textInput>
</channel>
</rss>
```

After the required Perl module declaration, you create a new instance of `XML::RSS`, like so:

```
my $rss = new XML::RSS (version => '2.0');
```

The new method function returns a reference to the new `XML::RSS` object. The function can take three arguments, two of which are of interest here:

```
new XML::RSS (version=>$version, encoding=>$encoding);
```

The version attribute refers to the version of RSS you want to make (either `'2.0'` or `'1.0'`, or, if you fancy being a bit retro, `'0.91'`), and the `encoding` attribute sets the encoding of the XML declaration. The default encoding, as with XML, is UTF-8.

The rest of the script is quite self-explanatory. The methods `channel`, `image`, `textinput`, and `add_item` all add new elements and associated values to the feed you are creating, and the `print $rss->as_string;` prints out the result. You can also call the `$rss->save` method to save the created feed as a file.

guid, Permalink or not

`XML::RSS` does support the two `guid` `isPermalink` options but in a slightly less predictable way than the other element functions. To set `guid isPermalink="true"`, you should do this:

```
$rss->add_item(
    title       => "Example Entry 1",
    link        => "http://www.oreilly.com/example/entry1",
    description => 'blah blah',
    permaLink   => "http://www.oreilly.com/example/entry1",
);
```

However, to set guid `isPermalink="false"`, you should do this:

```
$rss->add_item(
    title       => "Example Entry 1",
    link        => "http://www.oreilly.com/example/entry1",
    description => 'blah blah',
    guid        => "http://www.example.com/guidsRus/348324327",
);
```

Module support under XML::RSS

As you can see, `XML::RSS` always includes the namespace declaration for the `blogChannel` module. You can also use it to include other modules within your feed.

In Example 4-4, we passed known strings to the module. It's really not of much use as a script, you need to add a more dynamic form of data, or the feed will be very boring indeed. We do an awful lot of this sort of thing in Chapter 10, so let's leave Perl until then, and move on to another language.

Creating RSS 2.0 with PHP

Great RSS 2.0 support for PHP is to be found in the `feedcreator.class` by Kai Blankenhorn at *http://www.bitfolge.de*. Unlike the previous section's `XML::RSS`, `feedcreator.class` can only create RSS feeds; it can't parse them. No matter: it's very good at that indeed.

As illustrated in Example 4-10, the function for each feed element is named after the element, so it behaves pretty much as you would expect.

Example 4-10. A PHP script using FeedCreator that produces RSS 2.0

```
<?php
include("feedcreator.class.php");

$rss = new UniversalFeedCreator();
$rss->title = "Example Feed";
$rss->description = "This is the feed description";
$rss->link = "http://www.example.com/";
```

Example 4-10. A PHP script using FeedCreator that produces RSS 2.0 (continued)

```
// Image section
$image = new FeedImage( );
$image->title = "example logo";
$image->url = "http://www.example.com/images/logo.gif";
$image->link = "http://www.example.com";
$image->description = "Visit Example.com!";
$rss->image = $image;

// Item Loop
$item = new FeedItem( );
$item->title = "Entry one";
$item->link = "http://www.example.com/entryone";
$item->description = "This is the content of the first entry";
$item->author = "Ben Hammersley";
$rss->addItem($item);
// End Item Loop

?>
```

This is a very simple script. As you can see from the resulting feed, Example 4-11, it produces only one item. We'll be using it for more complicated things later on in the book, so in the meantime, once we've passed over the example output, we'll take a quick look at some of the special features.

Example 4-11. An RSS 2.0 feed created with PHP

```
<?xml version="1.0" encoding="ISO-8859-1"?>
<!-- generator="FeedCreator 1.7.1" -->
<rss version="2.0">
    <channel>
        <title>Example Feed</title>
        <description>This is the feed description</description>
        <link>http://www.example.com/</link>
        <lastBuildDate>Thu, 16 Sep 2004 20:16:22 +0100</lastBuildDate>
        <generator>FeedCreator 1.7.1</generator>
        <image>
            <url>http://www.example.com/images/logo.gif</url>
            <title>example logo</title>
            <link>http://www.example.com</link>
            <description>Visit Example.com!</description>
        </image>
        <item>
            <title>Entry one</title>
            <link>http://www.example.com/entryone</link>
            <description>This is the content of the first entry</description>
            <author>Ben Hammersley</author>
        </item>
    </channel>
</rss>
```

Caching and saving

One advantage that the FeedCreator class has over Perl's `XML::RSS` is the built-in caching mechanism. PHP is mostly used, in this case, as a way of dynamically building a feed upon request, perhaps from a database. However, when a feed gets too popular, that might cause too much of a server load. You can have your script store a cache file and serve that instead of running itself by adding this line:

```
$rss->useCached( );
```

This saves the dynamically created feed to a cache, serving that instead if it is less than one hour old. Remember, you need to place this line right underneath the `$rss = new UniversalFeedCreator( );`, or you'll waste precious processor cycles.

You can also explicitly save the file with a command like this:

```
echo $rss->saveFeed("RSS2.0", "index.xml");
```

Dates

Because, caching not withstanding, the feeds are usually produced dynamically, FeedCreator declares the `channel/lastBuildDate` element automatically at the time of creation. You can, of course, specify it explicitly, as you can with `pubDate`. FeedCreator allows the use of RFC 822 (`Mon, 20 Jan 03 18:05:41 +0400`), ISO 8601 (`2003-01-20T18:05:41+04:00`), and Unix (`1043082341`) time values.

Namespaced modules

This is the major drawback with the class. You can't, as of Version 1.71 at least, create a feed with modules in it. If you're set on doing that—perhaps with some groovy special in-house application in mind—you'll need to hack at the class's code. It is licensed under the GPL, so go right ahead.

Creating RSS 2.0 with Ruby

Since Version 1.8.2, Ruby has shipped with Kouhei Sutou's RSS parsing and creation library. At time of writing, however, Ruby has only reached 1.8.2.preview.3, and documentation is hard to come by. The only documentation for the new RSS classes is found at:

http://www.cozmixng.org/~rwiki/?cmd=view;name=RSS+Parser%3A%3ATutorial.en

in a potentially unreliable translation from the Japanese original.

Having said that, the library does seem very complete indeed, with support for the parsing and writing of both RSS 1.0 and 2.0. At time of writing, the tutorial just mentioned was growing rapidly and being completed by the library's author. Ruby programmers should check the URL for changes.

Serving RSS 2.0

Although, or perhaps because, there is no official word within the specification regarding this, the growing standard for serving RSS 2.0 is with a MIME type of `application/xml`. Dave Winer prefers `text/xml` for the way that it causes the file to display itself nicely inside Internet Explorer. Using `application/xml` is more correct, but it causes browsers to download the file instead of displaying it. Really advanced users are looking at `application/rss+xml`, but currently no standard exists. It's up to you, but certainly, it should not be served with any other MIME type. `text/plain` is right out.

CHAPTER 5
RSS 1.0

You see, I needed to go to hell. I was, you might say, homesick.

—Nick Tosches, *The Last Opium Den*

Most of the feeds we've seen so far have been very simple. They provide little information beyond what is needed for the instant gratification of displaying the feed in a human-readable form. Of course, this isn't such a bad deal; many people only want to display the feeds as they come.

Others, however require a far richer set of feeds. For this, many people are using the RSS 1.0 flavor of the Resource Description Framework (RDF). In this chapter, we'll look at the metadata options RSS 2.0 provides and why you might want (or need) more. Then I'll give a basic overview of RDF and a thorough rundown of RSS 1.0 itself.

Metadata in RSS 2.0

As all good tutorials on the subject will tell you, metadata is data about data. In the case of RSS 2.0, this includes the name of the author of the feed, the date the `channel` was last updated, and so on. In Example 5-1, the bold code is the metadata. You can remove this data, and the feed itself will still both parse and be useful when displayed as HTML. Like a Hitchcock cameo, the metadata is in the background, silent, but meaningful to those who can see it.

Example 5-1. The metadata within an RSS 2.0 feed

```
<rss version="2.0">
<channel>
  <title>RSS2.0 Example</title>
  <link>http://www.oreilly.com/example/index.html</link>
  <description>This is an example RSS2.0 feed</description>
  <language>en-gb</language>
  <copyright>Copyright 2004, Oreilly and Associates.</copyright>
```

Example 5-1. The metadata within an RSS 2.0 feed (continued)

```
  <managingEditor>editor@oreilly.com</managingEditor>
  <webMaster>webmaster@oreilly.com</webMaster>
  <pubDate>03 Apr 04 1500 GMT</pubDate>
  <lastBuildDate>03 Apr 04 1500 GMT</lastBuildDate>
  <docs>http://backend.userland.com/rss091</docs>
  <skipDays>
    <day>Monday</day>
  </skipDays>
  <skipHours>
    <hour>20</hour>
  </skipHours>
  <cloud domain="http://www.oreilly.com" port="80" path=
"/RPC2"
registerProcedure="pleaseNotify" protocol="XML-RPC" />

  <image>
    <title>RSS0.91 Example</title>
    <url>http://www.oreilly.com/example/images/logo.gif</url>
    <link>http://www.oreilly.com/example/index.html</link>
    <width>88</width>
    <height>31</height>
    <description>The World's Leading Technical Publisher</description>
  </image>
  <textInput>
    <title>Search</title>
    <description>Search the Archives</description>
    <name>query</name>
    <link>http://www.oreilly.com/example/search.cgi</link>
  </textInput>

  <item>
    <title>The First Item</title>
    <link>http://www.oreilly.com/example/001.html</link>
    <description>This is the first item.</description>
    <source url="http://www.anothersite.com/index.xml">Another Site</source>

    <enclosure url="http://www.oreilly.com/001.mp3" length="54321" type"audio/mpeg"/>
<category domain="http://www.dmoz.org">
Business/Industries/Publishing/Publishers/Nonfiction/</category>

  </item>

  <item>
    <title>The Second Item</title>
    <link>http://www.oreilly.com/example/002.html</link>
    <description>This is the second item.</description>
    <source url="http://www.anothersite.com/index.xml">Another
;Site</source>
    <enclosure url="http://www.oreilly.com/002.mp3" length="54321"
type"audio/mpeg"/>
    <category domain="http://www.dmoz.org">
    Business/Industries/Publishing/Publishers/Nonfiction/</category>
```

Example 5-1. The metadata within an RSS 2.0 feed (continued)

```
  </item>
</channel>
</rss>
```

With this sort of simple metadata, written in the grammar of RSS 2.0's XML format, we are describing simple statements. Take the first line of metadata, for example, which focuses on the language aspect:

```
<channel>
...
<language>en-gb</language>
...
</channel>
```

Here is the `language` element with a value of `en-gb`. The `language` element is a subelement of `channel`, so a simple translation of the XML into English reads, "The object called `channel` has a subelement called `language` whose value is `en-gb`."

This phrase is grammatically and semantically correct, but it lacks a certain poetry. (The use of the term "object" is bound to confuse people when they have their programmer's hat on.) Here's a rewrite into something a little more friendly: "The `channel`'s `language` is `en-gb`."

Now that's more like it. It's a statement of fact from the metadata: "The language of the channel is British English."

So far, so easy, you say. Well, you're quite right; metadata is all about making statements. With the simple metadata present in RSS 2.0, we do it all the time:

```
<language>en-gb</language>
<copyright>Copyright 2004, O'Reilly Media, Inc.</copyright>

<managingEditor>editor@oreilly.com</managingEditor>
<webMaster>webmaster@oreilly.com</webMaster>
<pubDate>03 Apr 04 1500 GMT</pubDate>
<lastBuildDate>03 Apr 04 1500 GMT</lastBuildDate>
```

From this section, you can see the feed is in English; it is copyright 2004, O'Reilly Media, Inc.; the managing editor is *editor@oreilly.com*, and so on.

You will notice, alas, that all isn't perfect with this syntax. For example, the managing editor is defined as *editor@oreilly.com*. To you and me, it is obvious that this is an email address for a person, and you can act accordingly, but to a machine—a search engine, for example—it is a general email address at best and just a string at worst. Either way, no one can tell anything at all about the managing editor. Herein lies a classic problem.

Let's recap. The simple metadata found in RSS 0.9x makes a simple statement based on its element, the element's value, and the place of the element within the document. We know the `language` element refers to the `channel` that is one level above it within the XML document. We also know that in the example, the value of `language` is `en-gb`, and by understanding what the element and its value mean, we can make the statement that the channel is written in British English.

Going back to childhood grammar classes, it's apparent that this is a simple subject/predicate/object sentence:

> The channel (subject) has the language (predicate) British English (object).

This sort of statement is called a *triple*. Remember this word: you'll need it later. Now, these simple triples work well for most things within RSS 2.0, but they somewhat limit you to raw data values: things such as dates and language codes that are unambiguous and easily understood. Triples don't help one bit when you're talking about abstract concepts, such as subjects, or when referring to other entities, such as people. Plus, and this is key, without human interaction, the combination of an arbitrary element name, value, and position within the document is meaningless. If you disregard the ability to read English, you can't tell what any of the element names refer to, and you can't understand their values. As it stands, RSS 2.0's metadata can't be understood by machines, and the triples there are, though elegant, are limited when you take the human out of the equation. Without machine comprehension, you lose a great deal of potential utility from RSS feeds.

To start rectifying this situation, we need to define exactly what every word in the statement means. To do this, let's study the Uniform Resource Identifier (URI).

Using URIs in RSS

A URI is a string of characters using a particular syntax that identifies a resource. This resource can be anything that has an identity, whether it is tangible or not: a person, a book, a standard, a web site, a service, an email address, and so on. For example:

`mailto:ben@benhammersley.com`
: My URI

`http://www.w3.org/1999/xhtml`
: The URI for the concept of XHTML

`pop://pop.example.org`
: An example POP mailbox URI

You'll notice that these look very similar to URLs—the standard hyperlinks. You're right; URLs are a subset of URIs. There are, however, some major differences between the two.

Primarily, even though many URIs are named after, and closely resemble, network-contactable URLs, this doesn't mean that the resources they identify are retrievable via that network method: a person can be represented by a URI that looks like a URL, but pointing a browser at it doesn't retrieve the person. A concept—the XML standard, for example—has its own URI that starts with `http://`, but typing it into your address bar won't make your computer understand the XML standard. In fact, there is a whole debate, that we need not detain ourselves with in this book, over exactly what the URI represents: the thing, or a representation of the thing. It gets very philosophical and can be very interesting. But it's also well beyond the scope of actual useful code.

So, a URI simply provides a unique identifier for the resource, whatever it is. Granted, wherever possible, the URI gives you something useful (documentation on the resource, usually) if it is treated like a URL, but this isn't necessary.

Now, by allowing resources to be defined, we can make our metadata more robust. Let's reconsider the `managingEditor` example:

```
<managingEditor>editor@oreilly.com</managingEditor>
```

At the moment, we can't make any form of definitive statement about this, except what can be understood from being able to read English. We can't say for sure what `managingEditor` actually means (what context is this in?), nor can we understand what the value denotes. Is it an email address you can freely contact, or is it something else? You just can't tell.

If you assign URIs to each resource in this statement, you can give it more meaning:

```
<rdf:RDF xmlns:rdf="http://www.w3.org/1999/02/22-rdf-syntax-ns#"
         xmlns:RSS091="http://purl.org/rss/1.0/modules/rss091#"
         xmlns:rss="http://purl.org/rss/1.0/">

  <rss:channel rdf:about="http://www.example.org/example.rss">

    <RSS091:managingEditor>ben@benhammersley.com</RSS091:managingEditor>

  </rss:channel>

</rdf:RDF>
```

This example introduces a few more concepts, which we'll discuss in the next section. In the meantime, if you look at the emphasized code, you'll see that the `channel` gains a URI, denoted by the `rdf:about=""` attribute, and the `managingEditor` element becomes `RSS091:managingEditor`.

This immediately gives more context to the metadata. For one, the `channel` is uniquely defined. Second, the `managingEditor` element is associated with a concept of `RSS091`, which itself is given a URI to identify it uniquely. Third, the concept of a `channel` is associated with its own URI. From this information, you can make the following assertion:

> The channel (where the concept of channel is identified by the URI `http://purl.org/rss/1.0/`, and the channel itself is identified by the URI `http://www.example.org/example.rss`) has an attribute called `managingEditor` (which is part of a concept as defined by the URI `http://purl.org/rss/1.0/modules/rss091#`), whose value is `ben@benhammersley.com`.

Because you can know what the `managingEditor` element means in the context of the resource represented by the URI `http://purl.org/rss/1.0/modules/rss091#` (it's the guy in charge of the site the feed is from, but you'll have to wait until Chapter 6 to see why), you can now understand what the statement means. Even better than that, you can start to make definitive statements about the metadata within a document, and hence about the document itself. We, and other machines, can definitively state that the managing editor of this feed has the email address *ben@benhammersley.com*, because we've defined all the terms we are using. There is no ambiguity as to what each phrase means or to what it refers.

You probably noticed the additional lines of code within the example. This was your first look at RDF. The rest of this chapter deals with RDF, so let's take a look at it in some detail.

Resource Description Framework

This system of defining everything with URIs, and using this to describe the relationships between things, has been formalized in a system known as the Resource Description Framework (RDF). In this section, we'll look at enough RDF to give you a head start on the rest of the book. For a much deeper insight into RDF, take a look at *Practical RDF* (O'Reilly).

Because RDF is quite abstract—its ability to be written in different ways notwithstanding—in this chapter, we are going to look at what the RDF developers call the "data model," which we can call "the really simple version, in pictures."

Resources, PropertyTypes, and Properties

As before, within the data model, anything (an object, a person, a document, a concept, a section of a document, etc.) can have a URI. In RDF anything addressable with a URI is called a *resource*.

Some resources can be used as properties of other resources. For example, the concept of "Author" has a URI of its own (all concepts can), and other resources can have a property of "author." Such resources are called *PropertyTypes*.

A *property* is the combination of a resource, a PropertyType, and a value. For example, "The Author of *RSS and Atom* is Ben Hammersley." The value can be a string ("Ben Hammersley" in the previous example), or it can be another resource—for example, "Ben Hammersley (resource) has a home page (PropertyType) at *http://www.benhammersley.com* (resource)."

Nodes and Arcs

RDF's data model is most easily understood with diagrams, called *RDF graphs*, that show the relationships between resources, PropertyTypes, and properties. In these diagrams, the RDF world is split into nodes and arcs.

The resources and the values are the nodes, identified by their URIs. The PropertyTypes are the arcs, representing connections between nodes. The arcs themselves are also described by a URI.

Figure 5-1 is an RDF graph that shows the previous `managingEditor` example as three nodes connected by two arcs—two separate RDF triples. By convention, the subject is at the blunt end of the arrow, the property (or predicate) is the arrow itself, and the object is at the pointy end of the arrow.

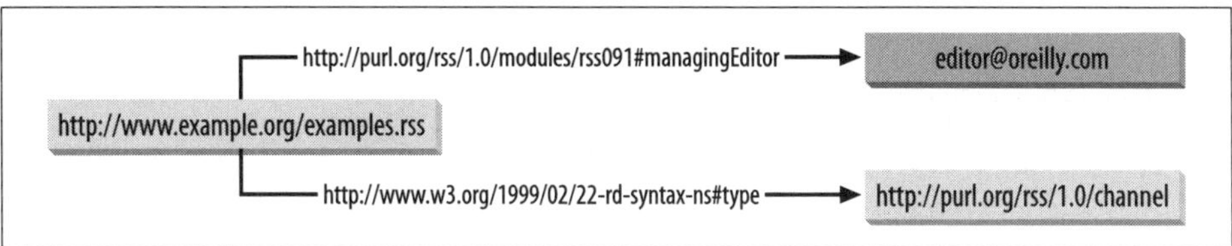

Figure 5-1. A simple RDF graph

In Figure 5-1, the subject node on the left, representing the URI `http://www.example.org/example.rss`, has a relationship with the object node on the right, representing the URI `editor@oreilly.com`, and this relationship is defined by the URI `http://purl.org/rss/1.0/modules/rss091#managingEditor`. The subject node also has a relationship with another object node, representing the URI `http://purl.org/rss/1.0/channel`, and that relationship is defined by the URI `http://www.w3.org/199/02/22-rdf-syntax-ns#type`.

What makes things interesting with RDF is that, as I've said before, a node can be both a subject and an object in a chain of node, arc, node, arc, node, and so on (or, to put it another way, resource, PropertyType, resource, PropertyType, resource, and so on). Consider the graph in Figure 5-2.

In this example, we've taken the RDF graph a step further. We've created a resource to represent the managing editor (you'll notice that the managing editor resource itself is anonymous—we haven't defined it with a URI yet, hence the empty rectangle—this isn't a problem), but have given it resources of its own, with PropertyType arcs whose URIs represent the managing editor's full name, home page, and email address.

This allows some definitive statements:

> The channel (where the concept of "channel" is identified by the URI `http://purl.org/rss/1.0/` and the channel itself is identified by the URI `http://www.example.org/example.rss`) has a resource called `managingEditor` (which is part of a concept defined

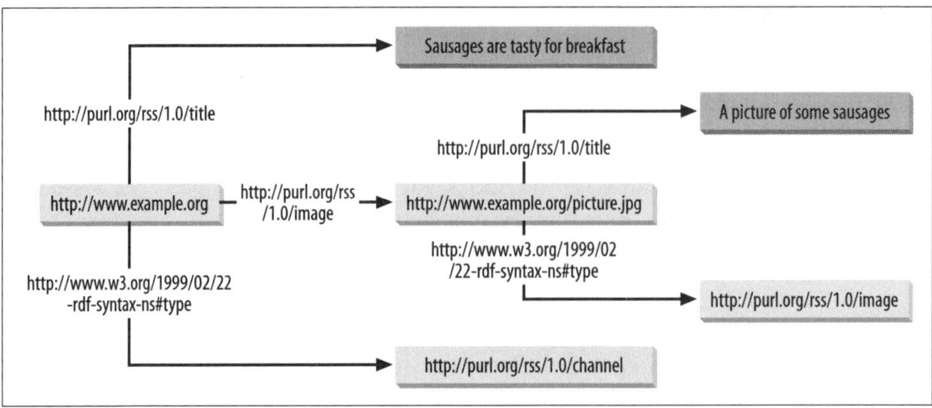

Figure 5-2. An RDF graph of the continuing example

> by the URI `http://purl.org/rss/1.0/modules/rss091#`), which in turn has one resource of its own, identified as a "home page" in the context of the URI `http://example.org/stuff/1.0/`, which is itself identified with the URI `http://jorge.oreilly.com/`. It also has two properties, `fullName` and `email`, both in the context of the URI `http://example.org/stuff/1.0/`, with the values `Jorge Grandehoncho` and `mailto:editor@oreilly.com`, respectively.

Or to put it simply:

> This channel has a managing editor whose name is `Jorge Grandehoncho`, whose home page is `http://jorge.oreilly.com/`, and whose email address is `editor@oreilly.com`.

You should bear two things in mind. First, the continuation of the RDF graph doesn't have to be constrained to one RDF document. The preceding example can be extended by including more RDF data at the network-retrievable version of the resource's URIs. So, while the RDF data for this book may refer to me solely by author, PropertyType, and a URI, the RDF at that URI can also refer to other things I have written, and those articles can contain RDF data that refers to the subjects of the articles. This distributed nature of RDF allows for vast fields of statements to be made definitively, and every additional set of RDF data increases the power of the whole considerably. RDF data is designed with aggregation in mind.

Second, and this will become key later on, because the PropertyTypes—the possible relationships between nodes—are represented by a URI, anyone can develop a set of elements. RDF vocabularies, therefore, can be developed to describe anything. And, as long as the URI is unique, RDF parsers won't get confused. Your descriptive powers, therefore, are endless: either an RDF vocabulary exists, or it is simple to make up your own.

Outside the scope of this book, there are also various languages for describing RDF vocabularies, or *ontologies*. When you add all of these together, you have what is called the *Semantic Web*.

Fitting RDF to RSS

This system for creating definitive statements from metadata fits perfectly with the aims of RSS. RSS feeds are, at their core, collections of resources with implicit relationships, and RDF is designed to describe these relationships. Also, and most powerfully, RDF makes these relationships explicit in a way that allows them to be used.

For example, the RDF graph can be traveled in any direction. The statement "This document (subject/resource) was written (predicate/PropertyType) by Ben Hammersley (object/resource)" can be read from the other end of the graph: "Ben Hammersley (subject/resource) wrote (predicate/PropertyType) this document (object/resource)."

So, you can query a database of RDF-based documents for "all the documents written by Ben Hammersley." If more triples are declared within the documents, you can query for "all the documents written by the man with the email address *ben@benhammersley.com*," or even "all the documents written by the man with the email address *ben@benhammersley.com*, and which are on the subject of dates." To take it even further, you can query for "all the documents written by the man with the email address *ben@benhammersley.com*, and which are on the subject of dates (in the context of small fruits, but not romantic encounters)." By taking different paths through an RDF graph, you can extract all sorts of data quite easily. You can also, by adding in RDF vocabularies not covered by RSS, do even more complicated searches, such as, "Find me all the articles written by any friend of Ben Hammersley, during any year that Manchester United won the English Premier League," and searches that are much more complex and interesting.

The ability of RDF to allow complex querying is one definite attraction, but the implications go further than that. Because RDF works just as well distributed as in a database, publishing an RDF version of RSS provides a remarkably useful entry point for the RDF world to access your site. Also, because the RDF vocabularies are easily definable, anyone can invent one. This makes RDF both wide ranging and fast growing, but in a way that doesn't require a single standards overlord. In the language of RSS 1.0, RDF is *extensible*.

RDF in XML

In preparation for the rest of this chapter, we need to look at how RDF is written in XML.

The Root Element

In all the examples in this book, I have given the RDF attributes a prefix of `rdf:`. This isn't necessary in many RDF documents, but it is the way they appear in RSS 1.0. For the sake of clarity, I will leave them in here too. Therefore, for reasons we will discuss later, the root element of an RDF document is:

```
<rdf:RDF xmlns:rdf="http://www.w3.org/1999/02/22-rdf-syntax-ns#">
...
</rdf:RDF>
```

As you will see further on, the root element can also contain the URIs of additional RDF vocabularies. The following examples use elements from the RSS 1.0 vocabulary.

<element rdf:about="URI OF ELEMENT">

The `rdf:about` attribute defines the URI for the element that contains it. Remember, it is like the subject in a sentence: everything else refers to it. For example:

```
<rdf:RDF xmlns:rdf="http://www.w3.org/1999/02/22-rdf-syntax-ns#"
        xmlns="http://purl.org/rss/1.0/"
>
<channel rdf:about="http://www.example.org/">
...
</channel>
</rdf:RDF>
```

means the `channel` resource is identified by the URI `http://www.example.org/`. Or, more to the point, everything within the `channel` element is referred to by `http://www.example.org`.

The contents of the element then describe the object referred to by the URI:

```
<rdf:RDF xmlns:rdf="http://www.w3.org/1999/02/22-rdf-syntax-ns#">
        xmlns="http://purl.org/rss/1.0/" >
<channel rdf:about="http://www.example.org">
<title>Sausages are tasty for breakfast</title>
<channel>
</rdf:RDF>
```

In this example, the resource `channel` identified by the URI `http://www.example.org` has a PropertyType `title` whose value is `Sausages are tasty for breakfast`. Nothing to object to there, then.

Remember, RDF describes the relationship between resources, their attributes, and other resources. You have to define all the resources, and the relationship PropertyTypes, before the RDF is valid and meaningful. The different objects are distinguished by unique URIs. So, every resource must have an `rdf:about` attribute when it is described.

<element rdf:resource="URI" />

Sometimes, the value of a property is another resource. To describe this, you can't just use the URI of the resource as the value of the element describing the

PropertyType, because nothing identifies it as a URI and not just as a string or a hyperlink. Instead, use the `rdf:resource` attribute:

```
<rdf:RDF xmlns:rdf="http://www.w3.org/1999/02/22-rdf-syntax-ns#">
         xmlns="http://purl.org/rss/1.0/" >

<channel rdf:about="http://www.example.org">
<title>Sausages are tasty for breakfast</title>
<image rdf:resource="http://www.example.org/picture.jpg" />
</channel>

</rdf:RDF>
```

In this example, the `channel` resource has a PropertyType `image` whose value is a resource, `http://www.example.org/picture.jpg`.

If you then want to describe the image itself, you need to create a description using the `rdf:about` attribute, as follows:

```
<rdf:RDF xmlns:rdf="http://www.w3.org/1999/02/22-rdf-syntax-ns#">
         xmlns="http://purl.org/rss/1.0/">

<channel rdf:about="http://www.example.org">
<title>Sausages are tasty for breakfast</title>
<image rdf:resource="http://www.example.org/picture.jpg" />
</channel>

<image rdf:about="http://www.example.org/picture.jpg">
<title>A picture of some sausages</title>
</image>

</rdf:RDF>
```

You can now begin to see the way RDF documents are structured. In this example, every concept, object, or thing is defined with reference to a URI. Figure 5-2 shows this example as an RDF graph, using the data model. Table 5-1 shows the relationships between subjects, predicates, and objects in Figure 5-2.

Table 5-1. The relationship illustrated in Figure 5-2

Subject	Predicate	Object
`http://www.example.org`	`http://purl.org/rss/1.0/title`	Sausages are tasty for breakfast
`http://www.example.org`	`http://purl.org/rss/1.0/image`	`http://www.example.org/picture.jpg`
`http://www.example.org`	`http://www.w3.org/1999/02/22-rdf-syntax-ns#type`	`http://purl.org/rss/1.0/channel`
`http://www.example.org/picture.jpg`	`http://purl.org/rss/1.0/title`	A picture of some sausages
`http://www.example.org/picture.jpg`	`http://www.w3.org/1999/02/22-rdf-syntax-ns#type`	`http://purl.org/rss/1.0/image`

RDF Containers

We've seen that RDF resources can also be used as properties with the use of the `rdf:resource` attribute. But what if you need to list more than one resource? For this, you need RDF containers. There are three to choose from, each with its own purpose.

rdf:Bag

`rdf:Bag` denotes an unordered list of resources. It is used like this:

```
<rdf:Bag>
  <rdf:li rdf:resource="URI" />
  <rdf:li rdf:resource="URI" />
  <rdf:li rdf:resource="URI" />
</rdf:Bag>
```

As you can see, each list item within the `rdf:Bag` is denoted with an `rdf:li` element, which takes the `rdf:resource` attribute. The order of the list items is unimportant and is ignored.

rdf:Seq

`rdf:Seq` denotes an ordered list of resources. The syntax is similar to `rdf:Bag`, but the order of the list is considered important:

```
<rdf:Seq>
  <rdf:li rdf:resource="URI Number 1" />
  <rdf:li rdf:resource="URI Number 2" />
  <rdf:li rdf:resource="URI Number 3" />
</rdf:Seq>
```

rdf:Alt

`rdf:Alt` describes a list of alternatives. The order is unimportant, except that the first list item is considered the default. The list items can contain other attributes to differentiate between them. For example, the `xml:lang` attribute denotes the language of the resource:

```
<rdf:Alt>
  <rdf:li xml:lang="en" rdf:resource="URI of English Version" />
  <rdf:li xml:lang="fr" rdf:resource="URI of French Version" />
  <rdf:li xml:lang="de" rdf:resource="URI of German Version" />
</rdf:Alt>
```

So, to continue our example, let's give the `channel` some `items`. Example 5-2 shows the first stage: you declare the items as resources connected to the `channel`. Example 5-3 includes the `items` themselves. Note how the URIs match correctly and pay attention to the position of the `items` and `item` elements with respect to the `channel`.

Example 5-2. A document with references to items

```
<rdf:RDF xmlns:rdf="http://www.w3.org/1999/02/22-rdf-syntax-ns#">
         xmlns="http://purl.org/rss/1.0/">
<channel rdf:about="http://www.example.org">
  <title>Sausages are tasty for breakfast</title>
  <image rdf:resource="http://www.example.org/picture.jpg" />

  <items>
    <rdf:Seq>
      <rdf:li rdf:resource="http://www.example.org/item1"/>
      <rdf:li rdf:resource="http://www.example.org/item2"/>
      <rdf:li rdf:resource="http://www.example.org/item3"/>
    </rdf:Seq>
  </items>
</channel>

<image rdf:about="http://www.example.org/picture.jpg">
  <title>A picture of some sausages</title>
</image>

</rdf:RDF>
```

Example 5-3. A document with the detailed items themselves

```
<rdf:RDF xmlns:rdf="http://www.w3.org/1999/02/22-rdf-syntax-ns#">
         xmlns="http://purl.org/rss/1.0/">
<channel rdf:about="http://www.example.org">
  <title>Sausages are tasty for breakfast</title>
  <image rdf:resource="http://www.example.org/picture.jpg" />

  <items>
    <rdf:Seq>
      <rdf:li rdf:resource="http://www.example.org/item1"/>
      <rdf:li rdf:resource="http://www.example.org/item2"/>
      <rdf:li rdf:resource="http://www.example.org/item3"/>
    </rdf:Seq>
  </items>
</channel>

<image rdf:about="http://www.example.org/picture.jpg">
  <title>A picture of some sausages</title>
</image>

<item rdf:about=" http://www.example.org/item1">
<title>This is item 1</title>
</item>

<item rdf:about=" http://www.example.org/item2>"
<title>This is item 2/title>
</item>

<item rdf:about=" http://www.example.org/item3>"
<title>This is item 3/title>
```

Example 5-3. A document with the detailed items themselves (continued)

```
</item>
</rdf:RDF>
```

Do you see the resemblance between Example 5-3 and a RSS 2.0 document? In this section, we have made something very close to RSS that has been depicted using RDF. This leads us to RSS 1.0, which is exactly that: RSS written as RDF.

Introducing RSS 1.0

Now that we're steeped in metadata and RDF syntax, it's time to move on to RSS 1.0. This standard, released in December 2000, brought two major changes to the RSS world: the reintroduction of RDF and with it an introduction of *namespaces*.

Nowadays, of course, both flavors of RSS have namespaced modules. But only RSS 1.0 is in RDF. Example 5-4 shows what it looks like.

Example 5-4. A sample RSS 1.0 document

```
<?xml version="1.0" encoding="utf-8"?>

<rdf:RDF  xmlns="http://purl.org/rss/1.0/"
  xmlns:rdf="http://www.w3.org/1999/02/22-rdf-syntax-ns#"
  xmlns:dc="http://purl.org/dc/elements/1.1/"
  xmlns:sy="http://purl.org/rss/1.0/modules/syndication/"
  xmlns:co="http://purl.org/rss/1.0/modules/company/"
  xmlns:ti="http://purl.org/rss/1.0/modules/textinput/"
>

<channel rdf:about="http://meerkat.oreillynet.com/?_fl=rss1.0">
  <title>Meerkat</title>
  <link>http://meerkat.oreillynet.com</link>
  <description>Meerkat: An Open Wire Service</description>
  <dc:publisher>The O'Reilly Network</dc:publisher>
  <dc:creator>Rael Dornfest (mailto:rael@oreilly.com)</dc:creator>
  <dc:rights>Copyright &#169; 2000 O'Reilly &amp; Associates, Inc.</dc:rights>
  <dc:date>2000-01-01T12:00+00:00</dc:date>
  <sy:updatePeriod>hourly</sy:updatePeriod>
  <sy:updateFrequency>2</sy:updateFrequency>
  <sy:updateBase>2000-01-01T12:00+00:00</sy:updateBase>

  <image rdf:resource="http://meerkat.oreillynet.com/icons/meerkat-powered.jpg" />
  <textinput rdf:resource="http://meerkat.oreillynet.com" />

  <items>
    <rdf:Seq>
      <rdf:li rdf:resource="http://c.moreover.com/click/here.pl?r123" />
    </rdf:Seq>
  </items>
</channel>
```

Example 5-4. A sample RSS 1.0 document (continued)

```
<image rdf:about="http://meerkat.oreillynet.com/icons/meerkat-powered.jpg">
  <title>Meerkat Powered!</title>
  <url>http://meerkat.oreillynet.com/icons/meerkat-powered.jpg</url>
  <link>http://meerkat.oreillynet.com</link>
</image>

<textinput rdf:about="http://meerkat.oreillynet.com">
  <title>Search Meerkat</title>
  <description>Search Meerkat's RSS Database...</description>
  <name>s</name>
  <link>http://meerkat.oreillynet.com/</link>
  <ti:function>search</ti:function>
  <ti:inputType>regex</ti:inputType>
</textinput>

<item rdf:about="http://c.moreover.com/click/here.pl?r123">
  <title>XML: A Disruptive Technology</title>
  <link>http://c.moreover.com/click/here.pl?r123</link>
  <dc:description>This the description of the article</dc:description>
  <dc:publisher>The O'Reilly Network</dc:publisher>
  <dc:creator>Simon St.Laurent (mailto:simonstl@simonstl.com)</dc:creator>
  <dc:rights>Copyright &#169; 2000 O'Reilly &amp; Associates, Inc.</dc:rights>
  <dc:subject>XML</dc:subject>
  <co:name>XML.com</co:name>
  <co:market>NASDAQ</co:market>
  <co:symbol>XML</co:symbol>
</item>
</rdf:RDF>
```

Walking Through an RSS 1.0 Document

At first glance, RSS 1.0 can look very complicated indeed. It isn't really, and breaking an example into chunks can help a great deal, so let's do that.

Throughout this section, we'll also examine RDF in XML syntax in general. An RSS 1.0 document is also a valid RDF document (though the reverse isn't always true, and you must not forget that RDF has many different ways of being written).

Example 5-4 is a simple RSS 1.0 feed with one item, an image, and a text-input section. The first line includes the standard XML declaration, declaring the document's encoding to be UTF-8:

```
<?xml version="1.0" encoding="utf-8"?>
```

The root element (the first line) is also the place to declare the additional namespaces that are used in the document, telling the parser that you're also going to use the vocabularies represented by these certain URIs. The required line already declares the namespace for all the core elements of RSS 1.0—the elements that appear without a colon—and the namespace for RDF:

```
<rdf:RDF xmlns="http://purl.org/rss/1.0/"
  xmlns:rdf="http://www.w3.org/1999/02/22-rdf-syntax-ns#"
```

```
    xmlns:dc="http://purl.org/dc/elements/1.1/"
    xmlns:sy="http://purl.org/rss/1.0/modules/syndication/"
    xmlns:co="http://purl.org/rss/1.0/modules/company/"
    xmlns:ti="http://purl.org/rss/1.0/modules/textinput/"
  >
```

Namespaces are represented by URIs. Nothing special needs to be at the namespace's URI (though by convention there is usually some documentation about the module);the only requirement is that the URI and the namespace are unique to each other. The syntax of a namespace declaration is simple and can be read aloud for greater understanding. For example, the line `xmlns:dc="http://purl.org/dc/elements/1.1/` is read as follows: "the XML namespace dc is associated with the URI `http://purl.org/dc/elements/1.1`."

Every namespace used in the RSS 1.0 document must be declared in the root element. For documents with many namespaces, this element can look very untidy, but a judicious application of spaces and new lines can make it easier to read.

Now let's look at the `channel` element:

```
<channel rdf:about="http://meerkat.oreillynet.com/?_fl=rss1.0">
  <title>Meerkat</title>
  <link>http://meerkat.oreillynet.com</link>
  <description>Meerkat: An Open Wire Service</description>
  <dc:publisher>The O'Reilly Network</dc:publisher>
  <dc:creator>Rael Dornfest (mailto:rael@oreilly.com)</dc:creator>
  <dc:rights>Copyright &#169; 2000 O'Reilly &amp; Associates, Inc.</dc:rights>
  <dc:date>2000-01-01T12:00+00:00</dc:date>
  <sy:updatePeriod>hourly</sy:updatePeriod>
  <sy:updateFrequency>2</sy:updateFrequency>
  <sy:updateBase>2000-01-01T12:00+00:00</sy:updateBase>
```

In the first half of the `channel` element, you can see the main differences in structure between RSS 0.9x and RSS 1.0. First, every top-level element (`channel`, `item`, `image`, `text input`) has an `rdf:about` attribute. This denotes the URI of that resource in the scope of RDF.

Second, you can see subelements of the `channel` using namespaces. In this example, dc: and sy: (the Dublin Core and Syndication modules) are in use.

Next comes a major departure from RSS 0.9x. The `image` and `textinput` elements of RSS 1.0 aren't contained within the `channel`. Rather, `channel` contains a pointer to their objects, which are elsewhere in the RSS 1.0 document, at the same level as `channel`. The pointers are RDF notation, using the `rdf:resource` attribute:

```
<image rdf:resource="http://meerkat.oreillynet.com/icons/meerkat-powered.jpg" />

<textinput rdf:resource="http://meerkat.oreillynet.com" />
```

In the same way, within RSS 1.0 (unlike RSS 0.9x), `channel` doesn't contain any `item` elements. It does, however, contain an `items` element within which sits an RDF list of all the item elements that exist within the whole document. Again, these are simply pointers that provide the correct RDF descriptions:

```
<items>
  <rdf:Seq>
    <rdf:li rdf:resource="http://c.moreover.com/click/here.pl?r123" />
  </rdf:Seq>
</items>

</channel>
```

Note that the channel element is closed here. Unlike RSS 0.9x, in RSS 1.0, channel doesn't encompass the entire document. Once it has defined its own metadata and pointed to the items, image, and textinput objects, its job is done.

The image, textinput, and item elements are similar to the RSS 0.9x equivalents, differing only in that they declare the rdf:about attribute, as previously discussed, and allow for additional namespaced subelements from the optional modules:

```
<image rdf:about="http://meerkat.oreillynet.com/icons/meerkat-powered.jpg">
  <title>Meerkat Powered!</title>
  <url>http://meerkat.oreillynet.com/icons/meerkat-powered.jpg</url>
  <link>http://meerkat.oreillynet.com</link>
</image>

<textinput rdf:about="http://meerkat.oreillynet.com">
  <title>Search Meerkat</title>
  <description>Search Meerkat's RSS Database...</description>
  <name>s</name>
  <link>http://meerkat.oreillynet.com/</link>
  <ti:function>search</ti:function>
  <ti:inputType>regex</ti:inputType>
</textinput>

<item rdf:about="http://c.moreover.com/click/here.pl?r123">
  <title>XML: A Disruptive Technology</title>
  <link>http://c.moreover.com/click/here.pl?r123</link>
  <dc:description>This the description of the article</dc:description>
  <dc:publisher>The O'Reilly Network</dc:publisher>
  <dc:creator>Simon St.Laurent (mailto:simonstl@simonstl.com)</dc:creator>
  <dc:rights>Copyright &#169; 2000 O'Reilly &amp; Associates, Inc.</dc:rights>
  <dc:subject>XML</dc:subject>
  <co:name>XML.com</co:name>
  <co:market>NASDAQ</co:market>
  <co:symbol>XML</co:symbol>
</item>
</rdf:RDF>
```

The Specification in Detail

This section is based on the RSS 1.0 Specification, Version 1.3.4, dated May 30, 2001. The full document is available at *http://purl.org/rss/1.0/spec*.

The Basic Structure

As we've seen, RSS 1.0's structure differs from the earlier versions of RSS by bringing the item, image, and textinput elements to the same level as channel. Examples 5-5 and 5-6 show this difference in their basic structures.

Example 5-5. The basic structure of RSS 0.9x

```
<rss>
<channel>
   <image/>
   <textinput/>
   <item/>
   <item/>
   <item/>
</channel>
</rss>
```

Example 5-6. The basic structure of RSS 1.0

```
<rdf>
  <channel/>
  <image/>
  <textinput/>
  <item/>
  <item/>
  <item/>
</rdf>
```

This difference both results from, and necessitates, the use of RDF notation to define the relationships between the elements.

The Root Element

The root element of an RSS 1.0 document is always built upon this line:

```
<rdf:RDF xmlns="http://purl.org/rss/1.0/"
         xmlns:rdf="http://www.w3.org/1999/02/22-rdf-syntax-ns#">
```

Any additional namespace declarations are inserted within this line. When designing your feed, and again after creating it, it is worth checking that all the namespaces you use are declared in the root element.

<channel rdf:about=""> (a Subelement of rdf:RDF)

The next level begins with the required channel element. This element must look like this:

```
<channel rdf:about="
URI that identifies the channel">
```

```
Subelements

</content>
```

The contents of the rdf:about attribute must represent the feed itself. The specification states that this may be either the URL of the feed itself or the URL of the site it represents. Common usage seems to favor the URL of the feed itself—i.e., the URI.

Required subelements of channel

channel can contain many subelements. The additional modules, detailed in Chapter 6, define about 30 optional additions to these core subelements:

title
: The title of the feed, with a suggested maximum of 40 characters

description
: A summary of the feed, with a suggested maximum of 400 characters

link
: The URL of the site the feed represents

The following elements are required only if the feed contains the objects to which they refer. RSS 1.0 doesn't require an image, text input, or even any items to be present. However, the feed will be very dull indeed without at least one of these elements.

<image rdf:resource= *"URI of the image"* />
: This line creates the RDF relationship between the channel and any <image> within the RSS 1.0 feed. The URI within the rdf:resource must therefore be the same as the URI within the rdf:about element (which we'll discuss later) contained within the image element (i.e., the URL of the image file itself).

<textinput rdf:resource= *"URI of the text input"* />
: This line creates the RDF relationship between the channel and any <textinput> element within the feed. The URI within the rdf:resource must, again, be the same as the URI within the rdf:about element of the textinput element later in the feed. This URL should be the URL to which a text-input submission will be directed.

items
: The items element is tremendously important and pleasingly simple yet seemingly complicated. It defines the RDF relationship between the channel and any item found within the RSS 1.0 document. The URIs should be the same as the rdf:resource attribute of each of the items later in the document, so they should be identical to the value of the link subelement of the item element, if possible. For example:

```
<items>
<rdf:Seq>
<rdf:li resource="
URI of item 1" />
```

```
<rdf:li resource="
URI of item 2" />
...
</rdf:Seq>
</items>
```

<image rdf:resource=""> (a Subelement of rdf:RDF)

Although optional, image is used quite a bit. According to the specification, "this image should be of a format supported by the majority of web browsers. While the later 0.91 specification allowed for a width of 1–144 and height of 1–400, convention (and the 0.9 specification) dictate 88 × 31."

This element takes the rdf:resource attribute. This attribute should be the URL of the image file, and it should be mirrored within the image subelement of channel.

The element also takes three mandatory subelements in addition to the optional subelements available through the modules we will discuss in Chapter 6. The mandatory subelements are:

title
: The alternative text (alt attribute) associated with the channel's image tag when rendered as HTML. Text should be no more than 40 characters.

url
: The URL of the image file. This also appears within the rdf:resource attribute and is mirrored within the <image> subelement of the <channel>.

link
: The URL to which the image file will link when the feed is rendered in HTML. This link is normally to the page the feed represents, so it is usually identical to the link subelement of channel.

<textinput rdf:about=""> (a Subelement of rdf:RDF)

This element, like its RSS 2.0 counterpart, provides a way to describe a form of input for delivering data to a URL that can deal with an HTTP GET request (a CGI script, for example). It's entirely optional, however, as the specification states:

> The field is typically used as a search box or subscription form—among others. While this is of some use when RSS documents are rendered as channels and accompanied by human readable title and description, the ambiguity in automatic determination of meaning of this overloaded element renders it otherwise not particularly useful. RSS 1.0 therefore suggests either deprecation or augmentation with some form of resource discovery of this element in future versions while maintaining it for backward compatibility with RSS 0.9.

Nevertheless, it is still used. It takes an rdf:about attribute, which should point to the URL contained within its own link subelement, and requires four mandatory subelements:

title
: The label for the Submit button. It has a maximum of 40 characters.

description
: Text to explain what the textinput actually does. It has a maximum of 100 characters.

name
: The name of the text object that is passed to the CGI script. It has a maximum of 500 characters.

link
: The URL of the CGI script. It has a maximum of 500 characters.

<item rdf:about=""> (a Subelement of rdf:RDF)

The item subelement is where the real work gets done. Like its RSS 2.0 namesake, the item subelement contains the details of each URL listed within the feed, along with metadata, description, and so on. Unlike RSS 0.9x, however, RSS 1.0's item can point to many different things—basically anything that can be represented by a URL, even if it isn't an ordinary page.

Because of this capability, the item subelement is most affected by the use of optional modules. We'll deal with those in Chapter 6; for now, here are its core subelements:

title
: The title of the object. The maximum length is 100 characters.

link
: The URL of the object. The maximum is 500 characters.

description
: A synopsis of the object. This element is optional. The maximum length is 500 characters, and it must be plain text only (no HTML).

The Simplest Possible RSS 1.0 Feed

Whatever you do, when you produce an RSS 1.0 feed, it has to contain at least all of the fields in Example 5-7.

Example 5-7. The simplest possible RSS 1.0 feed

```
<?xml version="1.0" encoding="UTF-8"?>
<rdf:RDF xmlns:rdf="http://www.w3.org/1999/02/22-rdf-syntax-ns#">
  <channel rdf:about="http://example.org/index.html">
    <title>The Simplest Feed</title>
    <link>http://example.org/index.html</link>
    <description>The Simplest Possible RSS 1.0 Feed</description>

    <items>
      <rdf:Seq>
```

Example 5-7. The simplest possible RSS 1.0 feed (continued)

```
        <rdf:li rdf:resource="http://example.org/example_entry" />
      </rdf:Seq>
    </items>

  </channel>

  <item rdf:about="http://example.org/example_entry">
    <title></title>
    <link>http://example.org/example_entry</link>
  </item>
</rdf:RDF>
```

Creating RSS 1.0 Feeds

Despite the additional complexity of the RDF attributes, the methods for creating RSS 1.0 feeds are similar to those used to create RSS 2.0 feeds (discussed in Chapter 4).

Creating RSS 1.0 with Perl

The XML::RSS module used in Chapter 4 also works for RSS 1.0, with a few changes to the scripts. The script in Example 5-8 produces the feed shown, in turn, in Example 5-9.

Example 5-8. Creating RSS 1.0 with XML::RSS

```
#!/usr/bin/perl -w

use XML::RSS;

my $rss = new XML::RSS( version => '1.0' );

$rss->channel(
    title       => "The Title of the Feed",
    link        => "http://www.oreilly.com/example/",
    description => "The description of the Feed",
    dc          => {
        date      => "2000-08-23T07:00+00:00",
        subject   => "Linux Software",
        creator   => 'scoop@freshmeat.net',
        publisher => 'scoop@freshmeat.net',
        rights    => "Copyright 1999, Freshmeat.net",
        language  => "en-us",
    },
);

$rss->image(
    title => "Oreilly",
    url   => "http://meerkat.oreillynet.com/icons/meerkat-powered.jpg",
```

Example 5-8. Creating RSS 1.0 with XML::RSS (continued)

```
    link  => "http://www.oreilly.com/example/",
    dc    => { creator => "G. Raphics (graphics at freshmeat.net)", },
);

$rss->textinput(
    title       => "Search",
    description => "Search the site",
    name        => "query",
    link        => "http://www.oreilly.com/example/search.cgi"
);

$rss->add_item(
    title       => "Example Entry 1",
    link        => "http://www.oreilly.com/example/entry1",
    description => 'blah blah',
    dc          => { subject => "Software", },
);

$rss->add_item(
    title       => "Example Entry 2",
    link        => "http://www.oreilly.com/example/entry2",
    description => 'blah blah'
);

$rss->add_item(
    title       => "Example Entry 3",
    link        => "http://www.oreilly.com/example/entry3",
    description => 'blah blah'
);

$rss->save("example.rdf");
```

Example 5-9. The RSS feed produced by Example 5-8

```
<?xml version="1.0" encoding="UTF-8"?>

<rdf:RDF
 xmlns:rdf="http://www.w3.org/1999/02/22-rdf-syntax-ns#"
 xmlns="http://purl.org/rss/1.0/"
 xmlns:taxo="http://purl.org/rss/1.0/modules/taxonomy/"
 xmlns:dc="http://purl.org/dc/elements/1.1/"
 xmlns:syn="http://purl.org/rss/1.0/modules/syndication/"
 xmlns:admin="http://webns.net/mvcb/"
>

<channel rdf:about="http://www.oreilly.com/example/">
<title>The Title of the Feed</title>
<link>http://www.oreilly.com/example/</link>
<description>The description of the Feed</description>
<dc:language>en-us</dc:language>
<dc:rights>Copyright 1999, Freshmeat.net</dc:rights>
<dc:date>2000-08-23T07:00+00:00</dc:date>
```

Example 5-9. The RSS feed produced by Example 5-8 (continued)

```
<dc:publisher>scoop@freshmeat.net</dc:publisher>
<dc:creator>scoop@freshmeat.net</dc:creator>
<dc:subject>Linux Software</dc:subject>
<items>
 <rdf:Seq>
  <rdf:li rdf:resource="http://www.oreilly.com/example/entry1" />
  <rdf:li rdf:resource="http://www.oreilly.com/example/entry2" />
  <rdf:li rdf:resource="http://www.oreilly.com/example/entry3" />
 </rdf:Seq>
</items>
<image rdf:resource="http://meerkat.oreillynet.com/icons/meerkat-powered.jpg" />
<textinput rdf:resource="http://www.oreilly.com/example/search.cgi" />
</channel>

<image rdf:about="http://meerkat.oreillynet.com/icons/meerkat-powered.jpg">
<title>Oreilly</title>
<url>http://meerkat.oreillynet.com/icons/meerkat-powered.jpg</url>
<link>http://www.oreilly.com/example/</link>
<dc:creator>G. Raphics (graphics at freshmeat.net)</dc:creator>
</image>

<item rdf:about="http://www.oreilly.com/example/entry1">
<title>Example Entry 1</title>
<link>http://www.oreilly.com/example/entry1</link>
<description>blah blah</description>
<dc:subject>Software</dc:subject>
</item>

<item rdf:about="http://www.oreilly.com/example/entry2">
<title>Example Entry 2</title>
<link>http://www.oreilly.com/example/entry2</link>
<description>blah blah</description>
</item>

<item rdf:about="http://www.oreilly.com/example/entry3">
<title>Example Entry 3</title>
<link>http://www.oreilly.com/example/entry3</link>
<description>blah blah</description>
</item>

<textinput rdf:about="http://www.oreilly.com/example/search.cgi">
<title>Search</title>
<description>Search the site</description>
<name>query</name>
<link>http://www.oreilly.com/example/search.cgi</link>
</textinput>
</rdf:RDF>
```

The differences between creating RSS 2.0 and RSS 1.0 with `XML::RSS` are slight. Just make sure you declare the correct version, like so:

```
my $rss = new XML::RSS (version => '1.0');
```

The module takes care of itself, for the most part. If you use other namespaces, you must surround them with their namespace prefix. In this section, the script adds six elements that are part of the Dublin Core module into the `channel` section of the feed:

```
$rss->channel(
    title       => "The Title of the Feed",
    link        => "http://www.oreilly.com/example/",
    description => "The description of the Feed",
    dc          => {
        date       => "2000-08-23T07:00+00:00",
        subject    => "Linux Software",
        creator    => 'scoop@freshmeat.net',
        publisher  => 'scoop@freshmeat.net',
        rights     => "Copyright 1999, Freshmeat.net",
        language   => "en-us",
    },
);
```

`XML::RSS` comes with built-in support for the Dublin Core, Syndication, and Taxonomy modules. You can easily add support for any other module:

```
$rss->add_module(prefix=>'my', uri=>'http://purl.org/my/rss/module/');
```

This line does two things. First, it makes the module add the correct namespace declaration to the root element of the document (here, it adds the line `xmlns:my=http://purl.org/my/rss/module/`, but you should replace the prefix and the URI with the correct ones for your module). Second, it allows you to use the same syntax as the preceding Dublin Core example to add your elements to the feed.

```
$rss->channel(
    title       => "The Title of the Feed",
    link        => "http://www.oreilly.com/example/",
    description => "The description of the Feed",
    dc          => {
        date       => "2000-08-23T07:00+00:00",
        subject    => "Linux Software",
        creator    => 'scoop@freshmeat.net',
        publisher  => 'scoop@freshmeat.net',
        rights     => "Copyright 1999, Freshmeat.net",
        language   => "en-us",
    },
    my          => {
        element    => 'value',
    },
);
```

The rest of the script is identical to the RSS 2.0 creation script using the same module.

Producing RSS 1.0 with PHP

The FeedCreator class in Chapter 4 can produce RSS 1.0 documents. In fact, it's trivially easy to do so with the code in Chapter 4. Just change the last line in Example 5-10.

Example 5-10. A example of PHP code that produces an RSS 1.0 feed

```
<?
include("feedcreator.class.php");

$rss = new UniversalFeedCreator( );
$rss->title = "Example Feed";
$rss->description = "This is the feed description";
$rss->link = "http://www.example.com/";

// Image section
$image = new FeedImage( );
$image->title = "example logo";
$image->url = "http://www.example.com/images/logo.gif";
$image->link = "http://www.example.com";
$image->description = "Visit Example.com!";
$rss->image = $image;

// Item Loop
$item = new FeedItem( );
$item->title = "Entry one";
$item->link = "http://www.example.com/entryone";
$item->description = "This is the content of the first entry";
$rss->addItem($item);
// End Item Loop

echo $rss->saveFeed("RSS1.0", "news/feed.rdf");
?>
```

Once again, to remind you, the methods are named after the RSS elements, so it's easy to see what's happening. There's really very little extra to say that hasn't been covered in Chapter 4: namespaced modules are trickier, and require some extra code. We'll deal with this, and RSS 1.0 modules in great detail, in the next chapter.

CHAPTER 6

RSS 1.0 Modules

How can one conceive of a one-party system in a country that has 246 varieties of cheese?
—Charles de Gaulle

The modularization of RSS 1.0, and later of RSS 2.0, was the most important change the standard underwent since its inception. While the reintroduction of RDF into RSS 1.0 allowed you to create graphs of the relationships between RSS items and their attributes, modularization gives you many more attributes to play with in the first place. By using modules, both flavors of RSS can be extended without having to rewrite the core specification and without having to get consensus from the entire RSS community. It becomes a whole lot more useful. In this chapter, we will look at different modules available for RSS 1.0, by far the standard with the most module support.

Module Status

There is a great deal of confusion surrounding the status of individual modules within RSS 1.0. What, people often ask, makes a module "official" or not. The RSS 1.0 specification itself states that:

> Modules are classified as Proposed until accepted as Standard by members of the rss-dev working group or a sub-membership thereof focused on the area addressed by the module

However, this is overblowing the situation somewhat. The rss-dev working group, of which I am a member, has never actually considered the issue beyond this. Modules have, since the beginning of the specification, been allowed to flourish or die on their own merits and have never really undergone any form of accreditation process since the beginning.

So, currently there are only three modules classified as Standard—Dublin Core, Syndication, and Content—and more than 20 others that are Proposed. Considering that this indicates only the lack of a schedule for actually voting on the modules and that we have no real idea of what the voting really means anyway, you can safely consider all modules equally useful, at least in terms of some arbitrary rules body saying they're okay. In reality, working code trumps Working Groups: go ahead and use anything you like. RSS 2.0 never had this restriction, and the same philosophy applies.

Support for Modules in Common Applications

Although the modules mentioned herein are in use in at least one installation somewhere in the world, the vast majority of them aren't supported by the most common newsreader applications. Dublin Core is supported by most, but the others are variable in the extreme. This isn't to say that they aren't useful. Far from it. They are just used mostly within private organizations, with private software producing and parsing them. Just because you don't see many people using a module doesn't mean they aren't. But conversely, just because you produce data in a module doesn't mean the general public can read it. These things evolve.

mod_admin

The Administration module, written by Aaron Swartz and Ken Macleod, provides information about the feed's owner and the toolkit used to produce it. This helps the RSS user work with his provider to get things right, and it helps the RSS community at large identify problems with certain systems.

Recommended Usage

It is good manners to include this module as a matter of course. The data isn't dynamically created, so it can be included within a template and just left to do its job.

Namespace

The namespace prefix for this module is `admin:`, which should point to `http://webns.net/mvcb/`. Therefore, the root element and the RSS 1.0 module containing `mod_admin` should look like this:

```
<rdf:RDF xmlns:rdf="http://www.w3.org/1999/02/22-rdf-syntax-ns#"
xmlns="http://purl.org/rss/1.0/"
xmlns:admin="http://webns.net/mvcb/">
```

Elements

The `mod_admin` elements occur as subelements of `channel` only. They consist of:

`<admin:errorReportsTo rdf:resource="` *`URI`* `" />`
: The URI is typically a `mailto:` URL for contacting the feed administrator to report technical errors.

`<admin:generatorAgent rdf:resource=" URI" />`
: The URI is the home page of the software that generates the feed. If possible, this should be a page that specifies a version number within the URI—for example, `http://www.example.org/megaapp/version_1.0/index.html`.

Example

```
<?xml version="1.0" encoding="utf-8"?>
<rdf:RDF xmlns:rdf="http://www.w3.org/1999/02/22-rdf-syntax-ns#"
        xmlns="http://purl.org/rss/1.0/"
        xmlns:admin="http://webns.net/mvcb/">
  <channel rdf:about="http://rss.benhammersley.com/index.rdf">
    <title>Content Syndication with RSS</title>
    <link>http://rss.benhammersley.com</link>
    <description>Content Syndication with RSS, the blog</description>
    <admin:errorReportsTo rdf:resource="mailto:ben@benhammersley.com"/>
    <admin:generatorAgent rdf:resource="http://www.movabletype.org/?v=2.1"/>
...
```

mod_aggregation

The Aggregation module plays a small but useful part in the lifecycle of information passing through the Web. It allows news aggregators, such as those covered in Chapter 2, to display the sources of their items. These services gather `items` from many other sources and group them by subject. `mod_aggregation` lets you know where they originated.

This, of course, works over generations: as long as the `mod_aggregation` elements are respected, a Meerkat feed that uses a Snewp `item` from a Moreover feed that is itself an aggregation (for example) still has the original source credited. As long as the `mod_aggregation` elements are left in place, the information is preserved. There isn't, as yet, any feature for describing an aggregation history, however; you only know about the primary source. You also can't necessarily trust the contents of the element either, but this is more a social issue than a technological one.

Aggregators are the only people generating these elements; if you're building such a system, consider including them. The act of parsing such elements, however, is good for everyone. One can easily envisage an HTML representation of an RSS 1.0 feed with a "link via x" section. This is already done manually by many weblog owners, so why not include the feature in your RSS parsing scripts?

Namespace

`mod_aggregation` takes ag: as its prefix and `http://purl.org/rss/modules/aggregation` as its identifying URI. Therefore, an RSS 1.0 root element that uses it should look like this:

```
<?xml version="1.0"?>
<rdf:RDF xmlns:rdf="http://www.w3.org/1999/02/22-rdf-syntax-ns#"
        xmlns="http://purl.org/rss/1.0/"
        xmlns:ag="http://purl.org/rss/1.0/modules/aggregation/" >
```

Elements

mod_aggregation's elements are all subelements of item. There are three, and they are all mandatory if you are using the module:

ag:source
: The name of the source of the item (no character limit)

ag:sourceURL
: The URL of the source of the item (no character limit)

ag:timestamp
: The time the item was published by the original source, in the ISO 8601 standard (ccyy-mm-ddThh:mm:ss+hh:mm)

Example

```
<?xml version="1.0"?>
<rdf:RDF xmlns:rdf="http://www.w3.org/1999/02/22-rdf-syntax-ns#"
         xmlns="http://purl.org/rss/1.0/"
         xmlns:ag="http://purl.org/rss/1.0/modules/aggregation/"
>
    <channel rdf:about="http://meerkat.oreillynet.com/?_fl=rss1.0">
    <title>Meerkat</title>
    <link>http://meerkat.oreillynet.com</link>
    <description>Meerkat: An Open Wire Service</description>
  </channel>
    <items>
    <rdf:Seq>
      <rdf:li rdf:resource="http://c.moreover.com/click/here.pl?r123" />
    </rdf:Seq>
  </items>
   <item rdf:about="http://c.moreover.com/click/here.pl?r123" >
    <title>XML: A Disruptive Technology</title>
<link>http://c.moreover.com/click/here.pl?r123</link>
    <description>
    XML is placing increasingly heavy loads on the existing technical
    infrastructure of the Internet.
    </description>
    <ag:source>XML.com</ag:source>
    <ag:sourceURL>http://www.xml.com</ag:sourceURL>
    <ag:timestamp>2000-01-01T12:00+00:00</ag:timestamp>
  </item>
</rdf:RDF>
```

mod_annotation

mod_annotation is the smallest module. It consists of one element, which refers to a URL where a discussion of the item is being held. It might point to a discussion group, a commenting service, Usenet, an Annotea service, etc.

For sites that host such discussions, the addition of this module into the RSS feed should be simple and worthwhile. Weblogs, for example, might need to point the element only to the URL of the main entry page for a particular item.

If you want to parse this module into HTML, you should, as with many of these modules, have no problems simply assigning a separate div or span for the contents of the element, wrapping it within an <a href=" *URL* " >, and formatting it as you wish. This would probably make sense only if your parser is also taking notice of either the description element or the data provided by mod_content, simply because it is hard to have a discussion based solely on a headline.

Namespace

mod_annotation is identified by the namespace prefix annotate: and the URI http://purl.org/rss/1.0/modules/annotate/. Hence, the root element looks like this:

```
<rdf:RDF xmlns:rdf="http://www.w3.org/1999/02/22-rdf-syntax-ns#"
         xmlns="http://purl.org/rss/1.0/"
         xmlns:annotate="http://purl.org/rss/1.0/modules/annotate/"
>
```

Element

There's only one element, a subelement of item, and here it is:

<annotate:reference rdf:resource=" *URL* " />

The URL points to a discussion on the item.

However, this element can also take subelements of its own from the Dublin Core modules, mod_dublincore and mod_DCTerms. We'll see these modules soon, but Example 6-3 will give you an idea.

Do you see how the namespaces system works? Example 6-3 shows a feed using only the mod_annotation system. We've added one additional namespace and used the element correctly. In , we want to use another module to describe something in terms that the currently available elements can't. So we decide upon mod_dublincore, add in the namespace declaration, and go ahead.

Also notice that in Example 6-3, annotate is a one-line element, with a closing />, whereas in Example 6-4, annotate contains the mod_dublincore elements before closing. This means that the mod_dublincore elements refer to annotate, not to the item or channel. As you'll see, mod_dublincore can get addictive, and you might find yourself describing everything in your feed. This isn't bad at all, but it may get confusing. By paying attention to which elements are within which, you can see what is happening.

Examples

The following example shows mod_annotation in action:

```
<rdf:RDF xmlns:rdf="http://www.w3.org/1999/02/22-rdf-syntax-ns#"
         xmlns="http://purl.org/rss/1.0/"
         xmlns:annotate="http://purl.org/rss/1.0/modules/annotate/"
>
<item rdf:about="http://www.example.com/item1">
    <title>RSS 0.9 or RSS 1.0...Discuss</title>
    <link>http://www.example.com/item1</link>
    <annotate:reference rdf:resource="http://www.example.com/discuss/item1"/>
</item>
```

The following example shows mod_annotation inside an item element:

```
<rdf:RDF xmlns:rdf="http://www.w3.org/1999/02/22-rdf-syntax-ns#"
         xmlns="http://purl.org/rss/1.0/"
         xmlns:annotate="http://purl.org/rss/1.0/modules/annotate/"
         xmlns:dc="http://purl.org/dc/elements/1.1/"
>
. . .
<item rdf:about="http://www.example.com/item1">
    <title>RSS 0.9 or RSS 1.0...Discuss</title>
    <link>http://www.example.com/item1</link>
<annotate:reference rdf:resource="http://www.example.com/discuss/item1">
      <dc:subject>XML</dc:subject>
  <dc:description>A discussion group on the subject in hand</dc:description>
</annotate>
</item>
```

mod_audio

mod_audio is the first of the RSS 1.0 modules so far that points at something other than a text page. It is specifically designed for the syndication of MP3 files—its elements matching those of the ID3 tag standard—but it can be used for any audio format.

It was designed by Brian Aker, who also wrote the mp3 module for the Apache web server. That Apache module not only streams MP3s from a server, but also creates RSS playlists.

If you syndicate audio or point at feeds that syndicate audio, this is a must. Also, consider using mod_streaming, the module for streaming.

Namespace

mod_audio uses the prefix audio: and is indentified by the URI http://media.tangent.org/rss/1.0/. Hence:

```
<rdf:RDF xmlns:rdf="http://www.w3.org/1999/02/22-rdf-syntax-ns#"
          xmlns="http://purl.org/rss/1.0/"
          xmlns:audio="http://media.tangent.org/rss/1.0/" >
```

Elements

mod_audio elements are all subelements of item. None are mandatory to the module, but you should make an effort to include as many as possible per track.

audio:songname
: The title of the song

audio:artist
: The name of the artist

audio:album
: The name of the album

audio:year
: The year of the track

audio:comment
: Any text comment on the track

`audio:genre`
: The genre of the track (should match `genre_id`)

`audio:recording_time`
: The length of the track in seconds

`audio:bitrate`
: The bit rate of the track, in Kbps

`audio:track`
: The number of the track on the album

`audio:genre_id`
: The genre ID number, as defined by the ID3 standard

`audio:price`
: The price of the track, if you're selling it

Example

```
<item rdf:about="http://www.example.com/boyband.mp3" >
     <title>BoyBand's Latest Track!</title>
     <description>The latest track from the fab five.</description>
     <link>http://www.example.com/boyband.mp3</link>
     <audio:songname>One Likes to Get Funky</audio:songname>
     <audio:artist>BoyBand</audio:artist>
     <audio:album>Not Just Another</audio:album>
     <audio:year>2005</audio:year>
     <audio:genre>Top 40</audio:genre>
     <audio:genre_id>60</audio:genre_id>
</item>
```

Applications

It can be said that some of these elements are superfluous because they can be replaced by other elements (for example, `audio:songname` could be replaced by `title`). This is true in many cases, but it is much neater to use a simple MP3 tag-reading script to generate the RSS and map ID3 elements across directly. There are many ID3 tag-reading libraries available, including Chris Nandor's `MP3::Info` for Perl.

mod_changedpage

`mod_changedpage` does for RSS 1.0 what the `cloud` element does for RSS 0.9x: it introduces a form of Publish and Subscribe. We'll discuss Publish and Subscribe in detail in Chapter 9, but basically it enables a system in which you can "subscribe" to a feed and be notified when something new is published.

`mod_changedpage` uses only one element, which points to a *changedPage server*. Users wishing to be told when the feed has updated send an HTTP POST request of a certain format to this server. Upon updating, this server sends a similar POST request back to the user. The user's client then knows about the update. Again, Chapter 9 examines this in detail.

Namespace

mod_changedpage takes the namespace prefix cp: and is identified by the URI http://my.theinfo.org/changed/1.0/rss/. Hence, its declaration looks like this:

```
<rdf:RDF xmlns:rdf="http://www.w3.org/1999/02/22-rdf-syntax-ns#"
         xmlns="http://purl.org/rss/1.0/"
         xmlns:cp="http://my.theinfo.org/changed/1.0/rss/">
```

Element

mod_changedpage takes only one element, a subelement of channel :

<cp:server rdf:resource="URL" />
: The URL is the address of the changedPage server.

Example

```
<?xml version="1.0" encoding="utf-8"?>
   <rdf:RDF  xmlns:rdf="http://www.w3.org/1999/02/22-rdf-syntax-ns#"
        xmlns=http://purl.org/rss/1.0/
          xmlns:cp="http://my.theinfo.org/changed/1.0/rss/"
>
  <channel rdf:about="http://meerkat.oreillynet.com/?_fl=rss1.0">
  <title>Meerkat</title>
  <link>http://meerkat.oreillynet.com</link>
  <description>Meerkat: An Open Wire Service</description>
<cp:server rdf:resource="http://example.org/changedPage" />
</channel>
...
```

mod_company

mod_company allows RSS feeds to deliver business news metadata. Like mod_audio, this is another example of RSS 1.0 stretching the bounds of RSS functionality; this module could lead to RSS being used as a specialist business news vehicle rather than just a generalized list of links.

Namespace

mod_company takes the namespace prefix company: and is identified by the URI http://purl.org/rss/1.0/modules/company. By now, you'll realize that this means the root element of a RSS 1.0 document containing mod_company will resemble this:

```
<rdf:RDF xmlns:rdf="http://www.w3.org/1999/02/22-rdf-syntax-ns#"
          xmlns="http://purl.org/rss/1.0/"
          xmlns:company="http://purl.org/rss/1.0/modules/company/">
```

Elements

mod_company provides four elements, all of which are subelements of item. None are defined as mandatory, but there's little hassle and much reward in including all of them.

company:name
: The name of the company.

company:symbol
: The ticker symbol of the company's stock.

company:market
: The abbreviation of the market in which the stock is traded.

company:category
: The category of the company, expressed using the Taxonomy module. For more details, see mod_taxonomy later in this chapter.

Example

```
<item rdf:about="http://www.example.com/financial_news/00001.html">
    <title>Cisco Stock moves either up or down!</title>
<description>A brief story about a thing happening today</description>
<link>http://www.example.com/financial_news/00001.html<link>
   <company:symbol>CSCO</company:symbol>
    <company:market>NASDAQ</company:market>
    <company:name>Cisco Systems Inc.</company:name>
    <company:category>
    <taxo:topic rdf:resource="http://dmoz.org/Computers/Data_Communications/Vendors/
                                Manufacturers/">
    </company:category>
</item>
```

mod_content

mod_content is perhaps the most misunderstood module of all. Its purpose isn't only to allow much richer content—the entire site, images and all, for example—to be included within a RSS 1.0 item, but also to give a complete RDF description of this content. Now, not only can you make RDF graphs from channel to item, but you can also make them from item to an image within an item. An RDF query of "find all feeds that point to articles accompanied by a picture of an elephant" can now be executed easily because mod_content provides not just the content itself, but the relationship metadata as well. It can also be used to split the object to which an item points into smaller sections, from the standpoint of an RDF parser.

The syntax for this can look a little long-winded—RDF is rather verbose when written in XML—and, because of this, mod_content feeds can often look scary. They're not really, and reformatting them in a text editor can give you an idea of what is happening. Despite this apparent complexity, it is one of the only modules to have been officially accepted by the rss-dev working group.

It must be noted that mod_content isn't to be confused with the core specification's description subelement of item. Some RSS 1.0 feeds use description to contain the content the item represents. While this may be common practice with RSS 0.9x users, RSS 1.0 users may wish to do it properly. description is for a description of the content; mod_content is for the content itself.

Namespaces

mod_content is identified by the namespace prefix content: and the URI http://purl.org/rss/1.0/modules/content/. Hence, the root element looks like this:

```
<rdf:RDF  xmlns:rdf="http://www.w3.org/1999/02/22-rdf-syntax-ns#"
          xmlns="http://purl.org/rss/1.0/"
          xmlns:content="http://purl.org/rss/1.0/modules/content/">
```

Elements

mod_content is slightly more complex than the other modules; it has a specific structure that must be followed. It consists of one element with various subelements that have important attributes of their own, some of which are mandatory, while others aren't.

The first element, content:items, is a subelement of item. It consists of an rdf:Bag that contains as many content:items as needed, each enveloped in an rdf:li element, as shown in Example 6-1.

Example 6-1. The basic structure of a mod_content item

```
<item>
...
<content:items>
<rdf:Bag>
  <rdf:li>
      <content:item rdf:about=""/>
  </rdf:li>
  <rdf:li>
      <content:item />
  </rdf:li>
</rdf:Bag>
</content:items>
</item>
```

Notice that one of the content:item elements in Example 6-1 has an rdf:about attribute, but the other doesn't. This difference is to show that if the content is available on the Web at a specific address, the rdf:about attribute contains the URI of the content, including any part of the content that is directly addressable (an image, for example). Hence, a deeper RDF relationship level is declared.

Also notice that the content:item element in Example 6-1 is empty. This isn't particularly useful, so let's look into filling it. Content, as you know, can come in many formats: plain text, HTML 4.0, XHTML 1.1, and so on. What you do with such content depends on its format, so mod_content needs to be able to describe the format. It does this with a content:format subelement.

This element takes one attribute, rdf:resource, which points to a URI that represents the format of the content. Basically, this attribute declares the namespace of the content. For example, for XHTML 1.0 Strict, the URI is http://www.w3.org/TR/xhtml1/DTD/xhtml1-strict. The URI for HTML 4.0 is http://www.w3.org/TR/html4/. Further examples of URIs for different types of content can be found at http://www.rddl.org/natures/.

The content:format element is required. If you don't include it, you force anyone parsing your feed to guess your content's format.

Because you have declared the format of the content:item using an RDF declaration, you must now envelop the actual content inside an rdf:value element. Example 6-2 shows a simple version.

Example 6-2. A simple version of a mod_content item

```
<item>
...
<content:items>
  <rdf:Bag>
    <rdf:li>
      <content:item>
      <content:format rdf:resource="http://www.w3.org/TR/html4/" />
        <rdf:value>
          <![CDATA[<em>This is<strong>very</em> cool</strong>.]]>
        </rdf:value>
      </content:item>
</rdf:li>
</rdf:Bag>
</content:items>
```

Example 6-2 shows a single item that contains a single content:item that itself contains a line of HTML 4.0 reading `<em>This is<strong>very</em> cool</strong>`. Note that the HTML content is encased in a CDATA section. As with all XML (see Appendix A for details), non-XML-compliant content must be wrapped in this manner inside an RSS feed.

HTML, however, isn't the only content type, and newer content types are fully XML compliant. XHTML, for example, doesn't need to be wrapped, as long as the parser is made aware that the contents of the rdf:value element can be treated accordingly. For this, you use rdf:value's optional range of attributes, rdf:parseType and xmlns. Example 6-3 shows the same content as Example 6-2, but it's reformatted into XHTML. Note the differences in bold.

Example 6-3. A simple version of a mod_content item, with XHTML

```
<item>
...
<content:items>
  <rdf:Bag>
    <rdf:li>
      <content:item>
      <content:format rdf:resource="http://www.w3.org/1999/xhtml"/>
       <content:encoding rdf:resource="http://www.w3.org/TR/REC-xml#dt-wellformed"/>
        <rdf:value rdf:parseType="Literal" xmlns="http://www.w3.org/1999/xhtml">
           <em>This is <strong>very</strong> </em> <strong>cool</strong>.
        </rdf:value>
      </content:item>
</rdf:li>
</rdf:Bag>
</content:items>
```

In Example 6-3, we've told the `rdf:value` element that its contents are both parsable using the namespace represented by the URI `http://www.w3.org/1999/xhtml`. We declare all of this to prevent RDF parsers from getting confused. We humans, of course, are anything but.

The content itself is now well-formed XML. To show this, you can include a new subelement of `content:item`, the optional `content:encoding`. This points to the `rdf:resource` of the URI of well-formed XML, `http://www.w3.org/TR/REC-xml#dt-wellformed`.

If no `content:encoding` is present, assume that the content is plain character data, either enclosed in a `CDATA` section or surrounded by escaped characters such as `<b>`.

Here are `mod` content's subelements:

`content:items`
: Contains a subelement of `rdf:Bag`.

`rdf:Bag`
: Contains one or more subelements of `rdf:li`.

`rdf:li`
: Contains a mandatory subelement of `content:item`.

`content:item`
: Takes the mandatory subelements `content:format` and `rdf:value`, and the optional subelement `content:encoding`. `content:item` must take the attribute `rdf:about="` *`URI`*`"` if the object can be directly addressed.

`content:format`
: Takes the attribute `rdf:about="` *`URI`*`"`, in which the URI represents the format of the content.

`rdf:value`
: Contains the actual content. It can take two attributes. If its content is well-formed XML, it must take the attributes `rdf:Parsetype="literal"` and `xmlns="http://www.w3.org/1999/xhtml"`.

`content:encoding`
: Takes the attribute `rdf:about="` *`URI`*`"`, in which the URI represents the format in which the content is encoded.

Examples

```
<item rdf:about="http://example.org/item/">
 <title>The Example Item</title>
 <link>http://example.org/item/</link>
 <description>I am an example item</description>
 <content:items>
  <rdf:Bag>
      <rdf:li>
   <content:item>
   <content:format rdf:resource="http://www.w3.org/1999/xhtml" />
   <content:encoding rdf:resource="http://www.w3.org/TR/REC-xml#dt-wellformed" />
    <rdf:value rdf:parseType="Literal" xmlns="http://www.w3.org/1999/xhtml">
     <em>This is a <strong>very cool</strong> example of mod_content</em>
    </rdf:value>
   </content:item>
  </rdf:li>
```

```
    <rdf:li>
   <content:item>
    <content:format rdf:resource="http://www.w3.org/TR/html4/" />
    <rdf:value>
     <![CDATA[You can include content in lots of formats. <a
      href="http://www.oreillynet.com">links</a> too. ]]>
    </rdf:value>
   </content:item>
  </rdf:li>
 </rdf:Bag>
</content:items>
</item>
```

It may either amuse or terrify you to realize that because content:item can contain any XML-formatted content, it can itself contain other RSS feeds. This might be useful for a RSS tutorial web site, syndicating its lessons. The next example is an early version of this very section of this book, represented as an item, up to this paragraph to prevent a spiral of recursion.

```
<title>Examples</title>
<description>The text of the first part of the Examples section of the mod_content
bit of chapter 6 of Content Syndication with XML and RSS</description>
<content:items>
<rdf:Bag>
<rdf:li>
<content:item>
<content:format rdf:resource="http://www.w3.org/TR/html4/" />
<rdf:value>
<![CDATA[ <h2>Examples</h2>]]>
</rdf:value>
</content:item>
</rdf:li>
<rdf:li>
<content:item>
<content:format rdf:resource="http://purl.org/rss/1.0/" />
<content:encoding rdf:resource="http://www.w3.org/TR/REC-xml#dt-wellformed" />
<rdf:value rdf:parseType="Literal"
              xmlns="http://purl.org/rss/1.0/"
              xmlns:rdf="http://www.w3.org/1999/02/22-rdf-syntax-ns#"
              xmlns:content="http://purl.org/rss/1.0/modules/content/">
<item rdf:about="http://example.org/item/"><title>The Example Item</title>
<link>http://example.org/item/</link>
<description>I am an example item</description>
<content:items><rdf:Bag><rdf:li><content:item>
<content:format rdf:resource="http://www.w3.org/1999/xhtml" />
<content:encoding rdf:resource="http://www.w3.org/TR/REC-xml#dt-wellformed" />
<rdf:value rdf:parseType="Literal" xmlns="http://www.w3.org/1999/xhtml"><em>
This is a <strong>very cool</strong> example of mod_content</em></rdf:value></
content:item></rdf:li>
<rdf:li><content:item>
<content:format rdf:resource="http://www.w3.org/TR/html4/" />
<rdf:value><![CDATA[You can include content in lots of formats. <a href="http://www.
oreillynet.com">links</a> too. ]]></rdf:value></content:item></rdf:li></rdf:Bag></
content:items></item>
```

```
</rdf:value>
</content:item>
</rdf:li>
<rdf:li>
<content:item>
<content:format rdf:resource="http://www.w3.org/TR/html4/" />
<rdf:value><![CDATA[ <p><i> Example 6.12 A fully mod_contented &lt;item&gt;</i></p>
<p>
It may either amuse or terrify you to realize that as &lt;content:item&gt can contain
any XML-formatted content, it can itself contain other RSS feeds. This might be of
use for a RSS tutorial website, syndicating its lessons. Here, in example 6.13, is
this very section of this book, represented as an &lt;item&gt;, stopping right here
to prevent a spiral of recursion.</p>]]>
</rdf:value>
</content:item>
</rdf:li>
</rdf:Bag>
</content:items>
</item>
```

mod_dublincore

The second of the Standard modules to be examined in this chapter, mod_dublincore is the most-used of all the RSS 1.0 modules. It allows an RSS 1.0 feed to express the additional metadata formalized by the Dublin Core Metadata Initiative.

Namespace

mod_dublincore is identified by the prefix dc: and the URI http://purl.org/dc/elements/1.1/. So, in the grand tradition, the root element appears as:

```
<rdf:RDF xmlns:rdf="http://www.w3.org/1999/02/22-rdf-syntax-ns#"
         xmlns="http://purl.org/rss/1.0/"
         xmlns:dc="http://purl.org/dc/elements/1.1/"
>
```

Elements

mod_dublincore can be used in two ways: the simpler and the more RDF-based.

In either usage, mod_dublincore elements are entirely optional and can be applied to the channel, an item, an image, a textinput element, or all of them, as liberally as you wish, as long as the information you are relating makes sense. It is rather addictive, I must say, and I encourage you to put Dublin Core metadata all over your feeds. Here's what you can include:

dc:title
: The title of the item.

dc:creator
: The name of the creator of the item (i.e., a person, organization, or system). If the creator is a person, this information is customarily in the format *Firstname Lastname (email@domain.com)*.

`dc:subject`
: The subject of the item.

`dc:description`
: A brief description of the item.

`dc:publisher`
: The name of the publisher, either a person or an organization. If the publisher is a person, this information is customarily in the format *`Firstname Lastname`* (*`email @ domain. com`*).

`dc:contributor`
: The name of a contributor, customarily in the format *`Firstname Lastname`* (*`email @ domain. com`*).

`dc:date`
: The publishing date, in the W3CDTF format (e.g., `2000-01-01T12:00+00:00`).

`dc:type`
: The nature of the item, taken from the list of Dublin Core types at *http://dublincore.org/documents/dcmi-type-vocabulary/*:

  Collection
  : A collection is an aggregation of items, described as a group; its parts can be described and navigated separately (for example, a weblog).

  Dataset
  : A dataset is information encoded in a defined structure (for example, lists, tables, and databases), intended to be useful for direct machine processing.

  Event
  : According to the official definition of the Dublin Core authors, an event is a non-persistent, time-based occurrence. Examples include any exhibition, webcast, conference, workshop, open-day, performance, battle, trial, wedding, tea party, conflagration, or orgy. The soon-to-be-described `mod_event` has a lot to do with this sort of thing.

  Image
  : They are worth a thousand words, you know.

  Interactive resource
  : The official Dublin Core definition of an interactive resource is "a resource which requires interaction from the user to be understood, executed, or experienced. For example—forms on web pages, applets, multimedia learning objects, chat services, virtual reality." In the RSS world, resources could be either pointers to programs or the `textinput` element itself.

  Service
  : Technically, a service is a system that provides one or more functions of value to the end user. Assuming that just providing information doesn't count, a service can point to web applications or web services, as long as you create an RSS feed that provides the necessary details (using `mod_content` to syndicate WSDL files, for example).

Software
: You know what software is. In this case, it is distinguished from an interactive resource by being downloadable rather than run on a remote server.

Sound
: Officially, a sound is a resource with content primarily intended to be rendered as audio.

Text
: Plain-text content.

`dc:format`
: This differs from `dc:type` by a degree of sophistication. Whereas `dc:type` provides a top-level indication of the feed's nature, `dc:format` should point to the exact MIME type of the content itself.

`dc:identifier`
: The identifier should be an unambiguous reference to the resource within a given context. So, in RSS 1.0 terms, this is the same as the `item`'s `rdf:about` attribute.

`dc:source`
: In RSS 1.0 terms, this element can do the same job as the `ag:sourceURL` of the `mod_aggregation` module. It should point to an unambiguous reference to the source of the `item`. Unlike the `ag:sourceURL` element, however, `dc:source` isn't restricted to URLs. Any sufficiently unambiguous reference works (ISBNs, for example).

`dc:language`
: The language in which the item is written, using the standard language code, as covered in Appendix B.

`dc:relation`
: The URI of a related resource. See `mod_DCTerms` later in this chapter for more details.

`dc:coverage`
: According to the Dublin Core authors, "coverage will typically include spatial location (a place name or geographic coordinates), temporal period (a period label, date, or date range), or jurisdiction (such as a named administrative entity). Recommended best practice is to select a value from a controlled vocabulary (for example, the Thesaurus of Geographic Names [TGN]) and that, where appropriate, named places or time periods be used in preference to numeric identifiers such as sets of coordinates or date ranges."

`dc:rights`
: This element should contain any copyright, copyleft, public domain, or similar declaration. The absence of this element doesn't imply anything whatsoever.

The more complex version of `mod_dublincore` adds RDF and the `mod_taxonomy` module to give a richer meaning to `dc:subject`. For example, `dc:subject` can be used simply like this:

```
<dc:subject>World Cup</dc:subject>
```

or combined with a definition of a topic, in a richer RDF version:

```
<dc:subject>
  <rdf:Description>
    <taxo:topic rdf:resource="http://dmoz.org/Sports/Soccer/" />
    <rdf:value>World Cup</rdf:value>
  </rdf:Description>
</dc:subject>
```

This not only defines the subject but also provides it with a wider contextual meaning. In this example, we're saying the subject is "the World Cup of soccer" (or more correctly, we're saying that "this item is on the subject represented by the term 'World Cup' in the context provided by the URI http://dmoz.org/Sports/Soccer.") After all, there is more than one World Cup. This approach is especially useful for describing homonyms, such as:

```
<dc:subject>
  <rdf:Description>
    <taxo:topic rdf:resource="http://dmoz.org/Business/Industries/
Food_and_Related_Products/Beverages/Soft_Drinks" />
    <rdf:value>Coke</rdf:value>
  </rdf:Description>
</dc:subject>
```

as opposed to:

```
<dc:subject>
  <rdf:Description>
    <taxo:topic rdf:resource="http://dmoz.org/Health/Addictions/Substance_Abuse/
Illegal_Drugs/" />
    <rdf:value>Coke</rdf:value>
  </rdf:Description>
</dc:subject>
```

Example

```
<rdf:RDF xmlns:rdf="http://www.w3.org/1999/02/22-rdf-syntax-ns#"
  xmlns="http://purl.org/rss/1.0/"
  xmlns:dc="http://purl.org/dc/elements/1.1/"
>
<channel rdf:about="http://meerkat.oreillynet.com/?_fl=rss1.0">
  <title>Meerkat</title>
  <link>http://meerkat.oreillynet.com</link>
  <description>Meerkat: An Open Wire Service</description>
  <dc:publisher>The O'Reilly Network</dc:publisher>
  <dc:creator>Rael Dornfest (mailto:rael@oreilly.com)</dc:creator>
  <dc:rights>Copyright &#169; 2000 O'Reilly &amp; Associates, Inc.</dc:rights>
  <dc:date>2000-01-01T12:00+00:00</dc:date>
  <dc:type>Interactive Resource</dc:type>
  <image rdf:resource="http://meerkat.oreillynet.com/icons/meerkat-powered.jpg" />
  <textinput rdf:resource="http://meerkat.oreillynet.com" />
   <items>
    <rdf:Seq>
      <rdf:li resource="http://c.moreover.com/click/here.pl?r123" />
    </rdf:Seq>
  </items>
</channel>
<image rdf:about="http://meerkat.oreillynet.com/icons/meerkat-powered.jpg">
  <title>Meerkat Powered!</title>
  <url>http://meerkat.oreillynet.com/icons/meerkat-powered.jpg</url>
  <link>http://meerkat.oreillynet.com</link>
  <dc:creator> Rael Dornfest (mailto:rael@oreilly.com)</dc:creator>
  <dc:type>image</dc:type>
</image>
<textinput rdf:about="http://meerkat.oreillynet.com">
```

```
    <title>Search Meerkat</title>
    <description>Search Meerkat's RSS Database...</description>
    <name>s</name>
    <link>http://meerkat.oreillynet.com/</link>
  </textinput>
  <item rdf:about="http://c.moreover.com/click/here.pl?r123">
    <title>XML: A Disruptive Technology</title>
    <link>http://c.moreover.com/click/here.pl?r123</link>
    <dc:description>This the description of the article</dc:description>
    <dc:publisher>The O'Reilly Network</dc:publisher>
    <dc:creator>Simon St.Laurent (mailto:simonstl@simonstl.com)</dc:creator>
    <dc:rights>Copyright &#169; 2000 O'Reilly &amp; Associates, Inc.</dc:rights>
    <dc:subject>XML</dc:subject>
  </item>
  </rdf:RDF>
```

mod_DCTerms

Once Dublin Core metadata has sunk its I-must-add-metadata-to-everything addictive nature into your very soul, you soon realize that the core terms are lacking in depth. For example, dc:relation means "is related to," but in what way? You don't know unless you use mod_DCTerms.

mod_DCTerms introduces 28 new subelements to channel, item, image, and textinput, as appropriate. These subelements are related, within Dublin Core, to the core elements found within mod_dublincore, but mod_DCTerms doesn't express this relationship. For example, dcterms:created is actually a refinement of dc:date.

Namespace

mod_DCTerms takes the namespace prefix dcterms: and is identified by the URI http://purl.org/dc/terms/. So, the root element looks like this:

```
<rdf:RDF xmlns:rdf="http://www.w3.org/1999/02/22-rdf-syntax-ns#"
         xmlns="http://purl.org/rss/1.0/"
         xmlns:dcterms="http://purl.org/dc/terms/"
>
```

Elements

You have a lot to choose from with this module. As shown earlier, the elements can be subelements of channel, item, image, or textinput. Apply liberally and with gusto.

dcterms:alternative
: An alternative title for the item. For example:

```
<title>Programming Perl</title>
<dc:title>Programming Perl</dc:title>
<dcterms:alternative>The Camel Book</dcterms:alternative>
```

dcterms:created
: The date the object was created, in W3CDTF standard (YYYY-MM-DDTHH:MM:SS).

`dcterms:issued`
: The date the object was first made available. This should be used, for backward compatibility, with `dc:date`, and it should contain the same value. Again, the date must be in W3CDTF format.

`dcterms:modified`
: The date the content of the object last changed, in W3CDTF format. This can sit inside `channel`, `item`, or both.

`dcterms:extent`
: The size of the document referred to by the section of the feed in which the element appears, in bytes.

`dcterms:medium`
: The HTTP Content-Type of the object to which the parent element refers. The HTTP Content-Type is made up of the MIME type followed optionally by the character set, denoted by the string `;charset=`. For example:

```
<dcterms:medium>text/html; charset=UTF-8</dcterms:medium>
```

Paired Elements

Some `mod_DCterms` elements come paired together naturally. When talking about two separate `items`, it's important to remember that the following paired elements must work together:

`dcterms:isVersionOf` *and* `dcterms:hasVersion`
: This pair of elements works together to point to different versions of an object. For example, you can use it to list versions in different languages or different formats. Their values should point to each other, should be URIs, and, for complete RDF compatibility, should be encased in an `rdf:resource` attribute. There is also nothing to stop you from providing further information about the version via additional RDF markup, like so:

```
<dcterms:hasVersion rdf:resource="
URI of resource">
<dc:title>Title of other resource</dc:title>
</dcterms:hasVersion>
```

`dcterms:isReplacedBy` *and* `dcterms:replaces`
: Denotes an `item` that points to a more recent version of the object in question. The syntax is the same as the `dcterms:isVersionOf` pair; it takes an `rdf:resource` attribute that points to the URI of the object in question.

`dcterms:isRequiredBy` *and* `dcterms:requires`
: Denotes an object relationship in which, according to the Dublin Core specification, "the described resource requires the referenced resource to support its function, delivery, or coherence of content." As you might expect by now, this pair takes the attribute `rdf:resource` to denote the URI of the object to which you're pointing and may be augmented by additional RDF.

`dcterms:isPartOf` *and* `dcterms:hasPart`
: The `mod_DCTerms` elements have quite self-explanatory names, and this pair is no exception. It denotes objects that are subsections of other objects. It's the traditional syntax of an `rdf:resource` attribute with the option of additional RDF within the element.

`dcterms:isReferencedBy` *and* `dcterms:references`
: A pair in which one object refers to or cites the other. Its syntax is the usual drill—an `rdf:resource` attribute and some additional RDF if you're feeling generous.

`dcterms:isFormatOf` *and* `dcterms:hasFormat`
: This final pair of elements denotes two objects that contain the same intellectual content but differ in format. For example, one object could be a color PDF and the other a Word document. The syntax is the same as the other paired elements but with the additional recommendation that you include `dc:format`, `dc:language`, or another element that helps the end user tell the difference between the two separate versions. Also bear in mind that URIs must be unique, so anyone using content negotiation on his server must give different URIs for each format, whether or not it is actually necessary.

Using DCSV Values

There are three `mod_DCTerms` elements that take a special syntax to denote a timespan. This syntax, Dublin Core Structured Values (DCSV), represents complex values together in one simple string. It takes the following format (all the attributes are optional):

```
name=
Associated name; start=
Start time; end=
End time; scheme=W3C-DTF;
```

`dcterms:temporal`
: This element denotes any timespan of the `item`'s subject matter. For example:

```
<dcterms:temporal>
name=World War 2; start=1939; end=1945; scheme=W3C-DTF;
</dcterms:temporal>
```

`dcterms:valid`
: This denotes the timespan during which the `item`'s contents are valid. For example:

```
<dcterms:valid>start=20030101; end=200300201;  scheme=W3C-DTF;</dcterms:valid>
```

`dcterms:available`
: This denotes the timespan during which the object to which the `item` points is available (i.e., network-retrievable).

mod_event

`mod_event` really breaks RSS 1.0 out of the datacentric model and into the real world. It's purpose is to describe details of real-world events. You can then use this data in your calendar applications, display it on a page, email it; use it for whatever purpose you like.

According to Søren Roug, the module's author, "This specification isn't a reimplementation of RFC 2445 iCalendar in RDF. In particular, it lacks such things as TODO and repeating events, and there is no intention of adding those parts to the specification."

Namespace

The events module takes the shapely ev: as its namespace prefix, and it is identified by the pleasingly regular `http://purl.org/rss/1.0/modules/event/`. So, the root element looks like this:

```
<?xml version="1.0" encoding="utf-8"?>
   <rdf:RDF xmlns:rdf="http://www.w3.org/1999/02/22-rdf-syntax-ns#"
         xmlns="http://purl.org/rss/1.0/"
         xmlns:ev="http://purl.org/rss/1.0/modules/event/"
>
```

Elements

The `mod_events` elements are all subelements of `item`. None of them are mandatory, but common sense should prevail regarding usage: the more the better.

`ev:startdate`
: The time and date of the start of the event, in W3CDTF format.

`ev:enddate`
: The time and date of the end of the event, in W3CDTF format.

`ev:location`
: The location of the event. This can be a simple string or a URI, or it can be semantically augmented via RDF. For example:

```
<ev:location>At Ben's house</ev:location>
```

or:

```
<ev:location>http://www.example.org/benshouse</ev:location>
```

or:

```
<ev:location rdf:resource="http://www.mapquest.com">
<rdf:value>
http://www.mapquest.com/maps/map.adp?map.x=177&map.
y=124&mapdata=xU4YXdELrnB2xoPaJ66QjsffE4Zu%252bP6OZQy2y1Ah8EPehGZcP7zX7a3LAujflI
6g%252boY5z8%252b7lqnLexYmGmo96xAPLE%252bMe4H2TaNOPDMZ5pH9rjsN3owqiP9AOg8%252fOX
tNlI1FGCb4fddEaWl23DGyUhXfazgpROqIrCGP%252fmKvh2vwRsOlc8k9FOltIpaTc%252foiXwyvfB
CMSvv2EAvYEbNgn6ztUAlmEA%252bK2tqfR5jD9QRdgAOyRNovXEpgRakMia3g2jRzToO6OcbL8TDJru
fAn11sl6d5CQUD8xjR1nJj3ieObeWOVwRBOw8T4MSHFQLg9SoPaSN3LMG2PixeD2X5%252bs4Sg3K1JS
4LqmvDON%252bugHKDenLg%252b%252fxQhtVGFuhugqWLosZ%252fSo2wQ7Y%253d&click=center
</rdf:value>
</ev:location>
```

`ev:organizer`
: The name of the organizer of the event. Again, you can semantically augment this element to include more information. For example:

```
<ev:organizer>Ben Hammersley</ev:organizer>
```

`ev:type`
: According to the specification, this should be "the type of event, such as conference, deadline, launch, project meeting. The purpose is to promote or filter out certain types of events that the user has a particular (lack of) interest for. Avoid the use of subject-specific wording. Use instead the Dublin Core subject element."

Example

```
<rdf:RDF xmlns:rdf="http://www.w3.org/1999/02/22-rdf-syntax-ns#"
  xmlns:ev="http://purl.org/rss/1.0/modules/event/"
  xmlns:dc="http://purl.org/dc/elements/1.1/"
  xmlns="http://purl.org/rss/1.0/"
>
  <channel rdf:about="http://events.oreilly.com/?_fl=rss1.0">
    <title>O'Reilly Events</title>
    <link>http://events.oreilly.com/</link>
    <description>O'Reilly Events</description>
    <items>
      <rdf:Seq>
        <rdf:li resource="http://conferences.oreilly.com/p2p/" />
        <rdf:li resource="http://www.oreilly.com/catalog/progxmlrpc/" />
      </rdf:Seq>
    </items>
  </channel>
  <item rdf:about="http://conferences.oreilly.com/p2p/">
    <title>The O'Reilly Peer-to-Peer and Web Services Conference</title>
    <link>http://conferences.oreilly.com/p2p/</link>
    <ev:type>conference</ev:type>
    <ev:organizer>O'Reilly</ev:organizer>
    <ev:location>Washington, DC</ev:location>
    <ev:startdate>2001-09-18</ev:startdate>
    <ev:enddate>2001-09-21</ev:enddate>
    <dc:subject>P2P</dc:subject>
  </item>
  <item rdf:about="http://www.oreilly.com/catalog/progxmlrpc/">
    <title>Programming Web Services with XML-RPC</title>
    <link>http://www.oreilly.com/catalog/progxmlrpc/</link>
    <ev:startdate>2001-06-20</ev:startdate>
    <ev:type>book release</ev:type>
    <dc:subject>XML-RPC</dc:subject>
    <dc:subject>Programming</dc:subject>
  </item>
</rdf:RDF>
```

mod_rss091

The `mod_rss091` module is designed to give RSS 1.0 "sideways compatibility" with RSS 0.91. Because the three core subelements of the `item` element are the same in both standards, including `mod_rss091` elements in your RSS 1.0 feed allows for dynamic downgrading of the feed for parsers that can't be bothered with all the RDF stuff. Because the data is rather simple and mostly static, including this module within your RSS 1.0 feed is straightforward. With this in mind, it's worth doing.

Namespace

The prefix for this module is the self-explanatory `rss091:`, and the module is represented by the URI `http://purl.org/rss/1.0/modules/rss091#`. Hence:

```
<rdf:RDF xmlns:rdf="http://www.w3.org/1999/02/22-rdf-syntax-ns#"
         xmlns="http://purl.org/rss/1.0/"
         xmlns:rss091="http://purl.org/rss/1.0/modules/rss091/"
>
```

Elements

The `mod_rss091` elements represent the same elements within RSS 0.91. Chapter 4 provides details on those elements.

Subelements of channel

`rss091:language`
: The language of the feed

`rss091:rating`
: The PICS rating of the feed

`rss091:managingEditor`
: The managing editor of the feed

`rss091:webmaster`
: The webmaster of the feed

`rss091:pubDate`
: The publication date of the feed

`rss091:lastBuildDate`
: The date of the feed's last build

`rss091:copyright`
: The copyright notice of the feed

`rss091:skipHours rdf:parseType="Literal"`
: The `skipHours` element, with correct RDF syntax

`rss091:hour`
: The hours, in GMT, during which the feed shouldn't be retrieved

`rss091:skipDays rdf:parseType="Literal"`
: The `skipDays` element, with correct RDF syntax

`rss091:day`
: The days during which a feed shouldn't be retrieved (Monday is `1`, and Sunday is `7`)

Subelements of image

`rss091:width`
: The width of the image

`rss091:height`
: The height of the image

Subelement of item

`rss091:description`
: The description of the `item`. While this element is replicated by core RSS 1.0, it is listed here for the sake of completion.

Example

```
<rdf:RDF xmlns:rdf="http://www.w3.org/1999/02/22-rdf-syntax-ns#"
         xmlns="http://purl.org/rss/1.0/"
         xmlns:rss091="http://purl.org/rss/1.0/modules/rss091/"
>
  <channel rdf:about="http://www.xml.com/xml/news.rss">
    <title>XML.com</title>
    <link>http://xml.com/pub</link>
    <description>
    XML.com features a rich mix of information and services for the XML community.
    </description>
    <rss091:language>en-us</rss091:language>
    <rss091:rating>(PICS-1.1 "http://www.rsac.org/ratingsv01.html"
     l gen true comment "RSACi North America Server"
     for "http://www.rsac.org" on "1996.04.16T08:15-0500"
     r (n 0 s 0 v 0 l 0))</rss091:rating>
    <rss091:managingEditor>Edd Dumbill</rss091:managingEditor>
    <rss091:webmaster>(mailto:webmaster@xml.com)</rss091:webmaster>
    <rss091:pubDate>Sat, 01 Jan 2000 12:00:00 GMT</rss091:pubDate>
    <rss091:lastBuildDate>Sat, 01 Jan 2000 12:00:00 GMT</rss091:lastBuildDate>
    <rss091:skipHours rdf:parseType="Literal">
    <rss091:hour>12</rss091:hour>
    </rss091:skipHours>
    <rss091:skipDays rdf:parseType="Literal">
    <rss091:day>Thursday</rss091:day>
    </rss091:skipDays>
  </channel>
  <image rdf:about="http://xml.com/universal/images/xml_tiny.gif">
    <title>XML.com</title>
    <link>http://www.xml.com</link>
    <url>http://xml.com/universal/images/xml_tiny.gif</url>
    <rss091:width>88</rss091:width>
    <rss091:height>31</rss091:height>
    <rss091:description>XML.com...</rss091:description>
  </image>
  <item rdf:about="http://xml.com/pub/2000/08/09/xslt/xslt.html" position= "1">
     <title>Processing Inclusions with XSLT</title>
     <link>http://xml.com/pub/2000/08/09/xslt/xslt.html</link>
     <rss091:description>
     Processing document inclusions with general XML tools can be problematic.
     This article proposes a way of preserving inclusion information through
     SAX-based processing.
     </rss091:description>
  </item>
</rdf:RDF>
```

mod_servicestatus

mod_servicestatus is one of the latest RSS 1.0 modules. Its purpose is to allow RSS 1.0 to display details of the status and current availability of services and servers.

You should bear in mind the difference between services and servers. One service may rely on more than one server in the back end. For the user, however, such information is irrelevant: something either works or it doesn't. With mod_servicestatus, you can't differentiate between a virtual service and an actual physical server, but you can combine servers into services at the parsing stage. This means one feed can be used for multiple things: a detailed display for sysadmins and a simplified version for end users.

Namespace

The mod_servicestatus prefix is ss:, and the module is identified by the URI http://purl.org/rss/1.0/modules/servicestatus/. So, a mod_servicestatus feed starts like this:

```
<rdf:RDF xmlns:rdf="http://www.w3.org/1999/02/22-rdf-syntax-ns#"
       xmlns="http://purl.org/rss/1.0/"
         xmlns:ss="http://purl.org/rss/1.0/modules/servicestatus/"
>
```

Elements

The first element of mod_servicestatus is a subelement of channel:

ss:aboutStats
: A URI that points to a page explaining the results and methodology being used

All other elements within mod_servicestatus are subelements of item. As with many modules, all these elements are optional, but the more you include, the more fun you'll have.

ss:responding
: This can be either true or false, and it refers to whether the server is responding.

ss:lastChecked
: The date and time the server was last checked, in W3CDTF format.

ss:lastSeen
: The date and time the server last responded, in W3CDTF format. Used with ss:lastChecked, this enables you to work out down times.

ss:availability
: A figure that describes server availability. Usually an integer percentage, this should be explained in the document referenced by ss:aboutStats.

ss:averageResponseTime
: The average response time of the server, usually in seconds. This should also be explained in the ss:aboutStats document.

ss:statusMessage
: A message aimed at the end user. For example: "We know this is broken, and we're working on it," or "Please log out, pushing of the Big Red Button is imminent," or "Run for the door! Run! Run!"

Example

```
<rdf:RDF xmlns:rdf="http://www.w3.org/1999/02/22-rdf-syntax-ns#"
         xmlns="http://purl.org/rss/1.0/"
         xmlns:ss="http://purl.org/rss/1.0/modules/servicestatus/"
>
```

```
<channel rdf:about="http://my.organisation.com">
  <title>An Example</title>
  <description>Just an example of system statuses</description>
  <link>http://my.organisation.com</link>
<ss:aboutStats>http://my.organisation.com/status.html</ss:aboutStats>
  <items>
    <rdf:Seq>
      <rdf:li resource="http://my.organisation.com/website" />
      <rdf:li resource="http://my.organisation.com/database" />
    </rdf:Seq>
  </items>
</channel>
<item rdf:about="http://my.organisation.com/website">
  <title>Website</title>
  <link>http://my.organisation.com/website</link>
  <ss:responding>true</ss:responding>
  <ss:lastChecked>2002-05-10T19:20:30.45+01:00</ss:lastChecked>
  <ss:lastSeen>2002-05-10T19:20:30.45+01:00</ss:lastSeen>
  <ss:availability>85</ss:availability>
  <ss:averageResponseTime>5.2</ss:averageResponseTime>
</item>
<item rdf:about="http://my.organisation.com/database">
  <title>Database server</title>
  <link>http://my.organisation.com/database</link>
  <ss:responding>false</ss:responding>
  <ss:lastChecked>2002-05-10T19:20:30.45+01:00</ss:lastChecked>
  <ss:lastSeen>2002-05-09T13:43:56.24+01:00</ss:lastSeen>
  <ss:availability>77</ss:availability>
  <ss:averageResponseTime>12.2</ss:averageResponseTime>
  <ss:statusMessage>Engineers are investigating.</ss:statusMessage>
</item>
</rdf:RDF>
```

mod_slash

Slash is the software originally written to run the popular technology news site Slashdot. It has spread quite far lately, and now hundreds of sites use it for their content management system. Slash's unique features don't fit into the core RSS 1.0 specification, so Rael Dornfest and Chris Nandor wrote this module. The features are most easily understood after a look at a Slash-based site, so go over to *http://slashdot.org* to see what's happening.

Namespace

The namespace prefix is slash:, and the identifying URI is `http://purl.org/rss/1.0/modules/slash/`. Hence:

```
<rdf:RDF xmlns:rdf="http://www.w3.org/1999/02/22-rdf-syntax-ns#"
         xmlns="http://purl.org/rss/1.0/"
         xmlns:slash="http://purl.org/rss/1.0/modules/slash/"
>
```

Elements

All the mod_slash elements are subelements of item. They are all mandatory.

slash:section
: The title of the section in which the article appears.

slash:department
: The title of the department in which the article appears (in most Slash sites, this title is a joke).

slash:comments
: The number of comments attached to an article.

slash:hit_parade
: A comma-separated list of the number of comments displayable at each karma threshold (this will make sense if you look at a Slash-based site). There should be seven figures, matching karma thresholds of –1, 0, 1, 2, 3, 4, and 5.

Example

```
<item rdf:about="http://slashdot.org/article.pl?sid=02/07/01/164242">
<title>LotR Two Towers Trailer Online</title>
<link>http://slashdot.org/article.pl?sid=02/07/01/164242</link>
<dc:creator>CmdrTaco</dc:creator>
<dc:subject>movies</dc:subject>
<dc:date>2002-07-01T17:08:24+00:00</dc:date>
<slash:department>provided-you-have-sorenson-and-bandwidth</slash:department>
<slash:section>articles</slash:section>
<slash:comments>20</slash:comments>
<slash:hitparade>20,19,11,8,3,0,0</slash:hitparade>
</item>
```

mod_streaming

mod_streaming was designed by me (happily enough) to take care of the additional needs of anyone who wants to create a feed that points to streaming-media presentations. You will notice elements for the live events—start times, end times, and so forth. These can also split a single stream into chunks and provide associated metadata with each section.

Namespace

mod_streaming takes str: as its prefix, and http://hacks.benhammersley.com/rss/streaming/ is its identifying URI. So, its root element looks like this:

```
<rdf:RDF xmlns:rdf="http://www.w3.org/1999/02/22-rdf-syntax-ns#"
         xmlns="http://purl.org/rss/1.0/"
         xmlns:str="http://hacks.benhammersley.com/rss/streaming/"
>
```

Elements

All the elements within mod_streaming are subelements of item except str:type, which can be a subelement of channel as well. All elements are optional.

`str:type`
: This can take `audio`, `video`, or `both` as its value, and it can be a subelement of either `item` or `channel`. `video` implies a video, regardless of the presence of a soundtrack. `both` implies a mixture of video and audio items, and hence is used only within a `channel` description.

`str:associatedApplication`
: The name of any special application required to play back the stream.

`str:associatedApplication.version`
: The version number of the associated application, if applicable.

`str:associatedApplication.downloadUri`
: The URI for downloading the associated application.

`str:codec`
: The name of the codec in which the stream is encoded.

`str:codec.version`
: The version number of the codec, if applicable.

`str:codec.downloadUri`
: The URI for downloading the codec.

`str:codec.sampleRate`
: The value of any audio's sample rate, in kHz.

`str:codec.stereo`
: Either `stereo` or `mono`, depending on the audio being used.

`str:codec.ResolutionX`
: The number of pixels in the X axis (width).

`str:codec.ResolutionY`
: The number of pixels in the Y axis (height).

`str:duration`
: The length of the item, in the W3C format of `HH:MM:SS`.

`str: live`
: Either `live` or `recorded`, as applicable.

`str:live.scheduledStartTime`
: A W3CDTF-encoded date and time for the start of live broadcasts, or just `HH:MM:SS.ss` for the start time in the time code of a recording.

`str:live.scheduledEndTime`
: The end time of a live broadcast or recording, in the same format as `str:live.scheduledStartTime`.

`str:live.location`
: This can be a literal string, as per the Dublin Core location guidelines, or it can use RDF with additional location-specific namespaces.

`str:live.contactUri`
: A URI to contact the live show (e.g., `mailto`:, `http`:, `aim`:, or `irc`:). Think "radio phone-in show."

Example

```
<rdf:RDF xmlns:rdf="http://www.w3.org/1999/02/22-rdf-syntax-ns#"
         xmlns="http://purl.org/rss/1.0/"
         xmlns:str="http://hacks.benhammersley.com/rss/streaming/"
>
<channel rdf:about="http://www.streamsRus.com/">
  <title>Streams R Us</title>
  <link>http://www.streamsRus.com</link>
  <description>Streams R Us: An Entirely Fictional Site</description>
  <str:type>both</str:type>
  <image rdf:resource="http://www.streamsRus.com/icons/stream.jpg" />
<items>
  <rdf:Seq>
    <rdf:li rdf:resource="http://www.streamsRus.com/example.ram" />
    <rdf:li rdf:resource="http://www.streamsRus.com/example2.mp3" />
    <rdf:li rdf:resource="http://www.streamsRus.com/example3.mov" />
  </rdf:Seq>
</items>
</channel>
<item rdf:about="http://www.streamsRus.com/example.ram">
  <title>RSS Rocks Out</title>
  <link>http://www.streamsRus.com/example.ram</link>
  <str:associatedApplication>realplayer</str:associatedApplication>
  <str:associatedApplication.downloadUri>http://www.real.com/
  </str:associatedApplication.downloadUri>
  <str:duration>00:04:30</str:duration>
  <str:live>recorded</str:live>
</item>
<item rdf:about="http://www.streamsRus.com/example2.ram">
  <title>RSS Rocks Out Live</title>
  <link>http://www.streamsRus.com/example2.mp3</link>
  <str:associatedApplication>winamp</str:associatedApplication>
  <str:associatedApplication.downloadUri>http://www.winamp.com/
  </str:associatedApplication.downloadUri>
  <str:duration>00:04:30</str:duration>
  <str:live>live</str:live>
  <str:live.scheduledStartTime>2002:04:03T00:00:00Z</str:scheduledStartTime>
  <str:live.scheduledEndTime>2002:04:03T00:04:30Z</str:scheduledEndTime>
</item>
<item rdf:about="http://www.streamsRus.com/example3.mov">
  <title>RSS Rocks Out Live on Video</title>
  <link>http://www.streamsRus.com/example2.mov</link>
  <str:type>video</str:type>
  <str:codec>sorenson</str:codec>
  <str:associatedApplication>Quicktime</str:associatedApplication>
  <str:associatedApplication.downloadUri>http://www.apple.com/quicktime
  </str:associatedApplication.downloadUri>
  <str:duration>00:02:32</str:duration>
  <str:live>live</str:live>
  <str:live.scheduledStartTime>2002:04:03T00:00:00Z</str:scheduledStartTime>
  <str:live.scheduledEndTime>2002:04:03T00:02:32Z</str:scheduledEndTime>
  <str:codec.ResolutionX>600</str:codec.ResolutionX>
  <str:codec.ResolutionY>400</str:codec.ResolutionY>
```

```
  <str:live.ContactUri>mailto:ben@benhammersley.com</str:live.contact.Uri>
</item>
</rdf:RDF>
```

mod_syndication

mod_syndication gives aggregators and feed users an idea of how often the feed changes. By giving this information, you prevent everyone from wasting time and bandwidth by asking for your feed too often or, indeed, too seldom. It is the third module to achieve Standard status.

mod_syndication supersedes the skipHours and skipDays elements of mod_rss091. Clients usually prefer the mod_syndication values over mod_rss091.

Namespace

mod_syndication takes sy: as its prefix and http://purl.org/rss/1.0/modules/syndication as its identifying URI. Thus:

```
<rdf:RDF xmlns:rdf="http://www.w3.org/1999/02/22-rdf-syntax-ns#"
         xmlns="http://purl.org/rss/1.0/"
         xmlns:sy="http://purl.org/rss/1.0/modules/syndication/"
>
```

Elements

The mod_syndication elements are all subelements of channel:

sy:updatePeriod
: Takes a value of hourly, daily, weekly, monthly, or yearly.

sy:updateFrequency
: A number representing the number of times the feed should be refreshed during the updatePeriod. For example, an updatePeriod of hourly and an updateFrequency of 2 makes the aggregator refresh the feed twice an hour. If this element is missing, the default is 1.

sy:updateBase
: The date and time, in W3CDTF format, from which all calculations should originate.

Example

```
<channel rdf:about="http://meerkat.oreillynet.com/?_fl=rss1.0">
<title>Meerkat</title>
<link>http://meerkat.oreillynet.com</link>
<description>Meerkat: An Open Wire Service</description>
<sy:updatePeriod>hourly</sy:updatePeriod>
<sy:updateFrequency>2</sy:updateFrequency>
<sy:updateBase>2000-01-01T12:00+00:00</sy:updateBase>
```

mod_taxonomy

mod_taxonomy allows the classification of objects under a defined taxonomic scheme; basically, you describe the topics of your objects.

The object can be anything: a channel, an item, or a reference from another module. Because of this universality, mod_taxonomy can be used heavily throughout an RSS 1.0 feed, which may cause some confusion. As with many modules, a good bit of reformatting may help clarify things.

The taxonomic definitions are always given as URIs. As shown in Chapter 5, URIs are used, like namespaces, to differentiate between homonyms. Python (the language) and Python (the snake) need to be distinguished, because you may want to run away from one of them. Snakes are generally cuddly, after all.

The Open Directory Project, at *http://www.dmoz.org*, is a good source of taxonomic URIs. All the examples in this section originate from this source.

Namespace

mod_taxonomy takes the stylish moniker of taxo: and the identifying URI of http://purl.org/rss/1.0/modules/taxonomy/. Hence, the lovely root element:

```
<rdf:RDF xmlns:rdf="http://www.w3.org/1999/02/22-rdf-syntax-ns#"
  xmlns="http://purl.org/rss/1.0/"
  xmlns:taxo="http://purl.org/rss/1.0/modules/taxonomy/"
>
```

Elements

mod_taxonomy can be used in two ways: the simple and the more defined. The simple method uses one element, and it can be used as a subelement of item or channel:

```
<taxo:topics>
<rdf:Bag>
<rdf:li resource="
URI to taxonomic reference" /
<rdf:li resource="
URI to taxonomic reference" />
</rdf:Bag>
</taxo:topics>
```

This nesting of elements gives a list of topics that are associated with the channel or the item that contains it. This structure remains the same, with additional <rdf:li resource=""/> elements for every new topic.

This provides a straightforward method for giving a list of defining URIs for an RSS object. Sometimes, however, you might want to define more details of each of the topic URIs themselves. For this, use the taxo:topic element. This element is a subelement of rdf:RDF—i.e., on the same level as channel, item, and so on.

Within the grammar of RDF, taxo:topic allows you to assign metadata to the URI used elsewhere in the feed in taxo:topics. It takes one subelement of its own module, taxo:link, and then any other module's element that can be a subelement of channel. The most popular elements come from mod_dublincore:

```
<taxo:topic rdf:about="
URI of taxonomic resource">
<taxo:link>URL to taxonomic resource<taxo:link>
<dc:subject>Example</dc:subject>
Other elements here
</taxo:topic>
```

The taxo:topic element itself can contain taxo:topics, as shown in Example 6-11.

Example

```
<item rdf:about="http://c.moreover.com/click/here.pl?r123" position="1">
  <title>XML: A Disruptive Technology</title>
  <link>http://c.moreover.com/click/here.pl?r123</link>
  <description>
  XML is placing increasingly heavy loads on the existing technical
  infrastructure of the Internet.
  </description>
  <taxo:topics>
    <rdf:Bag>
     <rdf:li resource="http://meerkat.oreillynet.com/?c=cat23">
     <rdf:li resource="http://meerkat.oreillynet.com/?c=47">
     <rdf:li resource="http://dmoz.org/Computers/Data_Formats/Markup_Languages/XML/">
    </rdf:Bag>
  </taxo:topics>
</item>
<taxo:topic rdf:about="http://meerkat.oreillynet.com/?c=cat23">
  <taxo:link>http://meerkat.oreillynet.com/?c=cat23</taxo:link>
  <dc:title>Data: XML</taxo:title>
  <dc:description>A Meerkat channel</dc:description>
</taxo:topic>
<taxo:topic rdf:about="http://dmoz.org/Computers/Data_Formats/Markup_Languages/XML/">
  <taxo:link>http://dmoz.org/Computers/Data_Formats/Markup_Languages/XML/</taxo:link>
  <dc:title>XML</taxo:title>
  <dc:subject>XML</dc:subject>
  <dc:description>DMOZ category</dc:description>
  <taxo:topics>
   <rdf:Bag>
    <rdf:li resource="http://meerkat.oreillynet.com/?c=cat23">
    <rdf:li resource="http://dmoz.org/Computers/Data_Formats/Markup_Languages/SGML/">
    <rdf:li resource="http://dmoz.org/Computers/Programming/Internet/">
    </rdf:Bag>
  </taxo:topics>
</taxo:topic>
```

This example shows an item using taxo:topics to describe itself and a taxo:topic defining two of the taxonomic definitions used. The last taxo:topic uses taxo:topics itself to define its own subject with more finesse.

Note that the taxo:topic elements—which define the URIs we use within the <item><taxo:topics></taxo:topics></item> section—are on the same level as the item within the document. RSS 1.0's structure, unlike RSS 0.9x, gives them both equal weight.

mod_threading

mod_threading provides a system to describe the children of an item (for example, replies to a weblog entry). This module is still in a state of flux; a great deal of work is being done by many people on the idea of descriptions of message threads within RSS and RDF. This is one of the goals of the ThreadML development effort (*http://www.threadsml.org/*).

With this in mind, mod_threading can get complicated quickly. Unfortunately, as complex as you might logically make it, the lack of standardization means that anything but the simplest usage will likely be misunderstood by most parsers. Therefore, in this chapter we restrict ourselves to defining children only within the limited scope of a single document. If true message threading is your goal, check with the mailing lists and weblogs linked to by the ThreadsML effort for more details.

Namespace

mod_threading takes the prefix thr: and the identifying URI http://purl.org/rss/1.0/modules/threading/. Hence, the root element:

```
<rdf:RDF xmlns:rdf="http://www.w3.org/1999/02/22-rdf-syntax-ns#"
         xmlns="http://purl.org/rss/1.0/"
         xmlns:thr="http://purl.org/rss/1.0/modules/threading/"
>
```

Element

There's only one element within mod_threading; it's a subelement of item[*], and it contains an rdf:Seq containing rdf:li elements of URIs representing items that are children of the item:

```
<thr:children>
  <rdf:Seq>
    <rdf:li rdf:resource="URI OF CHILD ITEM" />
  </rdf:Seq>
</thr:children>
```

For simplicity's sake, the child item, and hence the URI, must be also contained within the same RSS 1.0 document.

Example

```
<item rdf:about="http://c.moreover.com/click/here.pl?r123">
    <title>XML: A Disruptive Technology</title>
    <link>http://c.moreover.com/click/here.pl?r123</link>
    <thr:children>
     <rdf:Seq>
       <rdf:li rdf:resource="http://www.example.com/child1"/>
       <rdf:li rdf:resource="http://www.example.com/child2"/>
       <rdf:li rdf:resource="http://www.example.com/child2"/>
     </rdf:Seq>
   </thr:children>
</item>
```

mod_wiki

Wikis—web pages that grant editing rights to everyone—are increasingly popular, but they give RSS feed creators plenty of special problems. Because wikis contain extensive information about how the page has been edited, and by whom, they require their own module to supply all the necessary elements.

Namespace

mod_wiki's prefix is wiki:, and the identifying URI is http://purl.org/rss/1.0/modules/wiki/. mod_wiki also uses mod_dublincore for some of its elements. Hence, the lovely root element:

```
<rdf:RDF xmlns:rdf="http://www.w3.org/1999/02/22-rdf-syntax-ns#"
         xmlns="http://purl.org/rss/1.0/"
         xmlns:dc="http://purl.org/dc/elements/1.1/"
         xmlns:wiki="http://purl.org/rss/1.0/modules/wiki/"
 >
```

Elements

wiki:interwiki
: An optional subelement of channel, wiki:interwiki refers to the moniker of the wiki in question if it is part of an interwiki setup. It can take two forms, between which you may choose—the simpler:

```
<wiki:interwifi>INTERWIKI MONIKER<wiki:interwiki>
```

or the more complex, which may be unparsable for simple parsers:

```
<wiki:interwiki>
  <rdf:Description link="URL TO WIKI">
    <rdf:value>WIKI NAME</rdf:value>
  </rdf:Description>
</wiki:interwiki>
```

wiki:version
: An optional subelement of item containing the version number of the page.

wiki:status
: An optional subelement of item denoting it as new, updated, or deleted.

wiki:importance
: An optional subelement of item describing the importance of the change to the page (either major or minor).

wiki:diff
: An optional subelement of item that provides a URL to the previous version of the page.

wiki:history
: An optional subelement of item that provides a URL to a list of changes to the page.

wiki:host
: A special optional subelement of the dc:contributor element from mod_dublincore. It contains the IP address of the person who made the change to the wiki page. It should be in the following format:

```
<dc:contributor>
  <rdf:Description wiki:host="192.168.1.10">
    <rdf:value>A.N.Person</rdf:value>
  </rdf:Description>
</dc:contributor>
```

Example

```
<item rdf:about="http://www.usemod.com/cgi-bin/mb2.
pl?action=browse&amp;id=JohnKellden&amp;revision=30">
  <title>JohnKellden</title>
  <link>http://www.usemod.com/cgi-bin/mb2.pl?JohnKellden</link>
  <description></description>
  <dc:date>2002-07-03T06:47:19+00:00</dc:date>
  <dc:contributor>
  <rdf:Description wiki:host="pc88-86.norrkoping.se" >
  <rdf:value>pc88-86.norrkoping.se</rdf:value>
  </rdf:Description>
  </dc:contributor>
  <wiki:status>updated</wiki:status>
  <wiki:importance>major</wiki:importance>
<wiki:diff>http://www.usemod.com/cgi-bin/mb2.
pl?action=browse&amp;diff=4&amp;id=JohnKellden</wiki:diff>
<wiki:version>30</wiki:version>
  <wiki:history>http://www.usemod.com/cgi-bin/mb2.
pl?action=history&amp;id=JohnKellden</
wiki:history>
</item>
```

mod_prism

The mod_prism module allows an RSS 1.0 feed to express metadata terms formalized by the PRISM initiative of IDEAlliance, a publisher and information technology forum. PRISM stands for Publishers Requirements for Industry Standard Metadata and aims to describe content assets from trade serial publications for syndication. PRISM defines a small set of vocabularies that work together to address industry requirements for resource discovery. Adopting the Dublin Core vocabulary (with certain qualifications), PRISM defines an additional basic vocabulary of some 50 terms, plus three smaller, more specialized vocabularies for dealing with rights, inline markup, and controlled vocabularies. This module defines the basic PRISM vocabulary and is frequently used together with the Dublin Core module.

It should be noted that this description of the mod_prism was kindly written by Tony Hammond, a coauthor of the specification itself. Many thanks to him.

Namespace

mod_prism is identified by the prefix prism: and the URI http://prismstandard.org/namespaces/1.2/basic/. Because PRISM uses Dublin Core, it is common practice (though by no means required) to see both the PRISM and Dublin Core namespaces declared together. So, the root element typically appears as:

```
<rdf:RDF xmlns:rdf="http://www.w3.org/1999/02/22-rdf-syntax-ns#"
         xmlns="http://purl.org/rss/1.0/"
```

```
        xmlns:dc="http://purl.org/dc/elements/1.1/"
        xmlns:prism="http://prismstandard.org/namespaces/1.2/basic/"
>
```

Elements

The basic PRISM vocabulary has some 50 terms, far too many to detail here. If you want to experience the full panoply of PRISM, see the actual module for a complete listing and explanation. (That module, in turn, references the PRISM specification, which is the authoritative source for all definitions.) What I'll try to do here is list a few common elements that occur in bibliographic citations and some basic rights terms, and show how these are being used in actual feeds from science publishers to disseminate tables of content alerts.

`prism:copyright`
: Copyright statement for the resource.

`prism:eIssn`
: ISSN for an electronic version of the issue in which the resource occurs.

`prism:issn`
: ISSN for the publication in which the resource was published.

`prism:number`
: Indication of the magazine issue. This element is intended to be used with the `prism:volume` element to specify the magazine issue using the common scheme of Volume and Number.

`prism:publicationDate`
: Announced date and time when the resource is released to the public.

`prism:publicationName`
: Title of the magazine, or other publication, in which a resource is/will be published.

`prism:rightsAgent`
: Name, and possibly contact information, for the person or organization that should be contacted to license the rights to use a resource.

`prism:section`
: Name of the magazine section in which the resource was categorized.

`prism:startingPage`
: Identifies the first page number for the published version of the resource.

`prism:volume`
: Additional identifier for the publication in which the resource appeared, providing the Volume portion of the common Volume/Number scheme.

Example

This example is taken from *Nature*, the well-known weekly scientific magazine. Note especially the use of the `rdfs:seeAlso` link, which points to the previous issue in the series. In this way, the complete collection of issues can be made available and linked together. RSS isn't just for breaking news but can also be used to deliver archival feeds. There is just as much value (and sometimes more) in the older stories.

```
<?xml version="1.0" encoding="utf-8"?>
<rdf:RDF
   xmlns:rdf="http://www.w3.org/1999/02/22-rdf-syntax-ns#"
   xmlns:rdfs="http://www.w3.org/2000/01/rdf-schema#"
   xmlns="http://purl.org/rss/1.0/"
   xmlns:dc="http://purl.org/dc/elements/1.1/"
   xmlns:prism="http://prismstandard.org/namespaces/1.2/basic/"
>
<channel rdf:about="http://www.nature.com/nature/journal/v432/n7013/rss.rdf">
  <title>Nature</title>
  <description>International weekly journal of science</description>
  <link>http://www.nature.com/nature/journal/v432/n7013/rss.rdf</link>
  <rdfs:seeAlso rdf:resource="http://www.nature.com/nature/journal/v431/
                                                               n7012/rss.rdf"/>
  <dc:publisher>Nature Publishing Group</dc:publisher>
  <dc:language>en</dc:language>
  <dc:rights>Copyright © 2004 Nature Publishing Group</dc:rights>
  <prism:publicationName>Nature</prism:publicationName>
  <prism:issn>0028-0836</prism:issn>
  <prism:eIssn>1476-4679</prism:eIssn>
  <prism:copyright>Copyright © 2004 Nature Publishing Group</prism:copyright>
  <prism:rightsAgent>permissions@nature.com</prism:rightsAgent>
  <image rdf:resource="http://nurture.nature.com/rss/images/nature_rss_logo.gif"/>
  <items>
    <rdf:Seq>
        <rdf:li rdf:resource="http://dx.doi.org/10.1038/432004a"/>
    </rdf:Seq>
  </items>
</channel>
<image rdf:about="http://nurture.nature.com/rss/images/nature_rss_logo.gif">
    <title>Nature</title>
    <url>http://nurture.nature.com/rss/images/nature_rss_logo.gif</url>
    <link>http://www.nature.com/nature/</link>
</image>
<item rdf:about="http://dx.doi.org/10.1038/432004a">
    <title>Climate change clouds commercial licence to krill</title>
    <link>http://dx.doi.org/10.1038/432004a</link>
    <description>Emma Marris</description>
    <dc:title>Climate change clouds commercial licence to krill</dc:title>
    <dc:creator>Emma Marris</dc:creator>
    <dc:identifier>doi:10.1038/432004a</dc:identifier>
    <dc:source>Nature 432, 4 (2004)</dc:source>
    <dc:date>2004-11-04</dc:date>
    <prism:publicationName>Nature</prism:publicationName>
    <prism:publicationDate>2004-11-04</prism:publicationDate>
    <prism:volume>432</prism:volume>
    <prism:number>7013</prism:number>
    <prism:section>News</prism:section>
    <prism:startingPage>4</prism:startingPage>
</item>
</rdf:RDF>
```

Other RSS 1.0 Modules

The use of RSS 1.0 is especially prevalent in the scientific and governmental fields. There are modules available there, too. They're a little too specialized for a complete rundown, but here's a short list:

CMLRSS (http://wwmm.ch.cam.ac.uk/moin/CmlRss)
: For chemists, CMLRSS enables RSS 1.0 to convey information about the structure of chemical molecules. Developed at the University of Cambridge, the authors have also made Java software available for producing visualizations of the molecules themselves.

The UK e-Government Metadata Standard (http://www.esd-toolkit.org/laws/)
: The U.K. government has mandated an RDF schema for its data, and this is also available as an RSS 1.0 feed. Andrew Green has created Perl modules specifically for creating such feeds, available at *http://search.cpan.org/~article/*.

Context (http://www2.elsevier.co.uk/~tony/spec/rss/mod_context.html)
: Supports applications that want to use the proposed OpenURL Framework for Context-Sensitive Services. More details are at *http://www.niso.org/committees/committee_ax.html*.

MPN-Interest (http://matrixpn.auriga.wearlab.de/interest-module/interest.html)
: Creates an automatic recommendation system between weblogs, perhaps further explained by this presentation: *http://matrixpn.auriga.wearlab.de/freeporter-mgain_presentation/freeporter-mgain_presentation.html*.

LiveJournal (http://www.livejournal.org/rss/lj/1.0/)
: A module that allows RSS 1.0 to include LiveJournal specific metadata to each entry.

RSSDiscuss (http://www.flutterby.com/software/rssdiscuss/)
: Displays information about message boards and other discussion areas.

photoAlbum (http://xml.innothinx.com/photoAlbum/)
: Displays information commonly found in a photo album application.

Ruby Application Archive (http://www.rubycolor.org/rss/1.0/modules/raa/)
: Displays information about applications within the Ruby Application Archive, *http://raa.ruby-lang.org/*.

Learning Object Metadata (http://www.downes.ca/xml/RSS_LOM.htm)
: Displays information about Learning Objects.

CHAPTER 7

The Atom Syndication Format

Nothing exists except atoms and empty space;
everything else is opinion.
—Democritus

Rising from the ashes of the years of civil war within the RSS world, the Atom project has gained considerable attention for its syndication format and publishing API. We won't be dealing with the API in this book, but the syndication format is increasingly important. In this chapter, you'll come up to speed with the latest developments, and learn how to build your own Atom feed.

Introducing Atom

When, in 2003, it became painfully clear that the RSS world was not going to declare a truce and agree to sort out the remaining problems—the competing formats being the biggest of them, the lack of documentation the second—a large group of interested developers split off to design a new format from the ground up. After much tooing, froing, cogitating, and argument, not least over the name of the thing, a format has arisen: the Atom Syndication Format.

At time of writing, the format is at Version 0.5, and this book is based on that version. It is hoped that by April 2005, the Atom format will reach a solid Version 1.0 and will be submitted to the Internet Engineering Task Force as a proposed standard. You should therefore, after reading this chapter, consult the necessary web pages for the latest details. Changes will have been made, but nothing too drastic, I believe. Nevertheless, it is safer to warn you that *what I am about to write may well be wrong by the time you come to read it.*

This chapter is based on the standard found at *http://www.ietf.org/internet-drafts/draft-ietf-atompub-format-05.txt*, and the mailing list for discussing the syntax of the specification itself is at *http://www.imc.org/atom-syntax/index.html*.

One key difference between the development of RSS and the development of Atom is that Atom's whole design process is held out in the open, on the Atom-Syntax mailing list just mentioned and on the Atom wiki. The wiki (*http://www.intertwingly.net/wiki/pie/FrontPage*) is a great place to find the latest developments, issues, ideas, and pointers to the latest specification documents. It is well worth exploring, once you've finished reading.

The Structure of an Atom Feed

Because Atom is really two standards, one for syndication and one for the remote retrieval, creation, and editing of online resources (or, to put it more simply, a weblog API), an Atom document is deeply structured. The syndication format, our bailiwick here, defines two document formats: the Atom feed and the Atom entry.

An Atom feed is made up of none or more Atom entries (although it's most probably going to have at least one entry), plus some additional metadata. An Atom entry is just that: one single indivisible piece of "content." This single indivisible piece of content is what gives Atom its name and is the key to understanding the whole Atom project.

The Atom entry

Before we get too excited, let's look at an Atom entry document (Example 7-1).

Example 7-1. An Atom entry document

```
<?xml version="1.0" encoding="utf-8"?>
<entry version="draft-ietf-atompub-format-05: do not deploy"
 xmlns="http://purl.org/atom/ns#draft-ietf-atompub-format-05">

<title>Example Entry Document</title>

<link
rel="alternate"
type="text/html"
href="http://example.org/example_entry"
hreflang="en"
title="Example Entry Document"
/>

<edit href="http://example.org/edit?title=example_entry">

<author>
        <name>Ben Hammersley</name>
        <uri>http://www.benhammersley.com</uri>
        <email>ben@benhammersley.com</email>
</author>

<contributor>
        <name>Albert Einstein</name>
```

Example 7-1. An Atom entry document (continued)

```
        <uri>http://example.org/~al</uri>
        <email>BigAl@example.org</email>
</contributor>

<id>http://example.org/2004/12345678</id>

<updated>2004-10-22T22:08:02Z</updated>
<published>2004-10-22T20:19:02Z</published>

<summary type="TEXT">This is an example of an Atom Entry Document.</summary>

<content type="HTML"><p><em>This</em> is an example of an Atom Entry Document.
It's rather nice, don't you think?</p></content>

<copyright type="TEXT">This example of an Atom Entry Document is hereby granted into the
Public Domain</copyright>

</entry>
```

I will address the finer details of the syntax in the next section. An Atom entry document contains, quite readably, a good deal of the information you can possibly say about an Internet resource, plus the content itself. It doesn't contain any metadata about the *meaning* of the content—leaving that to RDF and RSS 1.0—but it does give all the information you might need to display the content and the first order of information about that content: who wrote it, and when, for example.

The Atom Publishing API uses this exact same format to transfer documents around. The ramifications of this architecture will be examined later in this chapter after we've looked over the format more thoroughly. For now, let's look at feeds.

Combining entries to make a feed

A feed, happily enough, is just a collection of entry documents, wrapped up with some additional information. Example 7-2 shows a single entry feed using the example entry in Example 7-1.

Example 7-2. An example Atom feed document

```
<?xml version="1.0" encoding="utf-8"?>

<feed version="draft-ietf-atompub-format-05: do not deploy"
 xmlns="http://purl.org/atom/ns#draft-ietf-atompub-format-05">

<head>
        <title>An Example Feed</title>

        <link
        rel="alternate"
        type="text/html"
        href="http://example.org/index.html"
```

Example 7-2. An example Atom feed document (continued)

```
        hreflang="en"
        title="Example Page"
        />

        <introspection href="http://www.example.org/introspection.xml" />
        <post href="http://www.example.org/post" />

        <author>
                <name>Ben Hammersley</name>
                <uri>http://www.benhammersley.com</uri>
                <email>ben@benhammersley.com</email>
        </author>

        <contributor>
                <name>Albert Einstein</name>
                <uri>http://example.org/~al</uri>
                <email>BigAl@example.org</email>
        </contributor>

        <tagline>Two Atoms are Walking Down the Street.</tagline>
        <id>http://www.example.org/feed.xml</id>
        <generator
        uri="http://www.example.org/atomtool.html"
        version="1.0">Acme Atom Tool</generator>

        <copyright>Unless otherwise stated, this feed and its entries are all copyright
example.org 2004, and may not be reused under any circumstances
under pain of death.</copyright>

        <info>This is an example feed.</info>
        <updated>2004-10-22T22:08:02Z</updated>
</head>

<entry>

<title>Example Entry Document</title>

<link
rel="alternate"
type="text/html"
href="http://example.org/example_entry"
hreflang="en"
title="Example Entry Document"
/>

<edit href="http://example.org/edit?title=example_entry"/>

<author>
        <name>Ben Hammersley</name>
        <uri>http://www.benhammersley.com</uri>
        <email>ben@benhammersley.com</email>
</author>
```

Example 7-2. An example Atom feed document (continued)

```
<contributor>
        <name>Albert Einstein</name>
        <uri>http://example.org/~al</uri>
        <email>BigAl@example.org</email>
</contributor>

<id>http://example.org/2004/12345678</id>

<updated>2004-10-22T22:08:02Z</updated>
<published>2004-10-22T20:19:02Z</published>

<summary type="TEXT">This is an example of an Atom Entry Document.</summary>

<content type="HTML"><p><em>This</em> is an example of an Atom Entry Document.
It's rather nice, don't you think?</p></content>

<copyright type="TEXT">This example of an Atom Entry Document is hereby granted into the
Public Domain</copyright>

</entry>
</feed>
```

This too is simple enough. You have the entry document, changed only for the sake of XML syntax (moving up the namespace declaration), and the tiny issue of moving the `version` attribute to the root element. Other than that, it's unchanged. If there are more entries, they will just drop in below in a predictable manner, as you'll see later.

The Reusable Syntax of Constructs

Both types of document, feed and entry, are made up of standardized elements. Each element is blessed with content that has been organized into one of the options provided by the Reusable Syntax of Constructs. Apart from being a particularly good name for a modern jazz quintet, the idea behind the Reusable Syntax of Constructs is to make the discussion of elements, both established and proposed, much simpler.

All the elements in an Atom document, therefore, can be one of seven alternative Constructs: Text, Person, Date, Service, Link, Category, and Identity. Here's what they mean:

Text
: Human-readable text. This may have a type attribute, set to either `TEXT`, `HTML`, or `XHTML`, denoting its format. If the attribute is missing, it is assumed to be `TEXT`. If you have entity-encoded markup in a Text construct without declaring it as `HTML` or `XHTML`, the application reading the feed will display tags literally and won't render it as if the application were a web browser. This ability to categorically state what the content actually is, is a significant difference and improvement over RSS 2.0

If the type attribute is set to `HTML`, the markup must be entity-encoded like so: <em>this</em>. If you use entity codes within the content itself, they need to be double-encoded. So, if you want to include some HTML code that displays an ampersand, it needs to be marked as & within the Atom element.

With the type attribute set to `XHTML`, the markup isn't entity-encoded but must be valid and well-formed. Tags must balance and close; if they don't, it throws out the entire document, so great care must be used here.

Person

This construct describes a "person, corporation, or similar entity" according to the specification. It takes three subelements:

- `name` is mandatory and should contain a human-readable name for the entity.
- `uri` is optional, can occur only once if it occurs at all, and must be a standard URI associated with the entity.
- `email` is optional, can only occur once, and must be a valid email address.

The Person construct can also be extended by any namespace-qualified subelements. We will deal with those in Chapter 11.

Date

The simplest construct. Its content is a date/time value, conforming to RFC3339. It's in the format YYYY-MM-DDTHH:MM:SS.ss+HH:MM.

Service

The Service construct is a single empty element with an attribute, `href`, that points to the endpoint of the Atom Publishing API service denoted by the name of the element. For example, the `href` attribute of the `edit` element of an Atom entry document points to the endpoint of the `edit` service for that entry. The `href` attribute of the `post` element of a feed document points to the `post` endpoint of that particular feed's installation.

Link

The Link construct is the most complicated of the constructs but perhaps the most interesting and powerful. It denotes a connection from the Atom document to another web resource. It has five attributes:

- `rel` denotes what sort of relationship the link is. It's most commonly either `alternate` (for an alternatively formatted version of the same content) or `related`, and is optional. However, if it's left out, it is assumed to be `alternate`. I'll cover the many different types of `link` later in this chapter.
- `type` indicates the media type of the resource. This is optional and is only to be taken as a hint. It doesn't override the media type the server returns with the resource. No amount of wishful thinking on behalf of the feed can make a `text/plain` resource into an `audio/mpeg`. Its value must be a registered media type as detailed in RFC 2045.

- `length` indicates the size of the resource in octets. Again, like `type`, this is optional and is only to be taken as a hint: it doesn't override reality.
- `href` is the URI the link points to and so is compulsory and must be a URI. `xml:base` processing must be applied to the content of this attribute, which means that if the Atom document has declared an `xml:base` attribute in its root element, this must be taken into account. The lack of an `xml:base` declaration, too, is significant: relative URIs are meaningless and wrong without one.
- `hreflang` denotes the language of the resource found at the `href`. It's an optional attribute whose value must be a standard language tag as per RFC 3066. If this attribute is used with `rel="alternate"`, it implies that the resource referenced is a translation of the document in hand.

Category

The Category construct contains information that categorizes elements of an Atom document: the feed itself, or individual entries. It consists of three attributes:

- `term` is a string that identifies the category of the parent element within whatever taxonomy you are operating. If you use the Category construct, you must have a term attribute present.
- `scheme` is a URI that identifies a formal taxonomy within which the `term` attribute is found. It's optional.
- `label` provides a human-readable label for the `term` attribute for display by end-user applications. It's optional and allows an element using the Category construct to provide both nicely readable categorization as well as references to more unfriendly formal categories, which might be written as, say, numeric codes.

Identity

This contains a URI to represent the construct's parent for its entire existence. It must be permanent and universally unique, and *doesn't change*. No matter what happens to that Atom document—whether it's relocated, migrated, syndicated, republished, exported or imported, updated, downgraded, abused, folded, spindled, or mutilated—an Identity construct is unwavering. It stands by its man. It doesn't change. We salute it.

You should also bear in mind that the Identity construct is a URI, as defined by RFC 2396. This means that it isn't a simple string but is its own datatype with its own rules. See the sidebar "Dealing with URIs in Atom" for details.

Dealing with URIs in Atom

URIs are used in Atom to identify the feed or entry. They allow applications to keep track of things they have seen in order to flag new or changed content. Applications do this by comparing the URIs as strings. However, for various complex reasons, (as detailed by Mark Pilgrim at *http://www.xml.com/pub/a/2004/08/18/pilgrim.html*), this isn't simple. To avoid these problems, Atom specifies that URIs must be normalized by the document's publisher before they are published. Most standard publishing packages already produce normalized URIs, but here are the rules as per RFC 2396bis:

- Provide the scheme in lowercase characters: have `http://` rather than `HTTP://`.
- Provide the host, if any, in lowercase characters: have `www.example.org` instead of `WWW.EXAMPLE.ORG`.
- Perform percent-encoding only where essential and use only uppercase A through F characters; decode all percent-encoded characters to their ASCII equivalents if they have any. If not, you should write them like `%C3%87` rather than `%c3%87` (that's a capital C with a cedilla, by the way).
- For schemes that define a default authority, use an empty authority if the default is desired; some URI schemes allow you to pass a username and password within the URI. HTTP, for example, allows `http://username:password@www.example.org/` and rules that leave them off entirely, and so accessing the resource as the default user is the same as leaving them blank. (`http://@www.example.org/` is the same as `http://www.example.org/`). If this is the case, and you want to access the resource as the default user, leave off the authentication section entirely. So, use `http://www.example.org/`, not `http://@www.example.org/`.
- For schemes that define an empty path to be equivalent to a path of /, use /. Don't use `www.example.org` as shorthand for `www.example.org/`. With some URI schemes, in some circumstances, the presence or absence of the trailing slash changes the meaning. So, the rule is if you can add the slash without changing the meaning of the path, you should always add it.
- For schemes that define a port, use an empty port if the default is desired. As with the authentication, if you're using the default setting, leave it off entirely. So, instead of `http://www.example.org:80/` or `http://www.example.org:/`, use `http://www.example.org`.
- Preserve empty fragment identifiers and queries. With URIs that represent query strings or fragments, you should keep them there, even if they are empty. So `http://www.example.org/search?q=atom&x=` should remain so; don't change to `http://www.example.org/search?q=atom` even if the resultant query is exactly the same when dereferenced.
- Ensure that all portions of the URI are UTF-8-encoded NFC form Unicode strings. There are multiple ways to encode multibyte unicode characters. Use the form known as Normalized Form C, or the "composed" version.

Sam Ruby has published a Python script to do all this at *http://intertwingly.net/stories/2004/08/04/urlnorm.py*.

The Atom Entry Document in Detail

Now that you have the building blocks of Atom, let's move on to the details. We'll first look at the standard elements of an Atom entry document.

Atom entry documents not only make up the bulk of an Atom feed but are also used as the transport for the Atom Publishing API and as a format for web site archives. For example, using the Atom entry document format as an archive template for your weblog seems an increasingly good idea.

The Elements of Atom Entry

`entry`
: Within an Atom entry document, the `entry` element is the root, which must have a version attribute to denote the version of Atom you are deploying. This book is based on the draft-05, whose version identifier is `draft-ietf-atompub-format-05: do not deploy`. Subtlety isn't its strong point, you have to admit. This element may also contain any number of XML namespace declarations for the use of other XML vocabularies. I cover this in Chapter 11.

  If the entry is part of a feed document, this element has no attributes. Either way, the remainder of the elements are all children of `entry`.

`title`
: The `title` element is a Text construct that gives the title of the entry. The entry must have one, and only one.

`link`
: `link`, a Link construct, gives details of related URIs. There must be at least one with a `rel` attribute of `alternate`, but there can't be more than one of these with the same `type` value. This most commonly points to the HTML version of the resource, as with the `link` element in both flavors of RSS.

  You can have as many `link` elements as you wish with a `rel` of something other than `alternate`. We'll talk about those later on in this chapter.

`edit`
: The `edit` element is a Service construct pointing to the edit endpoint for this particular entry for use with the Atom Publishing API. You can only have one of these, but it is optional.

`author`
: `author` is mandatory, unless the document is within a feed that has already declared an `author` for everything. It's a Person construct, denoting the primary author of the entry, and you can only have one of them. For multiple authors, you have to decide who the most important one was and demote the others to `contributor`. If necessary, fight.

`host`
: `host` is optional and conveys the domain name, dotted IPv4 address, or IPv6 colon-delimited address associated with the origin of the entry document. Confused? Me too, until I saw it came from the need to give authorship details of posts from wikis. In many cases, the author of a wiki article isn't known by anything other than the IP address she posted from. This element is for that situation.

`contributor`
: `contributor` is a Person construct, entirely optional and unlimited in number, that denotes a contributor to the entry. You must have an `author` before you start talking about `contributors`, however.

`id`
: `id` is a URI construct that provides a URI for the entry. See the sidebar "Dealing with URIs in Atom" for more on this.

`category`
: `category` is a category construct that provides a category for the entry document.

`updated`
: A Date construct, the `updated` element must be present, once, within an entry. It denotes the last time the content changed in a way that the producer deems significant. So, you don't need to change this if you're fixing spelling mistakes, for example.

`published`
: `published` is a Date construct denoting "an instant in time associated with an event early in the lifecycle of the entry," according to the specification document. Basically, this means either when it was written or when it was made available to the public. These are different things, granted, but there is no way to tell the difference within Atom's standard elements as yet.

: You can, curiously, also set the `published` element to a value in the future. This suggests to applications that the entry shouldn't be displayed until that time, but applications don't have to pay any attention to this and can go ahead and display it anyway. No manners, some people.

`summary`
: The `summary` element, in brief, is a Text construct that gives a short summary or extract of the entry. It's optional if there is a `content` element, and, like the Highlander, there can be only one.

: If there is no `content` element, `summary` is mandatory. The `summary` is also mandatory if the `content` has an `src` attribute and is therefore empty, or if the `content` is encoded in Base64. As for that, we're just getting to it.

`content`
: The concept of content within an Atom entry document differs slightly from that within an RSS feed. Within Atom, as with RSS, you can include the content directly within the entry document, but you can also just link to the content placed within a different file. (Although, as detailed later, you're discouraged

from doing this with text content.) Furthermore, you can include any form of content (inside the feed, or linked to externally) and not just text or HTML.

The `content` element is its own construct, consisting of two attributes, `type` and `src`, and its own content:

- `type` may be either `TEXT`, `HTML`, or `XHTML`—following the same rules as the Text construct—or if none of these things, it must be a valid MIME media type as per RFC 2045. If the `type` attribute is missing, it is considered to be equal to `TEXT` with all of the ramifications detailed for the earlier Text construct.
- The `src` attribute may be a URI, which the application may dereference to retrieve the content. If the `src` attribute is present, the `content` element must be empty, and the `type` must be a MIME type and not `TEXT`, `HTML`, or `XHTML`. The MIME type returned by the server providing the resource is definitive, however. In other words, the feed might say something is x, but if the server says its y, you should treat it as y.

  Finally, if the value of `type` begins with "text/" or ends with "+xml", the content should be part of the feed as far as possible.

`copyright`
: This is a Text construct that conveys copyright information for the entry. It's optional, and only one can be present. If it's not there, the `copyright` of the feed document takes over. If it is there, it takes precedence over that of the feed.

The Atom Feed Document in Detail

So, armed with handfuls of entry documents, we can make a feed. Feeds have their own elements too. Here they are:

`feed`
: The `feed` element is always the root element of a feed document. Like the `entry` element within a standalone entry document, it takes a single attribute, `version`, which in the case of this version of the specification equals `draft-ietf-atompub-format-05: do not deploy`.

  Everything is a child of this element. It takes two children directly, one `head`, and zero or more `entrys`, containing the entry documents.

`head`
: The `head` element is a container for the metadata of a feed. The rest of the elements in this section are children of this `head` element. It may also contain properly namespace-qualified elements from other XML vocabularies, as you'll see in Chapter 11.

`title`
: A Text construct giving the title of the feed. It is mandatory.

`link`
: As with its namesake within the entry document, `link` is a Link construct, giving details of related URIs. If there is no `content` element within an entry, there must be at least one `link` with a `rel` attribute of `alternate`. There can't be more than one with the same `type` value. `link` is most commonly used to point to the HTML version of the resource, as with the `link` element in both flavors of RSS.

  We'll talk about the other types of `link` later on in this chapter.

  If a feed's `link rel="alternate"` element resolves to an HTML document, then that document should have an autodiscovery link element that reflects back to the feed. We discuss this in Chapter 9.

`introspection`
: The `introspection` element is a Service construct giving the URI of a site's introspection file. It's optional, and you can only have one.*

`post`
: This element is a Service construct that conveys the URI used to add entries to the feed, using the Atom Publishing API. It's optional, and, yes, only one is allowed.

`author`
: As with the Atom entry document, the `author` element is a Person construct to denote the primary author of the feed and the entries found within it. As noted in the entry document section, the person denoted by `feed/head/author` is overruled by anyone denoted by `feed/entry/author`. However, if the majority of your entries are authored by the same person, use of this element saves time. Either way, unless all your entries have their own `author` element, it is mandatory. You can, naturally, have only one.

`contributor`
: Basically, this is the same as the `author` element, it's used only to denote any other authors. The rules of precedence are exactly the same as those for `author`.

`category`
: `category` is a category construct that provides a category for the entire feed document.

`tagline`
: A Text construct giving a description or tagline for the feed. Optional; only one is allowed; brevity and wit are appreciated.

* The idea of an introspection file is also a matter of debate. It is used with the Atom API and is a separate file containing the URIs of the Atom API endpoints for all the sites within that domain, for each of the API methods. There is no current standard for the introspection file, and perhaps there never will be. Certainly, the presence of the `post edit` elements take much of its place. As I keep stressing, in using the Atom standards, you are on the bleeding edge of syndication technology, which is itself built on the bleeding edge of publishing technology. It's not inconceivable that things will drop off every so often.

`id` An Identity construct giving a unique, permanent identifier for this feed. The feed's URI, in other words. It's optional, but you can have only one.

`generator`
: An optional element denoting the software used to create the feed. This is useful for statistics and for error tracking. You can have only one of these elements, obviously. The specification document puts it succinctly:

> The content of this element must be a string that is a human-readable name for the generating agent. The element may have a "uri" attribute whose value must be a URI. When dereferenced, that URI should produce a representation that is relevant to that agent. The generator element may have a "version" attribute that indicates the version of the generating agent. When present, its value is unstructured text.

`copyright`
: A Text construct conveying human-readable copyright information for the entire feed and all its entries except those that contain their own `copyright` element. It's optional, and the feed itself can have only one. It shouldn't be used to convey machine-readable information.

`info`
: This is a Text construct giving a human-readable explanation of the format itself. It's optional and really just a place for people to leave notes to other developers. It isn't meant to be used by any application and is only viewable if you look directly at the source.

`updated`
: A Date construct, the `updated` element must be present, once, within a feed. As with the entry document equivalent, it denotes the last time the content changed enough for the publisher to want readers to know about it.

So there you go: the entire makeup of an Atom feed, as of January 2005. Again, be aware that Atom is a changing specification. I am judging, perhaps wrongly, that the specification won't change radically from the one detailed here—and if it does, you are now in a fine position to understand the changes—but before you deploy the format in anything resembling a permanent manner, go and check the latest documents.

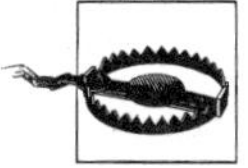

Atom documents should be served under a MIME type of `application/atom+xml` with the file extension *.atom*.

The Simplest Possible Thing That Will Actually Work

What, therefore, is the simplest possible Atom feed document? Technically speaking, you don't need to have any entries at all, but that's as close to useless as you're allowed to get. Assuming one entry, Example 7-3 shows the simplest possible Atom feed. If your feed is missing any of these elements, it is incomplete.

Alternate link Types

The link element allows entry and feed documents to be linked to others. The most common is to use the rel="alternate" attribute to point to an HTML version of the content within the Atom document. This, indeed, is mandatory.

There are many other types of link currently proposed within the Atom community. None of them are, as yet, part of the actual specification itself, and none of them are, again as yet, supported by the common newsreader applications. However they are popular, and the debate is raging around them.

The current guideline is that "implementations MUST consider the link relation type to be equivalent to the same name registered within the IANA Registry of Link Relations Section 10, and thus the URI that would be obtained by appending the value of the rel attribute to the string 'http://www.iana.org/assignments/relation/.'" The value of "rel" describes the meaning of the link but doesn't impose any behavioral requirements on implementations.

The discussion around this can be tracked on the atom-syntax list, and a series of examples can be found on the wiki at *http://intertwingly.net/wiki/pie/LinkTagMeaning*.

The upshot at the moment is that under draft-05, only two types of link are allowed: alterate and related.

A link rel="related" element, the only other type allowed, can appear only within entries, and should point to either web pages or other Atom entry documents that are related in some way to the entry in hand. For example:

```
<link rel="related" type="text/html" href="http://www.example.org/related.html"
hreflang="en"/>
```

Example 7-3. The simplest possible Atom feed, with one entry

```
<?xml version="1.0" encoding="utf-8"?>
<feed version="draft-ietf-atompub-format-05: do not deploy"
 xmlns="http://purl.org/atom/ns#draft-ietf-atompub-format-05">

<head>
<title>The Simplest Feed</title>
<link rel="alternate" type="text/html"   href="http://example.org/index.html"/>
<author><name>Ben Hammersley</name></author>
<updated>2004-10-25T15:07:02Z</updated>
</head>

<entry>
<title>The Simplest Entry Document</title>
<link rel="alternate" type="text/html" href="http://example.org/example_entry"/>
<author><name>Ben Hammersley</name></author>
<id>http://example.org/2004/12345679</id>
<updated>2004-10-25T15:07:02Z</updated>
```

Example 7-3. The simplest possible Atom feed, with one entry (continued)

```
<content type="TEXT">Simple Simple Simple</content>
</entry>
</feed>
```

Producing Atom Feeds

Because it is still in its infancy, the Atom Syndication Format has few libraries available to make its generation a simple matter. Unlike RSS, with its years of development, people haven't had the time or opportunity to build Perl modules or the like. The few that do exist are invariably out of date or will be by the time you read this book. With this in mind, therefore, there is little point in detailing those that do exist. By the time Atom goes to Version 1.0, there will be simpler alternatives, and we'll cover those in later editions of this book. Preorder now!

From that you'll see, of course, that using a library for the *creation* of Atom feeds is overkill. For most simple uses, you're perfectly well off using a series of `print` commands or using a templating system as if you were producing ordinary RSS.

Producing Atom with Perl

Perl is the one language with at least a framework of two Atom creation libraries. Ben Trott's `XML::Atom` and Tim Appnel's `XML::Atom::Syndication` are both very promising starts. But both are, at time of writing, either incomplete or out of date. Keep an eye on them, though, as they sport both good beginnings and fine authors.

Validating Atom Feeds

Atom's strict structure, and the fact that by the time the shouting is over, there will be only one version to get people's knickers in a twist, means that validation is easy. The Feed Validator, at *http://feedvalidator.org/*, is the one-stop shop for such needs. Written by Sam Ruby and Mark Pilgrim, both leading brains of the syndication world, it produces extremely useful results. Test your feeds often.

CHAPTER 8

Parsing and Using Feeds

The limits of my language mean the limits of my world.
—Ludwig Wittgenstein

By now you should be fully up to speed with both RSS 1.0 and 2.0 and Atom. You will also have seen, in Chapter 2, the most popular feed-reading applications. In this chapter, we deal with the consumption of the feeds, for either display on a web page or use within your own programs.

Important Issues

This is where it starts to get really messy. We have discussed the production of three standards in this book, but there are hundreds of variations in the wild. This chaos has arisen because of a combination of the confusion of standards development, common misunderstandings about what constitutes valid XML, and a general agreement among the developers of feed-reading applications that they would parse invalid feeds at all costs. Indeed, it is because of these clashing versions of the RSS family that the Atom project was started in the first place.

When it comes to parsing any given feed, therefore, you need to take one specific fact into account: the feed is probably invalid. This might seem harsh, but you have to remember that the RSS community went through a long period when the specifications were so loosely defined that it was hard to pin down exactly what was and wasn't valid. These feeds, and the systems that produce them, have not been revisited. Standards compliance aside, it's thought that at least 10% of feeds aren't even valid XML. This causes a lot of problems in itself.

The situation *is* improving, but you must remain aware of the problem. The most popular newsreader applications are built to be liberal parsers. That is, they act like modern web browsers and try to work round as many errors as they can. This tends to bring about a false sense of security that will betray you when you use your own parsing tools.

There is also a great deal of debate about whether or not it is *right* to use a liberal parser. The argument for strictness is that the RSS community would be better served by people's errors being pointed out to them. This may or may not be true, but it's a lost argument. The RSS community is now too big for any form of universal collaborative action, and no one is going to use a strict parser on a public web site and have it break in front of the rest of the world. The end user, after all, doesn't know or care about the technicalities discussed in this book. Liberal parsers, whether morally correct or not, have won the day.

Of course, there's only so far you can go with liberality, and even the most accepting of parsers will balk at the really badly formed feed. You are therefore advised to pay a lot of attention to generating well-formed feeds, despite the fact that if you do make a mistake, it will probably go unnoticed by the majority of your readers. The old adage to be strict in what you produce and liberal in what you accept has much application here.

The feed parsers available to us can be separated into two groups: those for display and those for programmatic use. The older, the Display Parsers, to coin a phrase, turn RSS and Atom into HTML. Programmatic Parsers, another neologism, turn RSS and Atom into internal structures within programs. There is only a little crossover.

Converting Atom to RSS

There really isn't a problem consuming both RSS and Atom in the same parser. By now, most of the useful libraries take both formats equally seriously. However, with Atom still in flux, there may be a time when the parsers' authors haven't caught up with a new specification. If you really must use a parser that supports only RSS or can't deal with the latest version of Atom, and yet you must also consume the latest Atom feeds, the only thing to do is convert the Atom feed to RSS. This can be done in two ways:

Third-party services
: Various people, for varying reasons, offer RSS-to-Atom conversion as an online service. Two examples are *http://www.2rss.com/software.php?page=atom2rss* and *http://www.feedburner.com*.

XSLT
: Because both formats are XML-based, you can use XSLT to convert between the two. Aaron Straup Cope makes some XSL stylesheets to do just this. They are available at *http://www.aaronland.info/xsl/atom/0.3/*.

I don't recommend either option; it's far preferable, if Atom is going to be presented, to use an Atom-capable parser from the start. RSS is certainly never going to go away, but then again, neither is Atom.

JavaScript Display Parsers

The original use for RSS was to allow Netscape to display headlines and links on its My Netscape portal pages, and this sort of use remains very popular. But because you don't need any programming skills to build a web site, nor a server that can run scripts to make it public, right from the beginning there has been a need for RSS parsers that live on other people's servers and that web site authors can use without much trouble.

These JavaScript Display Parsers are still very popular, and there are many to go round. Each works pretty much the same way: you edit a snippet of JavaScript slightly and then place it inside a web page. Let's look at one of these.

RSS XPress

Andy Powell and Pete Cliff's RSS XPress system, found at *http://rssxpress.ukoln.ac.uk/lite/*, is an excellent example. Hosted by the U.K. Office for Library Networking at the University of Bath, it takes a feed's URL and returns XHTML directly to the browser's rendering engine. Example 8-1 shows a listing of a very basic web page that displays the RSS 1.0 file from my own weblog. Figure 8-1 shows how it looks in the Safari browser on Mac OS X.

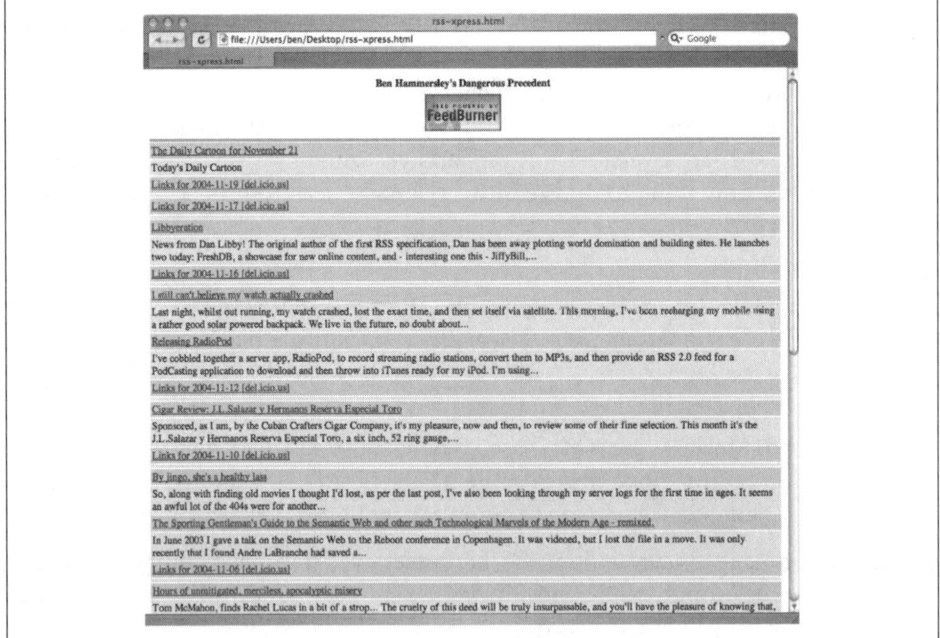

Figure 8-1. A very basic web page invoking RSS Xpress

Example 8-1. A very basic web page invoking RSS Xpress

```
<html>
<head></head>
<body>
 <script src="http://rssxpress.ukoln.ac.uk/lite/viewer/?rss=http%3A%2F%2Fwww.
    benhammersley.com%2Findex.rdf"></script>
</body>
</html>
```

The advantages of this sort of parser are plain to see. It's extremely easy to set up and doesn't require any more programming skill than a knowledge of cutting and pasting. It's also potentially much kinder on the publisher of the feed itself because sensible versions of this parser will include some form of caching at the server end. The disadvantages are that it is impossible to do anything other than display the data, and that you might not like the way the feed looks when you display it. The latter isn't too serious an objection, however, because most such parsers add `div` and `span` markup to the XHTML they return. You can, therefore, apply a stylesheet to them. In the case of the RSS Xpress service, this is very straightforward. Example 8-2 shows an HTML page with some CSS, and Figure 8-2 shows how that looks.

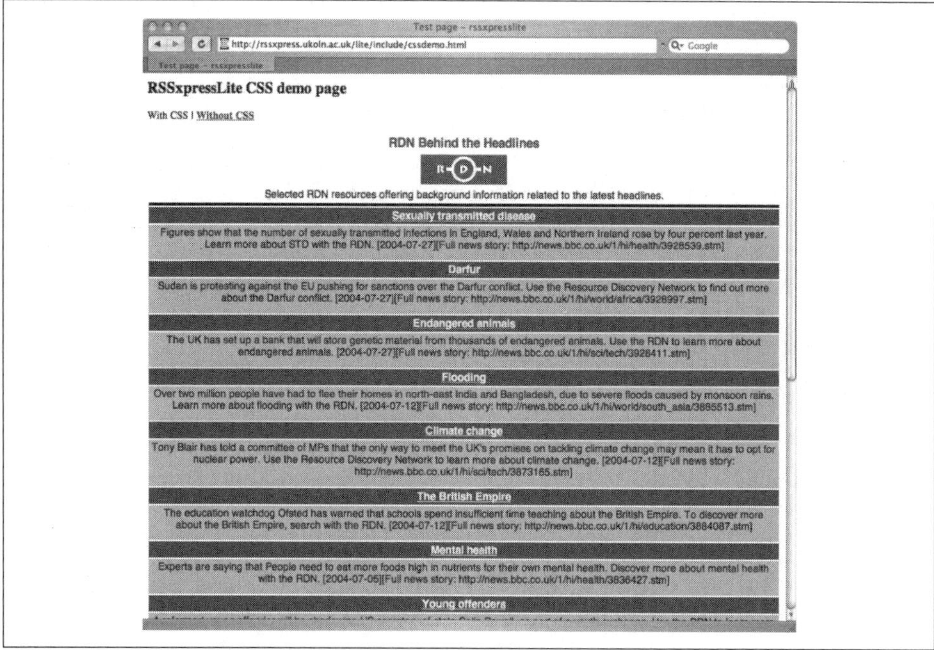

Figure 8-2. How the CSS changes the display of the feed

Example 8-2. An HTML listing to invoke RSS XPress, using CSS

```
<html>
  <head>
  <title>Test page - rssxpresslite</title>
  </head>
  <style>
  <!--
    /* A:link refers to all links on the page - not just the RSS content... */
    A:link { color : yellow; font-weight : bold; }
    A:visited { color : yellow; font-weight : bold; }

    /* these are the RSS classes - you can adapt them as you see fit
       values here override the defaults... */

    .rssxpresschannel {
      font-family : sans-serif;
      text-align : center;
    }

    .rssxpresschtitle {
      font-size : large;
      color : #006393;
    }

    .rssxpresschdesc {
      color : black;
      text-align : center;
    }

    .rssxpressittitle {
      font-size : 110%;
      line-height : 120%;
      background-color : #006393;
    }

    .rssxpressitdesc {
      background-color : #c6c6de;
      padding-bottom : 10pt;
    }

    .rssxpresstable {
      text-align : center;
    }

    /* rssxpressdivider is a special case - it is a single pixel, single column row on the
rssxpress channel - to alter its color just change the background-color image. */

    .rssxpressdivider {
      background-color : black;
    }

  //-->
  </style>
```

Example 8-2. An HTML listing to invoke RSS XPress, using CSS (continued)

```
  <body>
  <h2>RSSxpressLite CSS demo page</h2>
  <p><!-- <a href="cssdemo.html"> -->With CSS<!-- </a> --> | <a href=
"cssdemowithout.html"><font color="blue">Without CSS</a></p>

 <script src="http://rssxpress.ukoln.ac.uk/lite/viewers/rss.cgi?rss=http://www.rdn.ac.uk/
news/rdnheadlines.xml"></script>

  </body>
</html>
```

A full rundown of the service's CSS markup is available on the RSS Xpress site, once you have chosen which URL you wish to parse.

That really is that, as far as JavaScript parsers go. They are very simple and easy to use and do a perfectly good job of displaying headlines from other sites within your own pages. These pages, of course, needn't be served from a web browser. Indeed, Figure 8-1 shows Example 8-1 being viewed as a file on my desktop. This is perhaps the simplest possible personal aggregator you can build.

Other Examples to Try

RSS XPress isn't the only JavaScript parser around. They all do much the same thing, so it's nice to spread the love a little bit.

RSS to JavaScript.com (http://www.rss-to-javascript.com/)
: Despite the name, this system can deal with all the syndication formats, with tentative Atom support also available. It's an exceptionally straightforward form system for styling up and creating code for a JavaScript snippet.

Infinite Penguins RSS Viewer (http://infinitepenguins.net)
: Check out the Infinite Penguins waddling in action with RSS and Atom. Again, it offers a nice form to configure your JavaScript snippet. The code for this parser is also available for download, so you can use it on your own site if you like. It's based on the MagpieRSS parser, in PHP, which we'll visit later.

Feedroll.com (http://www.feedroll.com/rssviewer/)
: This system also supports Atom and offers a nice form to style up your feeds.

Feed2JS (http://jade.mcli.dist.maricopa.edu/feed/)
: The Feed2Js service comes courtesy of Alan Levine at the Maricopa Community Colleges. It is also based on MagpieRSS and offers styling options.

Parsing for Programming

The ability to display a feed on a web page is important, no doubt about it, but it's not going to really excite anyone. To do that, you need to be able to parse feeds inside your own programs. In this section, we'll look at the two major alternatives, MagpieRSS and the Ultraliberal Feed Parser. Both parsers are libraries; both convert feeds into native data structures; and neither cares whether a feed is RSS 1.0, RSS 2.0 or Atom. That, really, is the final word with respect to the Great Battle of the Standards; most of the time, at a programmatic level, no one cares.

PHP: MagpieRSS

The most popular parser in PHP, and arguably the most popular in use on the Web right now, is Kellan Elliott-McCrea's MagpieRSS. As I write this, it stands at version 0.7, a low number indicative of modesty rather than product immaturity. MagpieRSS is a very refined product indeed.

To use MagpieRSS, first download the latest build from its web page at *http://sourceforge.net/projects/magpierss/*. There is also a weblog at *http://laughingmeme.org/magpie_blog/*.

Once downloaded, you're presented with a load of *README*s and example scripts, plus five include files:

- *rss_fetch.inc* is the library you call from scripts. It deals with retrieving the feed, and marshals the other files into parsing it, before returning the results to your code.
- *rss_parse.inc* deals with the nitty gritty of feed parsing. MagpieRSS is a liberal parser, which means it doesn't validate the feed it is given. It can also deal with any arbitrarily invented element as long as it follows the right sort of format, meaning that it is quite futureproof.
- *rss_cache.inc* lets you make *rss_fetch.inc* cache feeds instead of continually requesting new ones.
- *rss_utils.inc* currently contains only one internal function, which converts a W3CDTF standard date to Unix epoch time.
- *extlib/Snoopy.class.inc* provides the network support for the other included functions.

To install these include files, place them in the same directory as the script that is going to use them.

Using MagpieRSS

MagpieRSS is simple to use and comes well-documented. Included in the distribution is an example script called `magpie_simple.php`. It looks like Example 8-3.

Example 8-3. magpie_simple.php

```
<?php

define('MAGPIE_DIR', '../');
require_once(MAGPIE_DIR.'rss_fetch.inc');

$url = $_GET['url'];

if ( $url ) {
        $rss = fetch_rss( $url );

        echo "Channel: " . $rss->channel['title'] . "<p>";
        echo "<ul>";
        foreach ($rss->items as $item) {
                $href = $item['link'];
                $title = $item['title'];
                echo "<li><a href=$href>$title</a></li>";
        }
        echo "</ul>";
}
?>

<form>
        RSS URL: <input type="text" size="30" name="url" value="<?php echo $url ?>"><br />

        <input type="submit" value="Parse RSS">
</form>
```

Running this on my own weblog's RSS 1.0 feed produces a page that looks like Figure 8-3.

As you can see, it's very straightforward. Taken line by line, the meat of the script goes like this:

```
define('MAGPIE_DIR', '../');
require_once(MAGPIE_DIR.'rss_fetch.inc');

$url = $_GET['url'];
```

Here, you tell PHP where Magpie's files are kept—in this case, in the parent directory to the script. Now, invoke the *rss_fetch.inc* library, retrieve the URL, and place it, as a string, into the variable `$url`:

```
if ( $url ) {
$rss = fetch_rss( $url );

echo "Channel: " . $rss->channel['title'] . "<p>";
echo "<ul>";
```

If the retrieval worked, you pass the contents of `$url` to the parser and print out a headline for the web page, containing the `<title>` of the <channel> and the start of an HTML list. (The HTML in this example isn't very compliant, but no matter.)

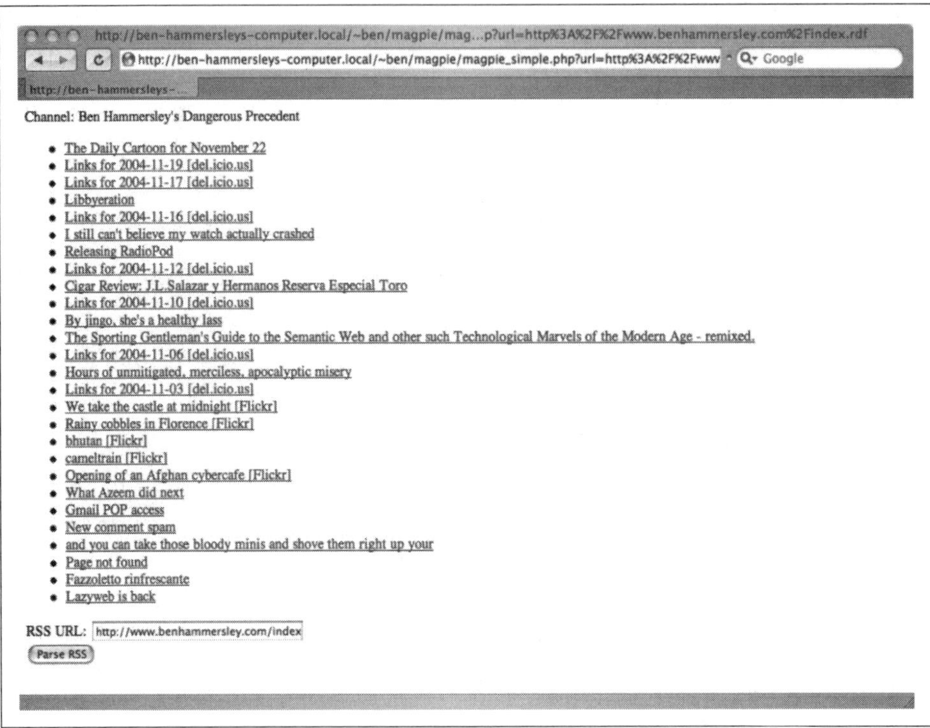

Figure 8-3. A very basic display using MagpieRSS

As you can see, the rest is easy to follow. It simply sets up a loop to run down the feed document and creates a link within an HTML list element from what it finds in the feed. This method of looping through the 15 or so elements in a feed is very typical.

```
foreach ($rss->items as $item) {
        $href = $item['link'];
        $title = $item['title'];
        echo "<li><a href=$href>$title</a></li>";
}
```

Once that's done, you can close off the list and get on with other things:

```
echo "</ul>";
```

Python: The Universal Feed Parser

Mark Pilgrim's Universal Feed Parser, hosted at *http://sourceforge.net/projects/feedparser/*, is perhaps the best feed application ever written. It is incredibly well-done and magnificently well-documented. Furthermore, it is released under the GPL and comes with over 2,000 unit tests. Those unit tests themselves are worth months of screaming from anyone writing their own parser; however, the question remains why would you when the UFP already exists?

It's well-documented, so the following sections will serve only to demonstrate its power.

A complete aggregator in 40 lines

To that end, here is a complete aggregator in only 40 lines, written by Jonas Galvez of *http://jonasgalvez.com*. Jonas released this underneath the GPL license, so it is free to use within the usual GPL bounds. Many thanks to him for that.

The full code is listed later in Example 8-4, but let's step through it section by section. The program stores the list of URLs to fetch and parse in a text file, *feeds.txt,* so to start, you import the required modules, pull in the contents of *feeds.txt,* and define an array to hold the items once you parse them:

```
import time
import feedparser

sourceList = open('feeds.txt').readlines( )
postList = [ ]
```

Next, define the Entry class to act as a wrapper for the entry object the Universal Feed Parser will return. The `modified_parsed` property contains the entry date in a tuple of nine elements, in which the first six are the year, month, day, hour, minute, and second. This tuple can be converted to Unix Epoch with the built-in time method `mktime( )`:

```
class Entry:
    def __init__(self, data, blog):
        self.blog = blog
        self.title = data.title
        self.date = time.mktime(data.modified_parsed)
        self.link = data.link
    def __cmp__(self, other):
        return other.date - self.date
```

The `__cmp__` method defines the standard comparison behavior of the class. Once you get an array with Entry instances and call `sort( )`, the `__cmp__` method defines the order.

Here is where the UFP comes in. Since we want to show entries ordered by date, it's prudent to at least verify if the entry actually includes a date. With UFP. you can also check for a "bozo bit" and refuse invalid feeds altogether. The package's documentation gives details on that:

```
for uri in sourceList:
    xml = feedparser.parse(uri.strip( ))
    blog = xml.feed.title
    for e in xml.entries[:10]:
        if not e.has_key('modified_parsed'):
            continue
        postList.append(Entry(e, blog))

postList.sort( )
```

To finish, print everything out as an XHTML list:

```
print 'Content-type: text/html\n'
print '<ul style="font-family: monospace;">'

for post in postList[:20]: # last 20 items
    date = time.gmtime(post.date)
    date = time.strftime('%Y-%m-%d %H:%M:%S', date)
    item = '\t<li>[%s] <a href=\"%s\">%s</a> (%s)</li>'
    print item % (date, post.link, post.title, post.blog)

print '</ul>'
```

Example 8-4 shows the entire aggregator.

Example 8-4. A 40-line aggregator in Python using the Universal Feed Parser

```
#!/usr/bin/python2.2
"""
License: GPL 2; share and enjoy!
Requires: Universal Feed Parser <http://feedparser.org>
Author: Jonas Galvez <http://jonasgalvez.com>
"""

import time
import feedparser

sourceList = open('feeds.txt').readlines( )
postList = [ ]

class Entry:
    def __init__(self, data, blog):
        self.blog = blog
        self.title = data.title
        self.date = time.mktime(data.modified_parsed)
        self.link = data.link
    def __cmp__(self, other):
        return other.date - self.date

for uri in sourceList:
    xml = feedparser.parse(uri.strip( ))
    blog = xml.feed.title
    for e in xml.entries[:10]:
        if not e.has_key('modified_parsed'):
            continue
        postList.append(Entry(e, blog))

postList.sort( )

print 'Content-type: text/html\n'
print '<ul style="font-family: monospace;">'

for post in postList[:20]:
    date = time.gmtime(post.date)
```

Example 8-4. A 40-line aggregator in Python using the Universal Feed Parser (continued)

```
    date = time.strftime('%Y-%m-%d %H:%M:%S', date)
    item = '\t<li>[%s] <a href=\"%s\">%s</a> (%s)</li>'
    print item % (date, post.link, post.title, post.blog)

print '</ul>'
```

Perl: XML::Simple

Because of the all-conquering success of Magpie and the UFP, Perl programmers haven't really moved on with the evolution of their feed-parsing tools. The UFP package can be called from Perl if need be, and many people have used the UFP as an excuse to try to learn Python anyway.

Certainly, there is no all-encompassing module for Perl that can parse all the flavors of RSS 1.0, RSS 2.0, and Atom with as much aplomb as the other scripting languages.

`XML::RSS` provides basic RSS parsing, as does Timothy Appnel's `XML::RAI` module framework, but neither support Atom. Ben Trott's `XML::Atom` is really designed for use with the Atom Publishing Protocol but can be used with the Syndication Format as well, once it is properly up to date. At time of writing, it is lagging the specification somewhat; this situation should improve once both Atom standards are at version 1.0. Timothy Appnel has also written an Atom module, `XML::Atom::Syndication`, which is very promising indeed.

With this mishmash of options for parsing feeds, and the necessity to write code to identify the feed's standard and pass it off to the correct functions, things can get too complicated too quickly with Perl. Let's take it back a notch, then, and resort to first principals. The following hasn't changed from the first edition of this book. I omit Atom to wait for the specification to settle down, but you will be able to see quite plainly how it would work with this structure.

Parsing RSS as simply as possible

The disadvantage of RSS's split into two separate but similar specifications is that we can never be sure which of the standards your desired feeds will arrive in. If you restrict yourself to using only RSS 2.0, it is very likely that the universe will conspire to make the most interesting stuff available solely in RSS 1.0, or vice versa. So, no matter what you want to do with the feed, your approach must be able to handle both standards with equal aplomb. With that in mind, simple parsing of RSS can be done with a standard general XML parser.

XML parsers are useful tools to have around when dealing with either RSS 2.0 or 1.0. While RSS 2.0 is quite a simple format, and using a full-fledged XML parser on it does sometimes seem to be overkill, it does have a distinct advantage over the other methods: futureproofing. Either way, for the majority of purposes, the simplest XML parsers are perfectly useful. The Perl module `XML::Simple` is a good example.

Example 8-5 is a simple script that uses `XML::Simple` to parse both RSS 2.0x and RSS 1.0 feeds into XHTML that is ready for server-side inclusion.

Example 8-5. Using XML::Simple to parse RSS

```
#!/usr/local/bin/perl

use strict;
use warnings;

use LWP::Simple;
use XML::Simple;

my $url=$ARGV[0];

# Retrieve the feed, or die gracefully
my $feed_to_parse = get ($url) or die "I can't get the feed you want";

# Parse the XML
my $parser = XML::Simple->new( );
my $rss = $parser->XMLin("$feed_to_parse");

# Decide on name for outputfile
my $outputfile = "$rss->{'channel'}->{'title'}.html";

# Replace any spaces within the title with an underscore
$outputfile =~ s/ /_/g;

# Open the output file
open (OUTPUTFILE, ">$outputfile");

# Print the Channel Title
print OUTPUTFILE '<div class="channelLink">'."\n".'<a href="';
print OUTPUTFILE "$rss->{'channel'}->{'link'}".'">';
print OUTPUTFILE "$rss->{'channel'}->{'title'}</a>\n</div>\n";

# Print the channel items
print OUTPUTFILE '<div class="linkentries">'."\n"."<ul>";
print OUTPUTFILE "\n";

foreach my $item (@{$rss->{channel}->{'item'}}) {
    next unless defined($item->{'title'}) && defined($item->{'link'});
    print OUTPUTFILE '<li><a href="';
    print OUTPUTFILE "$item->{'link'}";
    print OUTPUTFILE '">';
    print OUTPUTFILE "$item->{'title'}</a></li>\n";
        }

foreach my $item (@{$rss->{'item'}}) {
    next unless defined($item->{'title'}) && defined($item->{'link'});
    print OUTPUTFILE '<li><a href="';
    print OUTPUTFILE "$item->{'link'}";
    print OUTPUTFILE '">';
```

Example 8-5. Using XML::Simple to parse RSS (continued)

```
    print OUTPUTFILE "$item->{'title'}</a></li>\n";
            }

print OUTPUTFILE "</ul>\n</div>\n";

# Close the OUTPUTFILE
close (OUTPUTFILE);
```

This script highlights various issues regarding the parsing of RSS, so it is worth dissecting closely. Start with the opening statements:

```
#!/usr/local/bin/perl

use strict;
use warnings;

use LWP::Simple;
use XML::Simple;

my $url=$ARGV[0];

# Retrieve the feed, or die gracefully
my $feed_to_parse = get ($url) or die "I can't get the feed you want";
```

This is nice and standard Perl—the usual `use strict;` and `use warnings;` for good programming karma. Next, load the two necessary modules: `XML::Simple` (which you've been introduced to) and `LWP::Simple` retrieve the RSS feed from the remote server. This is indeed what to do next: take the command-line argument as the URL for the feed you want to parse. Place the entire feed in the scalar `$feed_to_parse`, ready for the next section of the script:

```
# Parse the XML
my $parser = XML::Simple->new( );
my $rss = $parser->XMLin("$feed_to_parse");
```

This section fires up a new instance of the `XML::Simple` module and calls the newly initialized object `$parser`. It then reads the retrieved RSS feed and parses it into a tree, with the root of the tree called `$rss`. This tree is actually a set of hashes, with the element names as hash keys. In other words, you can do this:

```
# Decide on name for outputfile
my $outputfile = "$rss->{'channel'}->{'title'}.html";

# Replace any spaces within the title with an underscore
$outputfile =~ s/ /_/g;

# Open the output file
open (OUTPUTFILE, ">$outputfile");
```

Here, you take the value of the `title` element within the `channel`, add the string `.html`, and make it the value of `$outputfile`. This is done for a simple reason: I wanted to make the user interface to this script as simple as possible. You can change it to allow the user to input the output filename himself, but I like the script to work one out automatically from the title element. Of course, many title elements use spaces, which makes a nasty mess of filenames, so you can use a regular expression to replace spaces with underscores. Now open up the file handle, creating the file if necessary.

With a file ready for filling, and an RSS feed parsed in memory, let's fill in some of the rest:

```
# Print the Channel Title
print OUTPUTFILE '<div class="channelLink">'."\n".'<a  href="';
print OUTPUTFILE "$rss->{'channel'}->{'link'}".'">';
print OUTPUTFILE "$rss->{'channel'}->{'title'}</a>\n</div>\n";
```

Here, you start to make the XHTML version. Take the link and title elements from the channel and create a title that is a hyperlink to the destination of the feed. Assign it a div, so you can format it later with CSS, and include some new lines to make the XHTML source as pretty as can be:

```
# Print the channel items
print OUTPUTFILE '<div class="linkentries">'."\n"."<ul>";
print OUTPUTFILE "\n";

foreach my $item (@{$rss->{channel}->{'item'}}) {
    next unless defined($item->{'title'}) && defined($item->{'link'});
    print OUTPUTFILE '<li><a href="';
    print OUTPUTFILE "$item->{'link'}";
    print OUTPUTFILE '">';
    print OUTPUTFILE "$item->{'title'}</a></li>\n";
        }

foreach my $item (@{$rss->{'item'}}) {
    next unless defined($item->{'title'}) && defined($item->{'link'});
    print OUTPUTFILE '<li><a href="';
    print OUTPUTFILE "$item->{'link'}";
    print OUTPUTFILE '">';
    print OUTPUTFILE "$item->{'title'}</a></li>\n";
        }

print OUTPUTFILE "</ul>\n</div>\n";

# Close the OUTPUTFILE
close (OUTPUTFILE);
```

The last section of the script deals with the biggest issue for all RSS parsing: the differences between RSS 2.0 and RSS 1.0. With XML::Simple, or any other tree-based parser, this is especially crucial, because the item appears in a different place in each specification. Remember: in RSS 2.0, item is a subelement of channel, but in RSS 1.0, they have equal weight.

So, in the preceding snippet you can see two foreach loops. The first one takes care of RSS 2.0 feeds, and the second covers RSS 1.0. Either way, they are encased inside another div and made into an ul unordered list. The script finishes by closing the file handle. Our work is done.

Running this from the command line, with the RSS feed from *http://rss.benhammersley.com/index.xml*, produces the result shown in Example 8-6.

Example 8-6. Content_Syndication_with_RSS.html

```
<div class="channelLink">
<a href="http://rss.benhammersley.com/">Content Syndication with XML and RSS</a>
</div>
<div class="linkentries">
<ul>
<li><a href="http://rss.benhammersley.com/archives/001150.html">PHP parsing of RSS</a></
li>

<li><a href="http://rss.benhammersley.com/archives/001146.html">RSS for Pocket PC</a></li>

<li><a href="http://rss.benhammersley.com/archives/001145.html">Syndic8 is One</a></li>

<li><a href="http://rss.benhammersley.com/archives/001141.html">RDF mod_events</a></li>

<li><a href="http://rss.benhammersley.com/archives/001140.html">RSS class for cocoa</a></
li>

<li><a href="http://rss.benhammersley.com/archives/001131.html">Creative Commons RDF</a></
li>

<li><a href="http://rss.benhammersley.com/archives/001129.html">RDF events in Outlook.</a>
</li>

<li><a href="http://rss.benhammersley.com/archives/001128.html">Reading Online News</a></
li>

<li><a href="http://rss.benhammersley.com/archives/001115.html">Hep messaging server</a></
li>

<li><a href="http://rss.benhammersley.com/archives/001109.html">mod_link</a></li>

<li><a href="http://rss.benhammersley.com/archives/001107.html">Individual Entries as RSS
1.0</a></li>
<li><a href="http://rss.benhammersley.com/archives/001105.html">RDFMap</a></li>

<li><a href="http://rss.benhammersley.com/archives/001104.html">They're Heeereeee</a></li>

<li><a href="http://rss.benhammersley.com/archives/001077.html">Burton Modules</a></li>

<li><a href="http://rss.benhammersley.com/archives/001076.html">RSS within XHTML documents
UPDATED</a></li>
</ul>
</div>
```

You can then include this inside another page using server-side inclusion (described later in this chapter).

After all this detailing of additional elements, I hear you cry, where are they? Well, including extra elements in a script of this sort is rather simple. Here I've taken another look at the second `foreach` loop from the previous example. Notice the sections in bold type:

```
foreach my $item (@{$rss->{'item'}}) {
    next unless defined($item->{'title'}) && defined($item->{'link'});
    print OUTPUTFILE '<li><a href="';
    print OUTPUTFILE "$item->{'link'}";
    print OUTPUTFILE '">';
    print OUTPUTFILE "$item->{'title'}</a>";
    if ($item->{'dc:creator'}) {
        print OUTPUTFILE '<span class="dccreator">Written  by';

        print OUTPUTFILE "$item->{'dc:creator'}";
        print OUTPUTFILE '</span>';
        }
    print OUTPUTFILE "<ol><blockquote>$item->{'description'}</blockquote></ol>";

    print OUTPUTFILE "\n</li>\n";
        }
```

This section now looks inside the RSS feed for a `dc:creator` element and displays it if it finds one. It also retrieves the contents of the `description` element and displays it as a nested item in the list. You might want to change this formatting, obviously.

By repeating the emphasized line, it is easy to add support for different elements as you see fit, and it's also simple to give each new element its own `div` or `span` class to control the onscreen formatting. For example:

```
if ($item->{'dc:creator'}) {
   print OUTPUTFILE '<span class="dccreator">Written  by';
   print OUTPUTFILE "$item->{'dc:creator'}";
   print OUTPUTFILE '</span>';
   }
if ($item->{'dc:date'}) {
   print OUTPUTFILE '<span class="dcdate">Date:';
   print OUTPUTFILE "$item->{'dc:date'}";
   print OUTPUTFILE '</span>';
   }
if ($item->{'annotate:reference'}) {
   print OUTPUTFILE '<span class="annotation"><a href="';
   print OUTPUTFILE "$item->{'annotate:reference'}->{'rdf:resource'}";
   print OUTPUTFILE '">Comment  on this</a></span>';
       }
```

Most XML parsers found in scripting languages (Perl, Python, etc.) are really interfaces for Expat, the powerful XML parsing library. They therefore require Expat to be installed. Expat is available from *http://expat.sourceforge.net/* and is released under the MIT License.

As you can see, the final extension prints the contents of the `annotate:reference` element. This, as mentioned in Chapter 7, is a single `rdf:resource` attribute. Note the way I get `XML::Simple` to read the attribute. It treats the attribute as just another leaf on the tree; you call the same way you would a subelement. You can use the same syntax for any attribute-only element.

Using Regular Expressions

Using regular expressions to parse feeds may seem a little brutish, but it does have two advantages. First, it totally negates the issues regarding the differences between standards. Second, it is a much easier installation: it requires no XML parsing modules or any dependencies thereof.

Regular expressions, however, aren't pretty. Consider Example 8-7, which is a section from Rael Dornfest's lightweight RSS aggregator, Blagg.

Example 8-7. A section of code from Blagg

```
# Feed's title and link
my($f_title, $f_link) = ($rss =~ m#<title>(.*?)</title>.*?<link>(.*?)</link>#ms);


# RSS items' title, link, and description

while ( $rss =~ m{<item(?!s).*?>.*?(?:<title>(.*?)</title>.*?)?(?:<link>(.*?)</link>.

*?)?(?:<description>(.*?)</description>.*?)?</item>}mgis ) {
     my($i_title, $i_link, $i_desc, $i_fn) = ($1||'', $2||'', $3||'', undef);

     # Unescape &amp; &lt; &gt; to produce useful HTML
     my %unescape = ('&lt;'=>'<', '&gt;'=>'>', '&amp;'=>'&', '&quot;'=>'"');

     my $unescape_re = join '|' => keys %unescape;
     $i_title && $i_title =~ s/($unescape_re)/$unescape{$1}/g;
     $i_desc && $i_desc =~ s/($unescape_re)/$unescape{$1}/g;

     # If no title, use the first 50 non-markup characters of the description
     unless ($i_title) {
          $i_title = $i_desc;
          $i_title =~ s/<.*?>//msg;
          $i_title = substr($i_title, 0, 50);
          }
          next unless $i_title;
```

While this looks pretty nasty, it is actually an efficient way of stripping the data out of the RSS file, even if it is potentially much harder to extend. If you are really into regular expressions and don't mind having a very specialized, hard-to-extend system, their simplicity may be for you. They certainly have their place.

Using XSLT

The transformation of RSS into another form of XML, using XSLT, isn't very common at the moment, but it may soon have its time in the sun. This is because RSS—especially RSS 1.0, with its complicated relationships and masses of metadata—can be reproduced in many useful ways.

While the examples in this book are text-based and mostly XHTML, there is no reason you can't render RSS into an SVG graphic, a PDF (via the Apache FOP tool), an MMS-SMIL message for new-generation mobile phones, or any of the hundreds of other XML-based systems. XSLT and the arcane art of writing XSLT stylesheets to take care of all of this is a subject too large for this book to cover in detail—for that, check out O'Reilly's *XSLT*.

Nevertheless, I will show you some nifty stuff. Example 8-8 is an XSLT stylesheet that transforms an RSS 1.0 feed into the XHTML produced in Example 8-7.

Example 8-8. Transforming RSS 1.0 into XHTML fragments

```
<?xml version="1.0"?>

<xsl:stylesheet version = '1.0'
xmlns:xsl="http://www.w3.org/1999/XSL/Transform"
xmlns:rdf="http://www.w3.org/1999/02/22-rdf-syntax-ns#"
xmlns:rss="http://purl.org/rss/1.0/"
exclude-result-prefixes="rss rdf"
>
<xsl:output method="html"/>

<xsl:template match="/">
 <div class="channellink">
  <a href="{rdf:RDF/rss:channel/rss:link}">
   <xsl:value-of select="rdf:RDF/rss:channel/rss:title"/>
  </a>
 </div>
 <div class="linkentries">
  <ul>
   <xsl:apply-templates select="rdf:RDF/*"/>
  </ul>
 </div>
</xsl:template>

<xsl:template match="rss:channel|rss:item">
 <li>
  <a href="{rss:link}">
```

Example 8-8. Transforming RSS 1.0 into XHTML fragments (continued)

```
    <xsl:value-of select="rss:title"/>
   </a>
  </li>
</xsl:template>
</xsl:stylesheet>
```

Again, just like the parsing code in Example 8-5, it is easy to extend this stylesheet to take the modules into account. Example 8-9 extends Example 8-8 to look for the `description`, `dc:creator`, and `dc:date` elements. Note the emphasized code: those are the changes.

Example 8-9. Making the XSLT stylesheet more useful

```
<?xml version="1.0"?>

<xsl:stylesheet version = '1.0'
xmlns:xsl="http://www.w3.org/1999/XSL/Transform"
xmlns:rdf="http://www.w3.org/1999/02/22-rdf-syntax-ns#"
xmlns:rss="http://purl.org/rss/1.0/"
xmlns:dc="http://purl.org/dc/elements/1.1/"
exclude-result-prefixes="rss   rdf
dc "
>
<xsl:output method="html"/>

<xsl:template match="/">
 <div class="channellink">
  <a href="{rdf:RDF/rss:channel/rss:link}">
   <xsl:value-of select="rdf:RDF/rss:channel/rss:title"/>
  </a>
 </div>
 <div class="linkentries">
  <ul>
   <xsl:apply-templates select="rdf:RDF/*"/>
  </ul>
 </div>
</xsl:template>

<xsl:template match="rss:channel|rss:item">
 <li>
  <a href="{rss:link}"><xsl:value-of select="rss:title"/></a>
   <ol>
     <xsl:value-of select="rss:description" />
   </ol>
   <ol>
    <xsl:text>Written  by: </xsl:text>
    <xsl:value-of select="dc:creator"/>
   </ol>
   <ol>
```

Example 8-9. Making the XSLT stylesheet more useful (continued)

```
    <xsl:text>Written  on: </xsl:text>
    <xsl:value-of select="dc:date"/>
   </ol>
 </li>
</xsl:template>
</xsl:stylesheet>
```

Client-Side Inclusion

Client-side inclusion is the way to go if you are setting up a third-party parsing service or hosting the majority of the site on a server that forbids server-side scripting. Doing this is very simple. All you need to do is create a script that returns a JavaScript script that displays the necessary XHTML. You've seen this earlier.

To do this, just wrap each line of the XHTML that your ordinary script would produce in a `document.writeln()` function:

```
document.writeln("<h1>This is the heading<h1>");
```

Now, have the script return this document as the result of a call by the `script` element from the HTML document. So, the HTML document contains this line:

```
<script src="Path to parsing script appended with feed URL" />
```

The CGI script returns the `document.writeln` script, which the browser executes, and then parses the resulting XHTML.

The upshot of this technique is that you can start a third-party RSS-parsing service with little effort. All you need to do is distribute the URL of the CGI script you are using and tell people to append the URL of the feed they want to the end of it. Give them the resulting `script` element to insert into their site code, and everyone is in business:

```
<script src="http://www.bensparsers.com?feed=http://bensfeed.com/index.xml"/>
```

Server-Side Inclusion

The more powerful method is server-side inclusion (SSI). It allows you to parse the feed using any technique and any language you like, and it allows greater flexibility for how the feed is used.

Let's look at an example of how it works. Example 8-10 produces an XHTML page with a server-side include directive.

Example 8-10. An XHTML page with a server-side include

```
<!DOCTYPE html PUBLIC "-//W3C//DTD XHTML 1.1//EN"
    "http://www.w3.org/TR/xhtml11/DTD/xhtml11.dtd">
<html xmlns="http://www.w3.org/1999/xhtml" xml:lang="en">
```

Example 8-10. An XHTML page with a server-side include (continued)

```
<head>
<title>An Example of a SSI</title>
</head>
<body>
<h1>This here is a News Feed from a really good site</h1>
<!--#include file="parsedfeed.html" -->
</body>
</html>
```

A server serving the page in Example 8-10 will, if the server is set up correctly, import the contents of *parsedfeed.html* and insert them in place of the SSI directive `<!--#include file="parsedfile.html" -->`.

So, by parsing RSS files into XHTML and saving them to disk, you can use SSI to place them within an existing XHTML page, apply formatting to change the way they look via the site's CSS stylesheet, and present them to the end user.

Enabling Server-Side Includes Within Apache 1.3.x

Turning on server-side includes within Apache is straightforward, but it involves delving into places where a wrong move can make a nasty mess. Have a coffee, then concentrate.

This section discusses Apache Version 1.3.x. Apache's configuration structure may change in later versions. Consult the documentation online at *http://www.apache.org*.

To permit SSI on your server, you must have the following directive either in your *httpd.conf* file or in a *.htaccess* file:

```
Options +Includes
```

This tells Apache you want to permit files to be parsed for SSI directives. Of course, real-world installations are more complicated than that; most Apache installations have multiple `Options` directives set: one for each directory in some cases. You will most likely want to apply the `Options` to the specific directory in which you want SSI enabled—where the document in which you want to include the RSS feeds resides.

Example 8-11 shows the relevant section of the *httpd.conf* file for my own server.

Example 8-11. A section of an Apache http.conf file that allows for CGI and SSI

```
<Directory "/usr/local/apache/htdocs/rss">
Options ExecCGI Includes
DirectoryIndex index.shtml
</Directory>
```

Note that this configuration defines the directory's index page as *index.shtml* because it isn't a good idea to make your browser seek out SSI directives in every page it serves. Rather, you should tell it to look for SSI directives solely in pages that end with a certain file extension by adding the following lines to your *httpd.conf* file

```
AddType text/html .shtml
AddHandler server-parsed .shtml
```

This makes Apache search any file ending in *.shtml* (the traditional extension for such things) for SSI directives and replace them with their associated files before serving them to the end user.

This approach has a disadvantage: if you want to add SSI directives to an existing page, you have to change the name of that page. All links to that page will therefore be broken in order to get the SSI directives to work. So, if you're retrofitting a site with RSS, the other method is to use the `XBitHack` directive within your *httpd.conf* file:

```
XBitHack on
```

`XBitHack` tells Apache to parse files for SSI directives if the files have the execute bit set. So, to add SSI directives to an existing page, rather than having to change the filename, you just need to make the file executable using `chmod`.

How Often to Read the Feed

Feeds do change, it is true. People update their sites at all hours, and it would be lovely to have the very latest headlines. Currently, however, it isn't a good idea to keep requesting a new feed every few minutes. Etiquette and convention limit requests for a new file to once every 60 minutes, unless the feed's publisher specifically allows you to grab it more often, or unless said publisher is using Publish and Subscribe (see Chapter 9).

In many cases, even requesting the feed every hour is too much. Feeds that change only once a day require downloading only once a day. It's a simple courtesy to pay attention to these conventions.

Server-Side Includes with Microsoft IIS

Microsoft's Internet Information Services (IIS) server package comes with server-side includes enabled: by default, it processes any file ending in *.stm*, *.shtm*, or *.shtml*. However, files are processed only if they're inside directories with Scripts or Execute access permissions.

Here's how to set these permissions:

1. Open *My Computer*, select the directory in which you want to allow SSI, and right-click to open its property menu.
2. On the Security property menu, select the Windows account for which you want to change permissions.
3. Under Permissions, select the types of access for the selected user or group. Use Allow to specifically allow access and Deny to specifically deny access. For more choices, click Advanced.

CHAPTER 9

Feeds in the Wild

When you have to kill a man, it costs nothing to be polite.
—Sir Winston Churchill

Now that we're fully capable of creating and consuming feeds, we can start to use them with a flourish. The final chapters of this book aim to help you do just that. This one deals with the place a feed has in the wider world of the Internet: how it should dress, talk, and hold itself in finer society.

Once You Have Created Your Simple RSS Feed

Once you have created your feed, there are just one or two more things to do. None of these are mandatory, but they are all so simple, and give so much to the richness of the Net, that you are encouraged to invest the little time needed. You can work through these one by one in about half an hour.

Publish a Link

Place a link to the RSS feed on your page! People regularly forget to do this and wonder why, after looking at their server logs, no one is subscribed to their feed. There are standard icons emerging from each of the news aggregators and desktop readers—some of these are freely available for this use, but even a simple text link is better than nothing at all. The original icon for RSS (see Figure 9-1) was the white-on-orange XML logo, produced by Userland Software. Most of the other logos (see Figures 9-2 and 9-3) stem artistically from this one vision. With the advent of Atom, the wording on the button is beginning to change. My prediction is that it will change to the word "Feed" over time, but the arguments over the standard syndication feed button have been almost as fraught as those over the standards themselves. At time of writing, for example, it looks as if the next version of Apple's Mac OS X will contain an RSS reader that uses a version of the button colored blue. A schism looms on the horizon for those who care about such things.

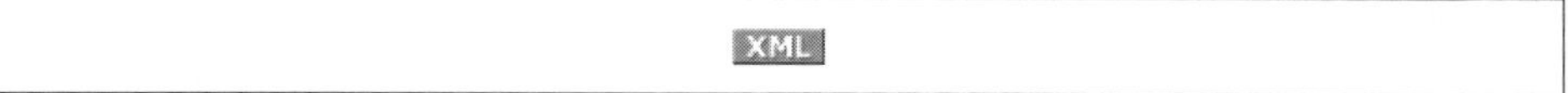

Figure 9-1. The original XML button

Figure 9-2. The XML button with the Radio Userland coffee cup logo

Figure 9-3. A further, very common development of an RSS button

Either way, it really does pay to make your feeds as noticeable as possible. One way to do this, of course, is to take the human out of the equation entirely and use autodiscovery.

Enabling Autodiscovery

Any web page with a corresponding feed document should contain an autodiscovery link pointing to said feed. This allows programs to determine the location of the feed even when they are only given the URL of the page itself. So the user doesn't really need to know about feeds at all. She can just point her feed application at the page she likes, and the rest happens automatically. Some browsers also automatically display the RSS badge, or a variant thereof, whenever you're looking at a page with an autodiscovery link.

To do this, simply add the relevant link from those in Example 9-1 to your HTML page inside the <head> section.

Example 9-1. Autodiscovery links

```
<link rel="alternate" type="application/rss+xml" title="RSS 2.0" href="url/to/rss2/file">
<link rel="alternate" type="application/rdf+xml" title="RSS 1.0" href="url/to/rss1/file">
<link rel="alternate" type="application/atom+xml" title="Atom" href="url/to/atom/file">
```

The top of my own weblog's source code looks like Example 9-2.

Example 9-2. Autodiscovery links in action

```
<!DOCTYPE html PUBLIC "-//W3C//DTD XHTML 1.0 Transitional//EN"
        "http://www.w3.org/TR/xhtml1/DTD/xhtml1-transitional.dtd">
<html xmlns="http://www.w3.org/1999/xhtml" xml:lang="en" lang="en">
<head>
<title>Ben Hammersley's Dangerous Precedent - The Weblog</title>
```

Example 9-2. Autodiscovery links in action (continued)

```
<link rel="alternate" type="application/atom+xml" title="Atom" href="http://www.
benhammersley.com/atom.xml"/>
<link rel="alternate" type="application/rdf+xml" title="RSS" href="http://www.
benhammersley.com/index.rdf"/>
```

Technically, the autodiscovery link is a standard element of the XHTML format and is used by many metadata standards to link documents to their XHTML partner. The `rel="alternate"` attribute cannot change in this context, but the others can. In particular, the type attribute shows the MIME type of the feed you are pointing to. If, in the future, the feed world decides on a different MIME type format, the autodiscovery link should be changed as well.

Serving a Feed Correctly

If you have wide enough access privileges to your server's configuration, a lot can be done to make your position in the Internet ecosystem a great deal more fruitful. You can make life easier on yourself, and others, by setting the correct MIME type and by using the features of HTTP 1.1.

MIME types

Here we must tread carefully. As much as can be said definitively here, the correct MIME types for RSS and Atom are as follows:

- RSS 1.0: `application/rdf+xml`
- RSS 2.0: either `application/rss+xml`, `application/xml`, or `text/xml`
- Atom: `application/atom+xml`

As you can see, RSS 2.0 is tricky. The specification gives no help on this matter at all, and there is as yet no consensus within the community. The problem stems from the way certain browsers deal with these values, downloading the file instead of displaying it on the screen. This might cause confusion for users, and so some people claim that serving all of them with a MIME type of `text/xml` is the more sensible choice. I personally disagree, and go with `application/rss+xml`. The other two formats strictly define their MIME type in the earlier list.

To set this up on an Apache server, you can include an *.htaccess* file within the directory you are serving from. Assuming you are creating feeds in every format, called `index.rdf`, `index.atom`, and `index.rss`, you would want lines in your *.htaccess* file that look like Example 9-3.

Example 9-3. An example .htaccess file to set the correct MIME types for feeds

```
AddType application/rdf+xml rdf
AddType application/atom+xml atom
AddType application/rss+xml rss
```

For more details on *.htaccess* files, see the official documentation at *http://httpd.apache.org/docs/howto/htaccess.html.*

HTTP 1.1

HTTP Version 1.1 has two features that can greatly reduce the amount of bandwidth used by your feeds. Bandwidth is an enormous problem for feed providers. Already, many of the more popular sites are restricting the number of times an individual IP address can request the feed per day. Others are reducing the size of the feed they provide. Certainly most webloggers will find that their feed makes up over half of their served bandwidth after a while. It is worth, therefore, trying to reduce this figure. It can be done with both compression and by enabling conditional GET.

Compression. Under the HTTP 1.1 specification, data sent via the protocol can be compressed using the `gzip` algorithm. This works wonders with big text documents like feeds, making them smaller and so faster and cheaper to serve. You should make sure compression is enabled wherever possible.

If your feeds are static files, served by Apache, you should install and use the necessary Apache modules. For Apache 1.x users, `mod_gzip` is found at *http://sourceforge.net/projects/mod-gzip/*, and good unofficial documentation for it sits at *http://www.schroepl.net/projekte/mod_gzip/index.htm*. For Apache 2.0 users, `mod_deflate` is included within the source package.

If you use Perl, PHP, or Python to dynamically create your feeds, Mark Nottingham's `cgi_buffer` libraries take care of the compression for you. See *http://www.mnot.net/cgi_buffer/* for more. It is highly recommended.

Conditional GET. The main problem with serving feed documents is that your consumers are liable to request the file whether it has changed or not. If all your readers are downloading the file once an hour, yet you're only updating it once a week, both you and they are wasting each other's bandwidth. This can cost you a lot of money.

Happily, the authors of the HTTP 1.1 standard came up with an answer to this: conditional GET. It works like this: when you request an RSS feed that you have seen before, you tell the server some details about the last version you saw, and if it has changed, the server will give you the new version. If not, however, the server replies that nothing is new in the world, and you can go about your merry way. Doing that only takes a few hundred bytes, as opposed to the 20,000 or so that a full feed might. Happy savings in bandwidth and speed all round.

Most people are already serving documents using conditional GET. The standard was written in 1999, and effectively every server application in use today supports it without your needing to worry about it. The problems come when you serve dynamically created feeds or write a feed-consuming application.

The handling of conditional GET with the common scripting languages has been covered across the Web by specialists in the field, and it's more productive to point you to their examples. Therefore, have a look at:

- Perl: Kellan Elliott-McCrea at *http://laughingmeme.org/archives/000479.html*
- PHP: Simon Willison at *http://simon.incutio.com/archive/2003/04/23/conditionalGet*
- Python: Jarno Virtanen at *http://www.hole.fi/jajvirta/weblog/20030928T2101.html*

Mark Nottingham's `cgi_buffer` libraries mentioned earlier also take care of conditional GET.

RSScache.com

As I finish this book, *http://www.rsscache.com* is being launched. The site promises to cut the amount of bandwidth that your feed uses by caching it and serving it for you.

Using the system is very simple. Just add the URL *http://my.rsscache.com/* in front of your own feed. For example:

> *http://my.rsscache.com/www.benhammersley.com/index.rdf*

The system works very well; however, it removes any relationship between your server's log files and the real number of subscribers you have. If you don't care about knowing how many people read your feeds and are worried about bandwidth use, this seems like a great service.

Registering with Aggregators

Registering your feed at the major aggregators helps people and automatic services find your information. For example, most of the desktop news readers available today use the lists of feeds available at Syndic8 as a menu of feeds available to their users. Being part of this is a good thing. Here are a few of the major aggregators and their URLs:

- Syndic8 (*http://www.syndic8.com/suggest_start.php*)
- Feedster (*http://www.feedster.com/add.php*)
- NewsIsFree (*http://www.newsisfree.com/contact.php*)

A very full, and constantly maintained, list of aggregators that take submissions of feed URLs for their catalogs can be found at *http://www.rss-specifications.com/rss-submission.htm*.

Metadata for the Main Page

Along with the autodiscovery links mentioned earlier, there are other lines of metadata that can be usefully added to your site. Syndic8 has a few other built-in features that aid with its cataloging and require just this sort of metadata to be added to your page. These features deal with the geographical origin of the feed and its subject's place within the Open Directory at *http://www.dmoz.org*. If you are registering your feed with Open Directory, it is worthwhile to add these lines:

```
<META NAME="dc.creator.e-mail" CONTENT="yourname@yourdomain.com">
<META NAME="dc.creator.name" CONTENT="Your Name">
```

Then find the correct place within the Open Directory (*http://www.dmoz.org*) and add it to your site's page like so (if your site is not in the Open Directory, take this opportunity to submit it!):

```
<META NAME="dmoz.id" CONTENT="Computers/Internet/On_the_Web/Weblogs/Tools">
```

Now visit the Getty Thesaurus of Geographical Names (TGN) at *http://www.getty.edu/research/tools/vocabulary/tgn/* and find the location that best represents your web site's location. Make a note of the name of the place, the name of the nation, the latitude, the longitude, and the TGN number.

Then go to the International Standards Organization web site at *http://www.iso.org/iso/en/prods-services/iso3166ma/02iso-3166-code-lists/list-en1.html* and find the country code of your nation. Use this information to add the following lines to your site (replace my information with yours):

```
<meta name="tgn.id" content="7011781" />
<meta name="tgn.name" content="London" />
<meta name="tgn.nation" content="United Kingdom" />

<meta name="geo.position" content="51.500;-0.167" />
<meta name="geo.placename" content="London, England" />
<meta name="geo.country" content="UK" />
```

Now post a message to the Syndic8 mailing list (*syndic8@yahoogroups.com*) asking for a Syndic8 editor to flick the proverbial metadata switch on your feed. People will now be able to search for you by location and subject.

Counting Hits and Clickthroughs

Completely new since the first edition of this book, and although still in beta as I write this, the services at *http://www.feedburner.com* are proving to be immensely popular. One of Feedburner's most popular features, the others being dealt with in Chapter 10, is its circulation data.

Circulation data is very hard to accurately determine on the Web. The layers of caching implemented within the larger ISPs mean that you may have many more readers than you think. But it's certainly useful to be able to get an accurate count, especially with information on which applications your readers are using.

Using FeedBurner will give you what appear to be, more or less, accurate results and an idea of which links in your feed people are clicking on the most.

Publish and Subscribe

The traditional guidelines for the use of syndication feeds present a small problem. There is always going to be a balance between the need to be up to date and the need to refrain from abusing the feed publisher's server by requesting the feed every few seconds. While the norm is to request the feed a maximum of once an hour, many feeds deserve to be followed much more closely. Conversely, many feeds update only once a day, or less often. Requesting those once an hour is a waste of time and resources and potentially expensive for the publisher. On top of the compressed feeds and conditional GET already discussed, one other idea has long existed within the feed world: Publish and Subscribe.

Let's think of the earlier situation. We have a feed, and this feed has its users. The users take the feed and do what they will—I've presented some examples of potential uses in the previous chapters—but each user depends on his copy of the feed (whether in memory, or converted to another format and saved) being up to date. In order for this to happen, the users *subscribe* to a system that watches the feed continuously. This system then *publishes* notifications to all of the users when the feed changes. The users are then responsible for updating their copies of the feed, ordinarily by requesting it from the server.

Currently, there is no Publish and Subscribe mechanism for Atom, but there are two ways to implement such a system within RSS: one with the relevant elements included in RSS 2.0, and the other suggested by an RSS 1.0 module. We will deal with these in turn.

Publish and Subscribe Within RSS 2.0

RSS 2.0's Publish and Subscribe system is the result of work by Userland Software and its CEO Dave Winer. It was introduced with, and perhaps inspired, the release of RSS 0.92 and features heavily in Userland products. Furthermore, its workings are based on XML-RPC and SOAP, two protocols that Winer was instrumental in starting. But that is not to say that RSS 2.0's Publish and Subscribe is in any way proprietary—it is not.

There are three characters to watch in this drama: the user, the feed, and the Publish and Subscribe system, itself better known as the *cloud*. Here is the process:

1. The user's system sends a message, via either XML-RPC, SOAP, or HTTP-POST, to the cloud to subscribe. This message contains five parameters:
    - The name of the procedure that the cloud should call to notify the user of changes.
    - The TCP port on which the user's system is listening.

- The path to the user's system. This is all that is needed because the user's system will be running either XML-RPC or SOAP, both of which use HTTP as their transport layer, and the cloud can determine the IP address of the caller from the initial request. This has a nice security benefit: one user cannot make a registration call on behalf of another.
- A string indicating which protocol to use, either XML-RPC or SOAP, when the cloud messages the user.
- A list of URLs of RSS files to be watched.

2. If the registration is successful, the cloud returns `true`; if not, it returns an error.
3. Somewhat later on, the cloud either detects or is informed of a change in the feed.
4. The cloud messages the user using the protocol requested, giving the URL of the changed feed.
5. The user requests the fresh feed from its server and does what she likes with it.

Note that by design, the RSS 2.0 Publish and Subscribe system expires subscriptions after 25 hours, forcing them to be renewed every day.

As I described in Chapter 4, the RSS 2.0 Publish and Subscribe system is denoted in the RSS feed with the `cloud` element:

```
<cloud domain="
Domain or IP address of the cloud"
       port="TCP port on which the cloud is listening"
       path="The path to the cloud's listener"
       registerProcedure="
The procedure name to register with the cloud"
       protocol="Either xml-rpc
or soap,
Case-sensitive" />
```

You see that we talk of passing messages via XML-RPC or SOAP? These may require some explanation. The two protocols are the basis of the fashionable technology known collectively as *web services*. We have already used some web services in previous chapters: getting information from Google using SOAP, for example. With those examples, we were passing a query, encoded in XML, and getting a set of results back, also encoded in XML. In the case of RSS 2.0 Publish and Subscribe, we are doing something similar: passing XML-encoded messages between systems. What makes the RSS 2.0 Publish and Subscribe system different from the other uses of web services you have already seen is that the user's system has to not only pass a message and wait for a reply, but also continually listen for other systems trying to talk to it. For this reason, it cannot be used with machines that reside behind Network Address Translation (NAT) systems. The user's machine must be directly addressable from the rest of the Internet, and it must be listening for people trying to do so.

O'Reilly publishes some very good books on the implementation of XML-RPC and SOAP. You may be interested in reading the following:

- *Programming Web Services with XML-RPC*
- *Web Services Essentials*
- *Programming Web Services with SOAP*

RSS 2.0 Publish and Subscribe has been publicly implemented at least twice. Userland Software incorporates it directly into its own products, and NewsIsFree (*http://www.newsisfree.com*), the RSS aggregator site run by Mike Krus, uses it as well. Both services produce feeds with a `cloud` element, and both run servers that will notify you of changes to the feeds.

These are both nice services, but what if you want to use your own Publish and Subscribe system to update, say, a web site's rendering of a feed? No problem: we'll just roll our own Publish and Subscribe system (see the section "Rolling Your Own: LinkPimp PubSub").

Publish and Subscribe with RSS 1.0

As it stands, the RSS 2.0 version of Publish and Subscribe is currently unavailable to standard RSS 1.0 users; it exists neither in the core specification nor in any published modules. But that is not to say that you cannot create a module to import the `cloud` element. You are, of course, at liberty to do so.

Meanwhile, the rest of us may be looking at the `mod_changedpage` module. This Publish and Subscribe module, written by Aaron Swartz, is fundamentally different from the system used with RSS 2.0. Where the latter uses web services protocols to communicate between systems, `mod_changedpage` uses simple HTTP POST procedures to handle the same job.

It works like this: the RSS 1.0 feed's `channel` contains the single element `cp:server`, which contains simply the URL of the Publish and Subscribe service for the feed. A user who wants to subscribe to notifications for this feed sends an HTTP POST request to that URL, taking two parameters:

- `responder`: The URL of the user's `mod_changedpage` system
- `target`: The URL of the feed to be monitored:

  responder=http%3A%2F%2FURL.
  OFUSERSSYSTEM&target=http%3A%2F%2FURL OF FEED

Note that the `://` of the URLs within the parameters are entity-encoded as `%3A%2F%2F`.

The original proposal document for this specification states:

> Additional attributes should be allowed before or after the URL. Implementations should ignore attributes they don't understand. The order of the attributes is not significant. Content-Type should be specified as "application/x-www-form-urlencoded."

If this sounds familiar, it should be. This is how HTML forms are encoded, as described in the HTML spec.

Either way, the URL is received at the Publish and Subscribe service, which returns a HTTP status code of `200` if the subscription is successful and an HTTP status code of `400` if the subscription failed (it is also recommended that a `400` code should be accompanied by a plain-text file explaining the error as thoroughly as possible).

When the feed updates, the Publish and Subscribe system sends a similar HTTP POST request, with one parameter—the URL of the changed feed:

url=http %3A%2F%2FURL.OF.CHANGEDFEED

The user's system can then do what it likes with that feed.

Rolling Your Own: LinkPimp PubSub

Having said all that, and given that there are currently no implementations of `mod_changedpage` to receive pages from, let's concentrate on working with `cloud`. What's more, every `cloud` implementation in the wild uses XML-RPC, so, for simplicity, this is all we will support here. Extending the script to support SOAP and HTTP-POST would not be hard, if necessary, but it probably won't be necessary.

The following Publish and Subscribe (PubSub) system is for web sites displaying various feeds, rendered into XHTML and inserted onto the page using a server-side include. It is currently working live on the test site: *http://www.benhammersley.com/linkpimp*.

This system also incorporates two other things we have already discussed. First, it renders the feed into XHTML—you can leave the onscreen formatting to a stylesheet—but the subroutine that does this is quite obvious in the code and can be turned to do something else: send IM notifications, for example.

Second, it uses Syndic8's API and subscription list service to tell it which feeds to examine. This allows you not only to play with the Syndic8 system, but also to add or remove feeds from the site without touching its code. I can merely log on to Syndic8 and subscribe to a feed there, and it should be incorporated into the site within the hour. It is rough and ready, but you will undoubtedly get ideas of your own from it.

The system comes in two parts:

LinkpimpClient.pl
: This script retrieves a subscription list from Syndic8, using that site's XML-RPC interface, checks to see if any of the feeds contain a `cloud` element, and subscribes, if necessary. It then renders the feeds into XHTML, if necessary, and saves them to disk. It then creates a new file called *feeds.shtml*, which contains the server-side include instructions to include the feeds. This script is run hourly. Example 9-4, later in this chapter, contains the complete listing.

LinkpimpListener.pl
: This script listens for PubSub notifications and refreshes the rendered feed when necessary. This script is run as a daemon. Example 9-5, later in this chapter, contains the complete listing.

Running the system creates three files internal to its working:

logfile.txt
: The system creates a verbose log to explain what is happening. You can disable this, if you wish.

pubsub.txt
: This file holds the URL and last-subscription-time of all the feeds to which you have PubSub subscriptions. It must not be deleted. *LinkpimpStrimmer.pl* keeps it healthy by stripping it of URLs older than 24 hours.

Feeds.shtml
: This file contains the server-side include instructions for displaying the feeds on your page. In turn, it should be called in with its own SSI directive from your customer-facing page, using the command:

```
<!--#include file="feeds.shtml" -->
```

LinkpimpClient.pl

LinkpimpClient.pl deals with the majority of the tasks needed for this system. Although feeds can be PubSub-enabled via XML-RPC, SOAP, HTTP POST, or not at all, and while for completeness we should be able to deal with all these situations to make a PubSub system fully spec-compliant, XML-RPC is the only system being used at the moment and the only one we will discuss here.

So, onward! Example 9-4, shown later, shows the entire program listing, but first, let's step through the interesting bits to illustrate a few points.

After setting up the necessary variables and loading the modules, we get to the section of the program that deals with the current subscriptions. When the program is run for the first time, this section is irrelevant, but since we'll probably run this script every hour from `cron`, it soon becomes necessary. Subscriptions last for 25 hours, so you need to make sure they are renewed in time.

```
logger ("  Program started. Let's go! ");

# First we need to strim the PubSub records and remove all the old entries.

# Work out the time 25 hours ago (1 hour = 3600 seconds, so 25 hours = 90000 seconds)
my $oldestpossibletime = time(  ) - 90000;

logger ("The oldest allowable  subscription  cannot have been made earlier
than $oldestpossibletime");
```

```
# Open the subscriber list created by pubSubListener and stick it in an array.
open (PUBSUBLIST, "<$pubsublog");
my @lines = <PUBSUBLIST>;
close (PUBSUBLIST);

# Clear the subscriber list.
unlink ($pubsublog) or die "Can't delete the data file ";
logger ("Old Subscription list deleted");

# We need to prevent the file being empty, even if there are no subscriptions, so:
open (NEWPUBSUBLIST, ">$pubsublog");
print NEWPUBSUBLIST "This holds the details of all your subscriptions , 0000001 ";

# Go through each line, splitting it back into the right variables.
foreach $line (@lines) {
               my ($rssUrl , $time) = split (/,/, "$line");

   # If the time the notification request was made ($time) is later than 25 hours ago
     # ($oldestpossibletime) then stick that line back into the data file.

                       if ($time > $oldestpossibletime)
                    {
                    print NEWPUBSUBLIST "$line ";
                                }; 
                      };
logger ("New PubSublist written");

close (NEWPUBSUBLIST);
```

The current subscriptions are stored in a file called *pubsub.txt*. This section opens the file, loads it into an array, and then deletes it. You then rewrite the file line by line if, and only if, the line is younger than the oldest possible time allowed (i.e., 24-hours old).

Now, open the new file and read the lines into another array, which we will work with later:

```
# Now, we reopen the pubsublog, and load it as a string for use later
open (PUBSUB, "$pubsublog");
$/ = '';
my $content_of_pubsublog  = <PUBSUB>;
```

Notice the `$/='';` line. This changes the delimiter for the line-input operator used in the next line. By default, saying `my$content_of_pubsublog=<PUBSUB>;` loads the file only until the first new line. By setting the delimiter to null, the operator scoops the whole file up in one swallow.

The next section then loads the subscription list from Syndic8 in the manner described in Chapter 10. Now, enter a loop, loading the RSS files one by one, and examine them for PubSub-related elements:

```
# Take the next line from the array of DataURLs
foreach $url (@edited_subscribed_feeds_list) {
```

```
                logger ("Now working with $url");
                # Check the feed is not on the list of subscribed-to feeds
                if ($content_of_pubsublog =~ m/$url/i ) {
                logger ("Subscription already present, it seems. Excellent.
I will get on with the next one.");
                #We leave the main loop and move onto the next URL
                } else {
                # Retrieve the RSS feed
                  $retrieved_feed = get ($url);
                  logger ("Retrieved Feed from $url");
                # Examine for <cloud>
                  if ($retrieved_feed =~ m/<cloud/) {
                   &there_is_a_cloud
                   } else {
                   logger("There is no cloud element");
                   # Stick it through print_html, with an error trap here
                   eval {&print_html};
                  logger ("The parsing choked on $url with this error  $@  ") if $@;
                   }
                  };
```

This section runs a series of tests. First, it checks to see if you've already subscribed to the feed. If so, move straight on to the next one. Why? Because one of the reasons for PubSub is to lessen the load on the publisher's server. If you were to retrieve the feed every hour anyway, this aspect of the idea would be ruined.

If you're not subscribed, retrieve the feed and run the other tests, using regular expressions to check for `cloud` elements. I realize the mention of regexps will have sent many of you into a swoon. They are here because they fulfill a very simple purpose (in other words: tough). Because these elements appear only when PubSub is allowed for, if they are found, you can spin the program off into the relevant subroutine. If no `cloud` element is found, you just go straight ahead and parse the feed using the subroutine `&print_html`. If you find a `cloud` element, spin the program off to the `there_is_a_cloud` subroutine

RSS 2.0's PubSub standard requires dealing with either XML-RPC or SOAP, depending on the whim of the publisher. Our system must be able to deal with both. Here it is:

```
sub there_is_a_cloud {

  logger ("We're not subscribed, so I will attempt to subscribe to the $url");

  # First we must parse the <cloud> element with $retrieved_feed. This is in a set
    format:
  # e.g <cloud domain="www.newsisfree.com" port="80" path="/RPC"
  registerProcedure="hpe.rssPleaseNotify" protocol="xml-rpc" />
  # We'll do this with XML::Simple.

  my $parsed_xml = XMLin($retrieved_feed);

  my $cloud_domain = $parsed_xml->{channel}->{cloud}->{domain};
  my $cloud_port = $parsed_xml->{channel}->{cloud}->{port};
```

```
    my $cloud_path = $parsed_xml->{channel}->{cloud}->{path};
    my $cloud_registerProcedure = $parsed_xml->{channel}->{cloud}->{registerProcedure};
    my $cloud_protocol = $parsed_xml->{channel}->{cloud}->{protocol};

    logger ("We have retrieved the PubSub data from the RSS 2.0 feed.");
    logger ("The cloud domain is $cloud_domain");
    logger ("The port is $cloud_port");
    logger ("The path is $cloud_path");
    logger ("The port is $cloud_registerProcedure");
    logger ("The protocol is $cloud_protocol");

    # The protocol is all important. We need to differentiate between SOAP users, those
      who like XML-RPC, and the big men of HTTP-POST.

    if ($cloud_protocol eq "xml-rpc") {
       # Marvellous. That done, we spawn a new xml:rpc client.
         my $pubsub_call = Frontier::Client -> new (  url => "http://$cloud_domain:
  $cloud_port$cloud_path",
                debug => 0,
                use_objects => 1);
       # Then call the remote procedure with the rss url, as per the spec.

       $pubsub_call->call($cloud_registerProcedure,$pubsub_listening_procedure,$pubsub_
  port,$pubsub_path,$cloud_protocol,$url);

       logger ("I've asked for the subscription");
           } else {
               logger ("The protocol requested is not yet supported");
               return 1;
                }

    # Now add the url and the time it was made to the pubsublog
    open (PUBSUBLOG, ">>$pubsublog");
    my $time = time(  );
    print PUBSUBLOG "$url , $time ";
    close PUBSUBLOG;

    # That's it: return to the next one in the list.
    };
```

This script checks for the protocol attribute of the cloud element and reacts accordingly. It then parses the feed for the first time in the usual way and moves on to the next URL.

The complete listing is shown in Example 9-4.

Example 9-4. LinkpimpClient.pl

```
#!/usr/bin/perl

use diagnostics;
use warnings;

use XML::RSS;
```

Example 9-4. LinkpimpClient.pl (continued)

```
use XML::Simple;
use LWP::Simple;
use Frontier::Client;
use Frontier::RPC2;
use File::Copy;
use SOAP::Lite;
use LWP::UserAgent;

# User changable variables

my $logging         = "1";
my $logfile         = "logfile.txt";
my $pubsublog       = "pubsub.txt";
my $includefile     = "feeds.shtml";
my $tempincludefile = "feeds.shtml.tmp";

my $syndic8_userid       = "XXXXXXXXXXXXXX";
my $syndic8_password     = "XXXXX";
my $syndic8_list_id      = "0";
my $syndic8_XMLRPC_path = "http://www.syndic8.com:80/xmlrpc.php";

my $pubsub_listening_procedure = "updatedFeed";
my $pubsub_port                = "8889";
my $pubsub_path                = "/RPC2";
my $pubsub_protocol            = "xml-rpc";

my $content;
my $file;
my $line;

our $url;
our $retrieved_feed;
our $feed_spec;

#####################################################

logger("\n Program started. Let's go!\n");

# First we need to strim the pubsub records and remove all the old entries.

# Work out the time 25 hours ago (1 hour = 3600 seconds, so 25 hours = 90000 seconds)
my $oldestpossibletime = time( ) - 90000;

logger(
"The oldest allowable subscription cannot have been made earlier than $oldestpossibletime"
);

# Open the subscriber list created by pubSubListener and stick it in an array.
open( PUBSUBLIST, "<$pubsublog" );
my @lines = <PUBSUBLIST>;
close(PUBSUBLIST);
```

Example 9-4. LinkpimpClient.pl (continued)

```
# Clear the subscriber list
unlink($pubsublog) or die "Can't delete the data file\n";
logger("Old Subscription list deleted");

# We need to prevent the file being empty, even if there are no subscriptions, so:
open( NEWPUBSUBLIST, ">$pubsublog" );
print NEWPUBSUBLIST
  "This holds the details of all your subscriptions , 0000001\n";

# Go through each line, splitting it back into the right variables.
foreach $line (@lines) {
    my ( $rssUrl, $time ) = split ( /,/, "$line" );

# If the time the notification request was made ($time) is later than 25 hours ago
# ($oldestpossibletime) then stick that line back into the data file.

    if ( $time > $oldestpossibletime ) {
        print NEWPUBSUBLIST "$line\n";
    }
}
logger("New PubSublist written");

close(NEWPUBSUBLIST);

# Now, we reopen the pubsublog, and load it as a string for use later
open( PUBSUB, "$pubsublog" );
$/ = '';
my $content_of_pubsublog = <PUBSUB>;

# and we finally close the filehandle.
close(PUBSUB);

##########

# Use xmlrpc to ask for list of feeds from syndic8, and create object from result.
my $syndic8_xmlrpc_call = Frontier::Client->new(
    url         => $syndic8_XMLRPC_path,
    debug       => 0,
    use_objects => 1
);

my $syndic8_xmlrpc_returned_subscriber_list = $syndic8_xmlrpc_call-> call(
    'syndic8.GetSubscribed', $syndic8_userid,
    $syndic8_password,       $syndic8_list_id
  )
  or die "Cannot retrieve Syndic8 list";
logger("Retrieved Syndic8 subscription list");

# Place the dataurls from the subscriber list into an array
my @edited_subscribed_feeds_list =
  map { $_->{dataurl} } @$syndic8_xmlrpc_returned_subscriber_list;
```

Example 9-4. LinkpimpClient.pl (continued)

```
# Take the next line from the array of DataURLs
foreach $url (@edited_subscribed_feeds_list) {
    logger("Now working with $url");

    # Check the feed is not on the list of subscribed-to feeds
    if ( $content_of_pubsublog =~ m/$url/i ) {
        logger(
"Subscription already present, it seems. Excellent. I shall get on with the next one."
        );

        #We leave the main loop and move onto the next URL
    }
    else {

        # Retrieve the RSS feed
        $retrieved_feed = get($url);
        logger("Retrieved Feed from $url");

        # Examine for <cloud>
        if ( $retrieved_feed =~ m/<cloud/ ) {
            &subscribetorss092feed;
        }
        elsif ( $retrieved_feed =~ m/<cp:server/ ) {
            &subscribetorss10feed;
        }
        else {
            logger("There is no cloud element");

            # Stick it through print_html, with an error trap here
            eval { &print_html };
            logger("The parsing choked on $url with this error\n $@ \n") if $@;
        }
    }

    # Go to the next url in the list
}

### Replace the include file with the temporary one, and do it fast!
move( "$tempincludefile", "$includefile" );

### Clean up and exit the program
logger("We're all done here for now. Exiting Program.\n\n");

END;

######
## THE SUBROUTINES
######

sub subscribetorss092feed {

    logger("We're not subscribed, so I shall attempt to subscribe to the $url");
```

Example 9-4. LinkpimpClient.pl (continued)

```
# First we must parse the <cloud> element with $retrieved_feed This is in a set format:
# e.g <cloud domain="www.newsisfree.com" port="80" path="/RPC" registerProcedure=
"hpe.rssPleaseNotify" protocol="xml-rpc" />
# We'll do this with XML::Simple

    my $parsed_xml = XMLin($retrieved_feed);

    my $cloud_domain            = $parsed_xml->{channel}->{cloud}->{domain};
    my $cloud_port              = $parsed_xml->{channel}->{cloud}->{port};
    my $cloud_path              = $parsed_xml->{channel}->{cloud}->{path};
    my $cloud_registerProcedure =
      $parsed_xml->{channel}->{cloud}->{registerProcedure};
    my $cloud_protocol = $parsed_xml->{channel}->{cloud}->{protocol};

    logger("We have retrieved the PubSub data from the RSS 0.92 feed.");
    logger("The cloud domain is $cloud_domain");
    logger("The port is $cloud_port");
    logger("The path is $cloud_path");
    logger("The port is $cloud_registerProcedure");
    logger("The protocol is $cloud_protocol");

# The protocol is all important. We need to differentiate between SOAP users and those who
like XML-RPC

    if ( $cloud_protocol eq "xml-rpc" ) {

        # Marvellous. That done, we spawn a new xml:rpc client
        my $pubsub_call = Frontier::Client->new(
            url         => "http://$cloud_domain:$cloud_port$cloud_path",
            debug       => 0,
            use_objects => 1
        );

        # Then call the remote procedure with the rss url, as per the spec

        $pubsub_call->call( $cloud_registerProcedure,
            $pubsub_listening_procedure, $pubsub_port, $pubsub_path,
            $cloud_protocol, $url );

        logger("I've asked for the subscription");
    }
    elsif ( $cloud_protocol eq "soap" ) {

        # Initialise the SOAP interface
        my $service =
          SOAP::Lite->uri("http://$cloud_domain:$cloud_port$cloud_path");

        # Run the search
        my $result = $service->call(
            $cloud_registerProcedure => (
                $pubsub_listening_procedure, $pubsub_port,
                $pubsub_path,                $cloud_protocol,
```

Example 9-4. LinkpimpClient.pl (continued)

```
                $url
            )
        );
    }
    else {
        logger("I can't work out what protocol this guy wants. ho hum");
        return 1;
    }

    # Now add the url, and the time it was made to the pubsublog
    open( PUBSUBLOG, ">>$pubsublog" );
    my $time = time( );
    print PUBSUBLOG "$url , $time\n";
    close PUBSUBLOG;

    # That's it: return to the next one in the list.
}

#######
#######

sub subscribetorss10feed {

    logger("We're not subscribed, so I shall attempt to subscribe to the $url");

    #We need to work out which URL to send the request to.

    my $request_url = $rss->{'channel'}->{'link'}->{'cp:server'};
    logger("The Request URL is $request_url");

    #We're going to use LWP::UserAgent for this
    #So, we need to fire up a new UserAgent implementation

    logger("Creating the UserAgent");
    my $ua = LWP::UserAgent->new;

    #and give it a nice name

    $ua->agent( Personal Pubsub 1.0 );

    #And then do the requesting,
    #Remembering that we only need to pass the URL of the listener,
    #and the URL of the feed we want to have running

    $ua->request( POST $request_url,
        [ responder => $responder, target => $url ] );
    logger("Subscription request made");

}

######
######
```

Example 9-4. LinkpimpClient.pl (continued)

```
sub logger {
    if ( $logging eq "1" ) {
        open( LOG, ">>$logfile" );
        print LOG @_, "\n";
        close LOG;
        return 1;
    }
    else {
        return 1;
    }
}

######
######

sub includefile {
    ## In order to prevent a race condition, or duplicate feeds, we can't just append
directly to the include file itself
    ## so we create a temporary include file, and then replace the real one with the
temporary one right at the end of the program
    open( INCLUDEFILE, ">>$tempincludefile" );
    print INCLUDEFILE '<!--#include file="'
      . $outputfile . '" -->' . "\n" . "<br/>" . "\n";
    close INCLUDEFILE;
    return 1;
}

#######
#######

sub print_html {

    # Create new instance of XML::RSS
    my $rss = new XML::RSS;

    # Parse the $url and stick it in $rss
    logger("Now trying to parse $url");
    my $feed_to_parse = get($url);
    $rss->parse($feed_to_parse);

    # Decide on name for outputfile
    our $outputfile = "$rss->{'channel'}->{'title'}.html";
    $outputfile =~ s/ /_/g;

    # Open the output file
    logger("I'm going to call the output file $outputfile");
    open( OUTPUTFILE, ">$outputfile" );

    # Print the Channel Title
    print OUTPUTFILE '<div class="channel_link">' . "\n" . '<a href= "';
    print OUTPUTFILE "$rss->{'channel'}->{'link'}";
```

Example 9-4. LinkpimpClient.pl (continued)

```
    print OUTPUTFILE '">';
    print OUTPUTFILE "$rss->{'channel'}->{'title'}</a>\n</div>\n";

    # Print channel image, checking first if it exists
    if ( $rss->{'image'}->{'link'} ) {
        print OUTPUTFILE '<div class="channel_image">' . "\n" . '<a href= "';
        print OUTPUTFILE "$rss->{'image'}->{'link'}";
        print OUTPUTFILE '">' . "\n";
        print OUTPUTFILE '<img src="';
        print OUTPUTFILE "$rss->{'image'}->{'url'}";
        print OUTPUTFILE '" alt="';
        print OUTPUTFILE "$rss->{'image'}->{'title'}";
        print OUTPUTFILE '"/>' . "\n</a>\n</div>";
        print OUTPUTFILE "\n";
    }

    # Print the channel items
    print OUTPUTFILE '<div class="linkentries">' . "\n" . "<ul>";
    print OUTPUTFILE "\n";

    foreach my $item ( @{ $rss->{'items'} } ) {
        next unless defined( $item->{'title'} ) && defined( $item->{'link'} );
        print OUTPUTFILE '<li><a href="';
        print OUTPUTFILE "$item->{'link'}";
        print OUTPUTFILE '">';
        print OUTPUTFILE "$item->{'title'}</a></li>\n";
    }
    print OUTPUTFILE "</ul>\n</div>\n";

    # Close the OUTPUTFILE

    close(OUTPUTFILE);
    logger("and lo $outputfile has been written.");

    # Add to the include-file
    includefile($outputfile);
}
```

LinkpimpListener.pl

The other half of a PubSub system is the listener. All the listener does is sit on a port—in this case, it is defaulting to port 8888, but you can change that—and wait for an update notification. It takes that notification and retrieves the refreshed feed, parsing it and saving it to disk, where the web server can retrieve it the next time someone requests the page. The complete listing is shown in Example 9-5.

Example 9-5. LinkpimpListener.pl

```
#!usr/bin/perl

use strict;
```

Example 9-5. LinkpimpListener.pl (continued)

```
use warnings;
use HTTP::Daemon;
use Frontier::RPC2;
use HTTP::Date;
use XML::RSS;
use LWP::Simple;

# ------USER CHANGABLE VARIABLES HERE -------

my $listeningport = "8888";

# ------------------------------------------

my $methods = { 'updateFeed' => \&updateFeed };
our $host = "";

# -------------- Start the server up -----------------------

my $listen_socket = HTTP::Daemon->new(
    LocalPort => $listeningport,
    Listen    => 20,
    Proto     => 'tcp',
    Reuse     => 1
);

die "Can't create a listening socket: $@" unless $listen_socket;

while ( my $connection = $listen_socket->accept ) {
    $host = $connection->peerhost;
    interact($connection);
    $connection->close;
}

# ------------ The Interact subroutine, as called when a peer connects

sub interact {
    my $sock = shift;
    my $req;
    eval { $req = $sock->get_request; };

    # Check to see if the contact is both xml and to the right path.
    if (   $req->header('Content-Type') eq 'text/xml'
        && $req->url->path eq '/RPC2' )
    {
        my $message_content = ( $req->content );
        if ($main::Fork) {
            my $pid = fork( );
            unless ( defined $pid ) {

                #  check this response
                my $res = HTTP::Response->new( 500, 'Internal Server Error' );
                $sock->send_status_line( );
```

Example 9-5. LinkpimpListener.pl (continued)

```
            $sock->send_response($res);
        }
        if ( $pid == 0 ) {
            $sock->close;
            $main::Fork->();
            exit;
        }

        $main::Fork = undef;
    }

    my $conn_host = gethostbyaddr( $sock->peeraddr, AF_INET )
      || $sock->peerhost;

    my $res = HTTP::Response->new( 200, 'OK' );
    $res->header(
        date         => time2str(),
        Server       => 'PubSubServer',
        Content_Type => 'text/xml',
    );

    $res->content($res_xml);
    $sock->send_response($res);

    # ---------------------------------------------------------------------

    # ---- updateFeed -----

    sub updateFeed {

        my ($url) = @_;

        # Create new instance of XML::RSS

        my $rss = new XML::RSS;

        # Parse the $url and stick it in $rss

        my $feed_to_parse = get($url);
        $rss->parse($feed_to_parse);

        # Decide on name for outputfile

        my $outputfile = "$rss->{'channel'}->{'title'}.html";
        $outputfile =~ s/ /_/g;

        # Open the output file

        open( OUTPUTFILE, ">$outputfile" );

        # Print the Channel Title
```

Example 9-5. LinkpimpListener.pl (continued)

```
print OUTPUTFILE '<div id="channel_link"><a href="';
print OUTPUTFILE "$rss->{'channel'}->{'link'}";
print OUTPUTFILE '">';
print OUTPUTFILE "$rss->{'channel'}->{'title'}</a></div>\n";

# Print channel image, checking first if it exists

if ( $rss->{'image'}->{'link'} ) {
    print OUTPUTFILE '<div id="channel_image"><a href= "';
    print OUTPUTFILE "$rss->{'image'}->{'link'}";
    print OUTPUTFILE '">';
    print OUTPUTFILE '<img src="';
    print OUTPUTFILE "$rss->{'image'}->{'url'}";
    print OUTPUTFILE '" alt="';
    print OUTPUTFILE "$rss->{'image'}->{'title'}";
    print OUTPUTFILE '"/></a>';
    print OUTPUTFILE "\n";
}

# Print the channel items

print OUTPUTFILE '<div id="linkentries">';
print OUTPUTFILE "\n";

foreach my $item ( @{ $rss->{'items'} } ) {
    next
      unless defined( $item->{'title'} )
      && defined( $item->{'link'} );
    print OUTPUTFILE '<li><a href="';
    print OUTPUTFILE "$item->{'link'}";
    print OUTPUTFILE '">';
    print OUTPUTFILE "$item->{'title'}</a><BR>\n";
}
print OUTPUTFILE "</div>\n";

# If there's a textinput element...

if ( $rss->{'textinput'}->{'title'} ) {
    print OUTPUTFILE '<div id="textinput">';
    print OUTPUTFILE '<form method="get" action="';
    print OUTPUTFILE "$rss->{'textinput'}->{'link'}";
    print OUTPUTFILE '">';
    print OUTPUTFILE "$rss->{'textinput'}->{'description'}<br/>/n";
    print OUTPUTFILE '<input type="text" name="';
    print OUTPUTFILE "$rss->{'textinput'}->{'name'}";
    print OUTPUTFILE '"><br/>/n';
    print OUTPUTFILE '<input type="submit" value="';
    print OUTPUTFILE "$rss->{'textinput'}->{'title'}";
    print OUTPUTFILE '"></form>';
    print OUTPUTFILE '</div>';
}
# If there's a copyright element...
```

Example 9-5. LinkpimpListener.pl (continued)

```
            if ( $rss->{'channel'}->{'copyright'} ) {
                print OUTPUTFILE '<div id="copyright">';
                print OUTPUTFILE "$rss->{'channel'}->{'copyright'}</div>";
            }
            # Close the OUTPUTFILE

            close(OUTPUTFILE);
        }
        # ----------------
    }
}
```

CHAPTER 10

Unconventional Feeds

Equation (1.2-9) is a second order, nonlinear, vector, differential equation which has defied solution in its present form. It is here therefore we depart from the realities of nature to make some simplifying assumptions...

—Roger R. Bate, Jerry E. White, and Donald Mueller
Fundamentals of Astrodynamics, 1971

By now you should be confident in your understanding of both RSS and Atom, how the standards work, how to parse them, and how to fit them into the rest of the Internet. Before we finish this book with an explanation of how the standards can be extended, we have a good opportunity to show our knowledge in action. This chapter, therefore, is a collection of recipes for creating and using feeds that do things slightly more interesting and useful than simply transporting headlines and articles.

Apache Logfiles

Like many people, I have a weblog and quite a considerable amount of other online writings sitting on my own web server. However once I've written something and it's been indexed by the search engines, people tend to find it, and I feel a vague social responsibility to keep it up there. But things being as they are, and me tinkering as I do, documents go missing. Keeping track of the "404 Page Not Found" errors spit out by your server is, therefore, a good thing to do.

This script, therefore, goes through a standard Apache logfile and produces an RSS 2.0 feed of pages other people have found to be missing.

Walking Through the Code

Let's start with the usual Perl good form of `strict;` and `warnings;` and then load up the marvellous `Date::Manip` module. This is perhaps a little overkill for its use here, but it does allow for some extremely simple and readable code. This is a CGI application, so we need that module, and we're producing RSS, so `XML::RSS` is naturally required too.

```
use strict;
use warnings;
use Date::Manip;
use XML::RSS;
use CGI qw(:standard);
```

First off, let's set up the feed. Because this is the simplest possible form of RSS— just a list, really—it is a perfect fit for RSS 2.0. Then we give it a nice title, link and description, as per the specification:

```
my $rss = new XML::RSS( version => '2.0' );
$rss->channel(
    title       => "Missing Files",
    link        => "http://www.example.org",
    description => "Files found to be missing from my server"
);
```

On my host at least, logfiles are split daily and named after the date. Since I'm fixing the missing files as they appear, I only want to parse yesterday's file. So let's use `Date::Manip`'s functions to return yesterday's date, then create the logfile path, and open a filehandle to it. You will need to change this line to reflect your own setup:

```
my $yesterdays_date = &UnixDate( "yesterday", "%Y%m%d" );
my $logfile_file = "/web/logs/ben/benhammersley.com/$yesterdays_date.log";
open( LOGFILE, "< $logfile_file" );
```

Now, go into a loop, taking the logfile line by line and using the mother of regular expressions to split it up into its requisite parts. This is a very useful line to take note of: you can change this section to convert this script to monitor your Apache logfiles for just about anything.

```
while (<LOGFILE>) {
    my (
        $host,      $ident_user, $auth_user, $date,     $time,
        $time_zone, $method,     $url,       $protocol, $status,
        $bytes,     $referer,    $agent
      )
      = /^(\S+) (\S+) (\S+) \[([^:]+):(\d+:\d+:\d+) ([^\]]+)\] "(\S+) (.+?) (\S+)" (\
S+) (\S+) "([^"]+)"
"([^"]+)"$/;
```

But today, we're interested in 404 errors. So, the script uses the `XML::RSS` module to add `items` for every error found:

```
my $cleaned_status = $status || "111";

if ( $cleaned_status == "404" ) {
    $rss->add_item(
        title       => "$url",
        link        => "$url",
        description => "$referer"
```

```
        );
    }
}
```

Then all that's left to do is to close the filehandle, print out the correct MIME type for RSS, and print out the feed we've built:

```
close(LOGFILE);
print header('application/xml+rss');
print $rss->as_string;
```

The Entire Listing

```
#!/usr/bin/perl
use strict;
use warnings;
use Date::Manip;
use XML::RSS;
use CGI qw(:standard);

my $rss = new XML::RSS( version => '2.0' );
$rss->channel(
    title       => "Missing Files",
    link        => "http://www.example.org",
    description => "Files found to be missing from my server"
);

my $yesterdays_date = &UnixDate( "yesterday", "%Y%m%d" );
my $logfile_file = "/web/logs/ben/benhammersley.com/$yesterdays_date.log";
open( LOGFILE, "< $logfile_file" );

while (<LOGFILE>) {
    my (
        $host,      $ident_user, $auth_user, $date,     $time,
        $time_zone, $method,     $url,       $protocol, $status,
        $bytes,     $referer,    $agent
      )
      = /^(\S+) (\S+) (\S+) \[([^:]+):(\d+:\d+:\d+) ([^\]]+)\] "(\S+) (.+?) (\S+)" (\
S+) (\S+) "([^"]+)"
"([^"]+)"$/;

    my $cleaned_status = $status || "111";

    if ( $cleaned_status == "404" ) {
        $rss->add_item(
            title       => "$url",
            link        => "$url",
            description => "$referer"
        );
    }
}

close(LOGFILE);
print header('application/xml+rss');
print $rss->as_string;
```

Code TODOs to RSS

I live by my to-do list. Without it, I'd be a drippy mess of procrastination, and you wouldn't be reading this book right now. It's good to be organized, and especially so with code. Working on the scripts and chapters in this book, I've started to leave messages to myself within them. I mark these out as a new line starting with TODO:.

I then have this script run over all of my working directories, parsing each file and looking for those lines. The result is a nice to-do list in my reader application and a morning's work all set out.

Walking Through the Code

We'll do the usual start, with strict;, warnings;, CGI and XML::RSS. Let's use the File::Find module to do the directory-traversing:

```
use strict;
use warnings;
use XML::RSS;
use CGI qw(:standard);
use File::Find;
```

Up near the top, we set the root directory, below which everything will be parsed. You need to change this to match your own setup, but remember that the script checks every file. Setting it to something too high up your filesystem tree might slow the script down magnificently.

```
my $start_directory = "/Users/ben/Code/";
```

Now, set up the RSS feed, as per usual. Here, we're using a cunning trick, technically against the RSS 2.0 specification, of making the link element a file:// URL. This usually works very well, bringing up your OS's file manager, or the application associated with that particular file, but remember that technically, it's not supposed to work at all. Still, for a locally produced, locally consumed feed, a little slackness on the specification is probably allowed.

```
my $rss = new XML::RSS( version => '2.0' );
$rss->channel(
    title       => "TODOs from $start_directory",
    link        => "file:/$start_directory",
    description => "Files with TODO messages, from $start_directory"
);
```

Now, use the File::Find module to traverse the directories, opening a filehandle for each one, slurping it in and searching each line with a regular expression for TODO. If it's found, add an item to the RSS feed.

```
find( \&search_and_rss, $start_directory );

sub search_and_rss {
```

```
    open( CODEFILE, "< $File::Find::name" );

    while (<CODEFILE>) {
        if ( $_ =~ m/TODO/ ) {
            $rss->add_item(
                title       => "$File::Find::name",
                link        => "file:\/\/$File::Find::name",
                description => "$_ at Line $. of $File::Find::name"
            );
```

As a test for the script, I've left a TODO line within itself. It's just a suggestion that a section of code to add the file's last modification date to the RSS feed might be a nice idea; I leave this as an exercise for the reader. Now, close the filehandle:

```
            #TODO: Put in date code here

        }
    }
    close(CODEFILE);
}
```

And finally, we serve up the feed:

```
print header('application/xml+rss');
print $rss->as_string;
```

The Entire Listing

```
#!/usr/bin/perl

use strict;
use warnings;
use XML::RSS;
use CGI qw(:standard);
use File::Find;

my $start_directory = "/Users/ben/Code/";

my $rss = new XML::RSS( version => '2.0' );
$rss->channel(
    title       => "TODOs from $start_directory",
    link        => "file:/$start_directory",
    description => "Files with TODO messages, from $start_directory"
);

find( \&search_and_rss, $start_directory );

sub search_and_rss {

    open( CODEFILE, "< $File::Find::name" );

    while (<CODEFILE>) {
        if ( $_ =~ m/TODO/ ) {
            $rss->add_item(
```

```
                title       => "$File::Find::name",
                link        => "file:\/\/$File::Find::name",
                description => "$_ at Line $. of $File::Find::name"
            );

            #TODO: Put in date code here
        }
    }
    close(CODEFILE);
}

print header('application/xml+rss');
print $rss->as_string;
```

Daily Doonesbury

The morning isn't quite the same without the daily dose of *Doonesbury*, the Pulitzer Prize winning cartoon strip by Garry Trudeau. But, frankly, the nearest newspaper stand is far too far to go before I've had morning coffee and typing in *http://www.doonesbury.com* on an empty stomach is a bit much. Why not have it delivered via RSS? You just need a web server, or a proper operating system capable of running CGI scripts, and the following code. This is tremendously simple stuff—but distinctly pleasing to have set up for your morning coffee.

Walking Through the Code

We'll go with the traditional start: `strict;`, `warnings;`, `CGI` with `DATE::Manip`, and the joy that is `XML::RSS` all being loaded for your coding pleasure. So far, so simple.

```
use strict;
use warnings;
use CGI qw(:standard);
use Date::Manip;
use XML::RSS;
```

The *Doonesbury* site, thankfully, names its image files after the date, in the format YYMMDD. So, first, you work out the date, then add a single entry containing escaped HTML that displays the image file you want.

```
my $todays_date = &UnixDate( "today", "%y%m%d" );
my $this_year = &UnixDate("today","%Y");

my $rss = new XML::RSS( version => '2.0' );

$rss->add_item(
    title => "Doonesbury for $todays_date",
    link  => "http://images.ucomics.com/comics/db/$this_year/db$todays_date.gif",
    description => '<img src="http://images.ucomics.com/comics/db/2004/'
      . "db$todays_date.gif"
      . '"/>'
);
```

Then it's just a matter of adding in the channel information and serving the thing out with the correct MIME type:

```
$rss->channel(
    title       => "Today's Doonesbury",
    link        => "http://www.doonesbury.com",
    description => "Doonesbury, by Garry Trudeau"
);

print header('application/xml+rss');
print $rss->as_string;
```

You can obviously use this sort of code to produce RSS feeds of any online comic strip. Do the author a favor, however: don't make the feed public, visit his site once in a while, and buy some schwag. You're getting great stuff for free—with the added convenience you've added, for sure—and it's nice to give something back.

The Entire Listing

```
#!/usr/bin/perl

use strict;
use warnings;
use CGI qw(:standard);
use Date::Manip;
use XML::RSS;

my $todays_date = &UnixDate( "today", "%y%m%d" );

my $rss = new XML::RSS( version => '2.0' );

$rss->add_item(
    title => "Doonesbury for $todays_date",
    link  => "http://images.ucomics.com/comics/db/2004/db$todays_date.gif",
    description => '&lt;img src="http://images.ucomics.com/comics/db/2004/'
      . "db$todays_date.gif"
      . '"/&gt;'
);

$rss->channel(
    title       => "Today's Doonesbury",
    link        => "http://www.doonesbury.com",
    description => "Doonesbury, by Garry Trudeau"
);

print header('application/xml+rss');
print $rss->as_string;
```

Amazon.com Wishlist to RSS

Being perfection herself, my wife loves books, and as a loving and dutiful husband, her Amazon wishlist is required reading for Christmas, birthdays, and all other occasions. But keeping track of the wishlist is a pain if I have to trudge over to Amazon every time. Far better to have my feed reader do it for me, with the help of a little script. Figure 10-1 shows my wishlist to give you an idea of what one looks like.

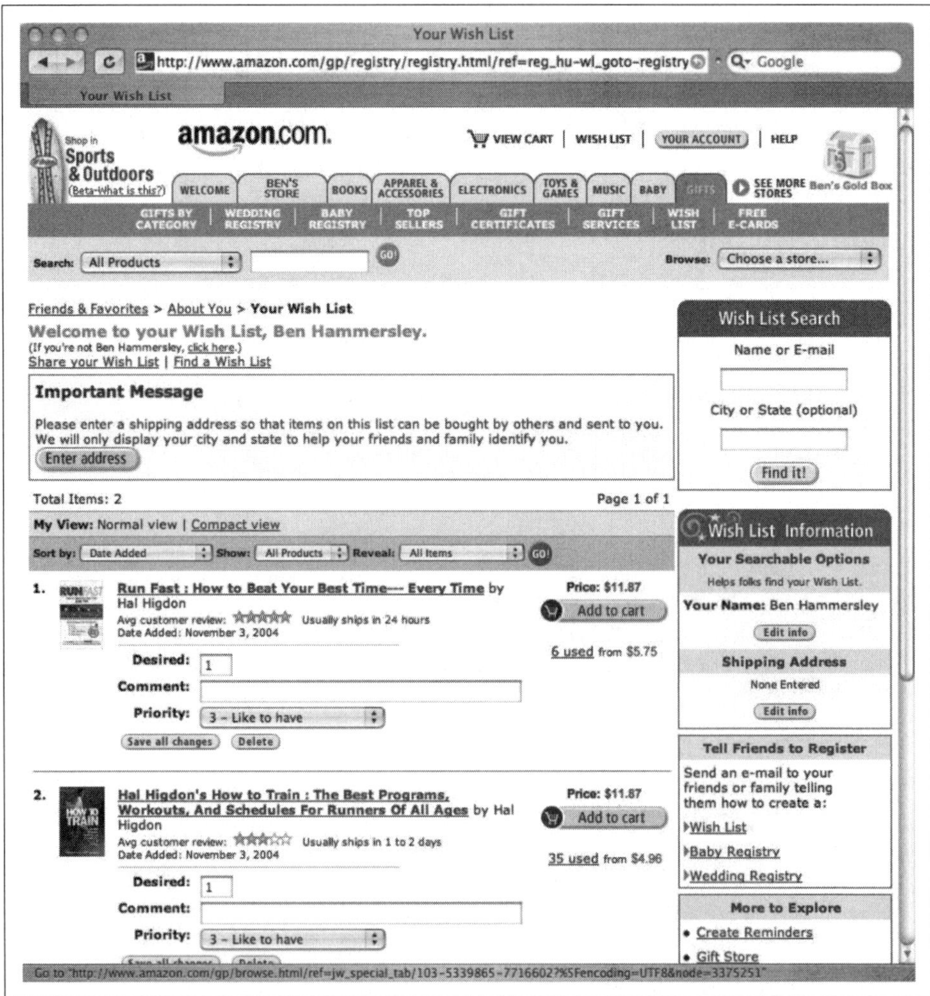

Figure 10-1. My Amazon.com wishlist page

This feed uses the Amazon Web Services API to do its evil work. This can be either REST- or SOAP-based, so you can choose your own preferred poison. For fun, I'll do this using the REST interface, and then using `XML::Simple` to parse the XML. My idea of fun might not be the same as yours, of course.

Walking Through the Code

As always, we fire up the script with the loading of the modules and the setting of some global variables: the obligatory `use strict;` and `use warnings;`, and the required Amazon API subscription key. You'll need to get your own from *http://www.amazon.com/gp/aws/landing.html.*

```
use strict;
use warnings;
use XML::RSS;
use XML::Simple;
use LWP::Simple qw(!head);
use CGI qw(:standard);
use Getopt::Long;
use Date::Manip;

my $amazon_subscription_id = "xxxxxxxxxxxxxxxxxx";
my $rss = new XML::RSS( version => '2.0' );
```

As this script is running as a CGI application, it requires the Amazon Wishlist ID as a parameter. This allows you to use the same script many times over for each of the lists you want to monitor. Let's make the parameter compulsory, naturally.

```
my $cgi = CGI::new( );
my $list_id = $cgi->param('list');
```

Now, run the query via the Amazon Web Services REST interface. This takes a specifically formed URI and returns an XML document. We'll retrieve this using the `LWP::Simple` module:

```
my $query_url =
"http://webservices.amazon.com/onca/
xml?Service=AWSProductData&SubscriptionId=$amazon_subscription_
id&Operation=ListLookup&ProductPage=15&ListType=WishList&ListId=$list_
id&ResponseGroup=Request,ListItems";

my $wishlist_in_xml = get("$query_url");
```

and place it into the Parser:

```
my $parser = XMLin("$wishlist_in_xml") or die ("Could not parse file");
```

This produces an array of the items within the wishlist, albeit still stored within the XML format returned by the REST query. That format looks like this:

```
&lt;ListItem&gt;
        &lt;ListItemId&gt;I2MNVARC9PUUA7&lt;/ListItemId&gt;
        &lt;DateAdded&gt;2004-11-03&lt;/DateAdded&gt;
        &lt;QuantityDesired&gt;1&lt;/QuantityDesired&gt;
        &lt;QuantityReceived&gt;0&lt;/QuantityReceived&gt;
        &lt;Item&gt;
```

```
                &lt;ASIN&gt;0875963528&lt;/ASIN&gt;
                &lt;ItemAttributes&gt;
                        &lt;Title&gt;Hal Higdon's How to Train&lt;/Title&gt;
                &lt;/ItemAttributes&gt;
        &lt;/Item&gt;
&lt;/ListItem&gt;
```

So now you need to take the relevant bits of that information and throw it into the feed. For the taking is the title, the date, and the ASIN number—Amazon's internal system for identifying its stock. Use this to provide a link. For a change of pace, let's use a different XML parsing method, too. `XML::Simple` is tremendously useful for this sort of thing.

Now, we'll add in some code to create the correct date, based on the date the item was added to the wishlist. Amazon returns the date in the format YYYY-MM-DD, but RSS 2.0 insists on the format `Sun, 19 May 2002 15:21:36 GMT`. For the sake of sanity, assume all the dates Amazon gives are at exactly midnight.

We need to do some date manipulation, and what better than `Date::Manip` to do this? Under its `UnixDate` function, the code %g is exactly the right format for RSS 2.0. Nifty, no?

```
foreach my $item (@{$parser->{'Lists'}->{'List'}->{'ListItem'}}) {

     #my $date = &UnixDate("midnight $item->{'Item'}->{'DateAdded'}","%c, %e %b %Y");

   $rss->add_item(
   title => "$item->{'Item'}->{'ItemAttributes'}->{'Title'}",
   link  => "http://www.amazon.com/exec/obidos/tg/detail/-/$item->{'Item'}->
{'ASIN'}",
    description => "$item->{'Item'}->{'ItemAttributes'}->{'Title'}",
    pubDate => &UnixDate("midnight $item->{'DateAdded'}","%g")

        );

}
```

Then, as ever, it's just a matter of adding in the channel information and serving the thing out with the correct MIME type:

```
$rss->channel(
    title       => "Amazon Wishlist, $list_id",
    link        => "http://www.amazon.com",
    description => "An RSS feed of the Amazon Wishlist, id number $list_id"
);

print header('application/xml+rss');
print $rss->as_string;
```

The Entire Listing

```
#!/usr/bin/perl

use strict;
use warnings;
use XML::RSS;
use XML::Simple;
use LWP::Simple qw(!head);
use CGI qw(:standard);
use Getopt::Long;
use Date::Manip;

my $amazon_subscription_id = "08R1SHPFGCA8VYT9P802";
my $rss = new XML::RSS( version => '2.0' );

my $cgi = CGI::new( );
my $list_id = $cgi->param('list');

my $query_url =
"http://webservices.amazon.com/onca/
xml?Service=AWSProductData&SubscriptionId=$amazon_subscription_
id&Operation=ListLookup&ProductPage=15&ListType=WishList&ListId=$list_
id&ResponseGroup=Request,ListItems";

my $wishlist_in_xml = get("$query_url");

my $parser = XMLin("$wishlist_in_xml") or die ("Could not parse file");

foreach my $item (@{$parser->{'Lists'}->{'List'}->{'ListItem'}}) {

    $rss->add_item(
    title => "$item->{'Item'}->{'ItemAttributes'}->{'Title'}",
    link  => "http://www.amazon.com/exec/obidos/tg/detail/-/$item->{'Item'}->
{'ASIN'}",
    description => "$item->{'Item'}->{'ItemAttributes'}->{'Title'}",
    pubDate => &UnixDate("midnight $item->{'DateAdded'}","%g")

        );

}

$rss->channel(
    title       => "Amazon Wishlist, $list_id",
    link        => "http://www.amazon.com",
    description => "An RSS feed of the Amazon Wishlist, id number $list_id"
);

print header('application/xml+rss');
print $rss->as_string;
```

FedEx Parcel Tracker

Christmas is coming, and Santa has outsourced his deliveries to Federal Express. Lucky us, as that means we can use FedEx's online shipment tracker to watch our parcels wend their merry way here. Except the tiresome chore of refreshing the FedEx site is just too much to handle. Let's let a nice script elf take care of it and create a feed for every parcel.

Although FedEx and its rivals do provide APIs, we won't be using them here. FedEx's page is easy enough to scrape by brute force, and it's fun to do so. Of course, when it next changes its page layout, this script will need rejigging. It's easy to see how to do that when it happens.

Walking Through the Code

So, starting with the usual Perl standards of `warnings;`, `strict;`, `XML::RSS`, and `CGI`, let's use `LWP::Simple` to retrieve the page and the marvellous `HTML::TokeParser` to do the dirty work. More on that anon.

```
use warnings;
use strict;
use XML::RSS;
use CGI qw(:standard);
use LWP::Simple 'get';
use HTML::TokeParser;
```

Now let's set up some variables to use later, then fire up the CGI module and grab the tracking number from the query string. To use this script, therefore, you need to request:

```
http://www.example.org/fedextracker.cgi?track=123456789
```

where `123456789` is the tracking number of the parcel:

```
my ( $tag, $headline, $url, $date_line );
my $last_good_date;
my $table_end_check;

my $cgi              = CGI::new();
my $tracking_number = $cgi->param('track');
```

Now we're ready to jingle. Using `LWP::Simple`'s get method, pull down the page from the FedEx site. FedEx, bless them, employ openly understandable URLs, so this is easy to set up. Once that's downloaded, throw it into a new instance of the `HTML::TokeParser` module, and we're ready for scraping:

```
my $tracking_page =
  get(
"http://fedex.com/Tracking?action=track&tracknumber_list=$tracking_number&cntry_
code=us"
  );

my $stream = HTML::TokeParser->new( \$tracking_page );
```

Now is as good a time as any to start off XML::RSS and fill in some channel details:

```
my $rss = XML::RSS->new( );

$rss->channel(
    title => "FedEx Tracking: $tracking_number",
    link  =>
"http://fedex.com/Tracking?action=track&tracknumber_list=$tracking_number&cntry_
code=us"
);
```

From now on, we're using the HTML::TokeParser module, skipping from tag to tag until we get to the section of the HTML to scrape. The inline comments say what we're up to.

```
# Go to the right part of the page, skipping 13 tables (!!!)
$stream->get_tag("table");
$stream->get_tag("table");
$stream->get_tag("table");
$stream->get_tag("table");
$stream->get_tag("table");
$stream->get_tag("table");
$stream->get_tag("table");
$stream->get_tag("table");
$stream->get_tag("table");
$stream->get_tag("table");
$stream->get_tag("table");
$stream->get_tag("table");
$stream->get_tag("table");

# Now go inside the tracking details table
$stream->get_tag("table");
$stream->get_tag("tr");
$stream->get_tag("/tr");
$stream->get_tag("tr");
$stream->get_tag("/tr");
```

By this point, you're at the table to parse, so loop through it, getting the dates and locations. You need to stop at the bottom of the table, so test for a closing /table tag. You can do so with a named loop and a last...if... command.

You'll notice that in this section, we use those mysterious variables from earlier. Because the table is displayed with the date mentioned only once per day, no matter how many stops the parcel makes on that day, you need to keep track of it.

```
PARSE: while ( $tag = $stream->get_tag('tr') ) {

    $stream->get_tag("td");
    $stream->get_tag("/td");

    # Test here for the closing /tr. If it exists, we're done.

    # Now get date text
    $stream->get_tag("td");
    $stream->get_tag("b");
```

```
my $date_text = $stream->get_trimmed_text("/b");

# The page only mentions the date once, so we need to fill in any blanks
# that might occur.

if ( $date_text eq "\xa0" ) {
    $date_text = $last_good_date;
}
else {
    $last_good_date = $date_text;
}

# Now get the time text
$stream->get_tag("/b");
$stream->get_tag("/td");
$stream->get_tag("td");
my $time_text = $stream->get_trimmed_text("/td");
$time_text =~ s/\xa0//g;

# Now get the status
$stream->get_tag("/td");
$stream->get_tag("/td");
$stream->get_tag("/td");
$stream->get_tag("/td");
$stream->get_tag("td");
my $status = $stream->get_trimmed_text("/td");
$status =~ s/\xa0//g;

# Now get the location
$stream->get_tag("/td");
$stream->get_tag("/td");
$stream->get_tag("/td");
$stream->get_tag("/td");
$stream->get_tag("td");
my $location = $stream->get_trimmed_text("/td");
$location =~ s/\xa0//g;

# Now get the comment
$stream->get_tag("/td");
$stream->get_tag("/td");
$stream->get_tag("/td");
$stream->get_tag("/td");
$stream->get_tag("td");
my $comment = $stream->get_trimmed_text("/td");
$comment =~ s/\xa0//g;

# Now go to the end of the block
$stream->get_tag("/td");
$stream->get_tag("/td");
$stream->get_tag("/tr");

# OK, now we have the details, we need to put them into a feed
# Do what you want with the info:
```

Still inside the loop, create an item for the RSS feed:

```
        if ($status) {
          $rss->add_item(
              title => "$status $location $date_text $time_text",
              link  =>
"http://fedex.com/us/tracking/?action=track&tracknumber_list=$tracking_number",
              description =>
"Package number $tracking_number was last seen in $location at $time_text on $date_
text, with the status,
$status. $comment Godspeed, little parcel! Onward, tiny package!"
          );
      }

      # Stop parsing after the pickup line.
      last PARSE if ( $status eq "Picked up " );
}
```

All that done, you can serve it up nice and festive:

```
print header('application/rss+xml');
print $rss->as_string;
```

The Entire Listing

```
#!/usr/bin/perl

use warnings;
use strict;
use XML::RSS;
use CGI qw(:standard);
use LWP::Simple 'get';
use HTML::TokeParser;

my ( $tag, $headline, $url, $date_line );
my $last_good_date;
my $table_end_check;

my $cgi             = CGI::new( );
my $tracking_number = $cgi->param('track');

my $tracking_page =
  get(
"http://fedex.com/Tracking?action=track&tracknumber_list=$tracking_number&cntry_
code=us"
  );

my $stream = HTML::TokeParser->new( \$tracking_page );

my $rss = XML::RSS->new( );

$rss->channel(
    title => "FedEx Tracking: $tracking_number",
    link  =>
```

```
"http://fedex.com/Tracking?action=track&tracknumber_list=$tracking_number&cntry_
code=us"
);

# Go to the right part of the page, skipping 13 tables (!!!)
$stream->get_tag("table");
$stream->get_tag("table");
$stream->get_tag("table");
$stream->get_tag("table");
$stream->get_tag("table");
$stream->get_tag("table");
$stream->get_tag("table");
$stream->get_tag("table");
$stream->get_tag("table");
$stream->get_tag("table");
$stream->get_tag("table");
$stream->get_tag("table");
$stream->get_tag("table");

# Now go inside the tracking details table
$stream->get_tag("table");
$stream->get_tag("tr");
$stream->get_tag("/tr");
$stream->get_tag("tr");
$stream->get_tag("/tr");

PARSE: while ( $tag = $stream->get_tag('tr') ) {

    $stream->get_tag("td");
    $stream->get_tag("/td");

    # Test here for the closing /tr. If it exists, we're done.

    # Now get date text
    $stream->get_tag("td");
    $stream->get_tag("b");

    my $date_text = $stream->get_trimmed_text("/b");

    # The page only mentions the date once, so we need to fill in any blanks
    # that might occur.

    if ( $date_text eq "\xa0" ) {
        $date_text = $last_good_date;
    }
    else {
        $last_good_date = $date_text;
    }

    # Now get the time text
    $stream->get_tag("/b");
    $stream->get_tag("/td");
    $stream->get_tag("td");
```

```
    my $time_text = $stream->get_trimmed_text("/td");
    $time_text =~ s/\xa0//g;

    # Now get the status
    $stream->get_tag("/td");
    $stream->get_tag("/td");
    $stream->get_tag("/td");
    $stream->get_tag("/td");
    $stream->get_tag("td");
    my $status = $stream->get_trimmed_text("/td");
    $status =~ s/\xa0//g;

    # Now get the location
    $stream->get_tag("/td");
    $stream->get_tag("/td");
    $stream->get_tag("/td");
    $stream->get_tag("/td");
    $stream->get_tag("td");
    my $location = $stream->get_trimmed_text("/td");
    $location =~ s/\xa0//g;

    # Now get the comment
    $stream->get_tag("/td");
    $stream->get_tag("/td");
    $stream->get_tag("/td");
    $stream->get_tag("/td");
    $stream->get_tag("td");
    my $comment = $stream->get_trimmed_text("/td");
    $comment =~ s/\xa0//g;

    # Now go to the end of the block
    $stream->get_tag("/td");
    $stream->get_tag("/td");
    $stream->get_tag("/tr");

    # OK, now we have the details, we need to put them into a feed
    # Do what you want with the info:

    if ($status) {
        $rss->add_item(
            title => "$status $location $date_text $time_text",
            link  =>
"http://fedex.com/us/tracking/?action=track&tracknumber_list=$tracking_number",
            description =>
"Package number $tracking_number was last seen in $location at $time_text on $date_
text, with the status,
$status. $comment Godspeed, little parcel! Onward, tiny package!"
        );
    }

    # Stop parsing after the pickup line.
    last PARSE if ( $status eq "Picked up " );
```

```
}

print header('application/rss+xml');
print $rss->as_string;
```

Google to RSS with SOAP

Google, the search engine of fashion these days, is as close to an authority as you can get on the Internet. If it's not mentioned on Google, the feeling is, it's not really online. And if it is, conversely, then people will find it. Keeping track of things in Google's database, therefore, is an important job. Whether you are trying to find things out or monitoring for other people's discoveries, an RSS feed is the perfect way to do it. Happily, Google provides a nice interface to work with its systems. This makes things very easy.

Walking Through the Code

We start, as ever, with the usual pragmas, `CGI` and `XML::RSS`. This time, you also need `SOAP::Lite` and `HTML::Entitie`.

```
use warnings;
use strict;
use XML::RSS;
use CGI qw(:standard);
use HTML::Entities ();
use SOAP::Lite;
```

We'll set up the query term, and the Google API key, from the CGI input. Then, we fire up the `SOAP::Lite` by pointing it at Google's WSDL file. WSDL files contain the finer details of a SOAP interface, telling the script exactly where to send commands and so on.

```
my $query = param("q");
my $key   = param("k");

my $service = SOAP::Lite -> service('http://api.google.com/GoogleSearch.wsdl');
```

Now, run the search using the SOAP interface we just set up; then set up the feed:

```
my $result = $service -> doGoogleSearch ($key, $query, 0, 10, "false", "",
"false","", "latin1", "latin1");

my $rss = new XML::RSS (version => '2.00');

$rss->channel( title  => "Google Search for $query",
               link => "http://www.google.com/search?q=$query",
               description => "Google search for $query",
                      language => "en",
                    );
```

Now, it's just a matter of going through the results and using them as values for the feed's items. To make it valid XML, use the HTML::Entities module to encode any stray characters that might need it:

```
foreach my $element (@{$result->{'resultElements'}}) {
        $rss->add_item(
                title    => HTML::Entities::encode($element->{'title'}),
                link     => HTML::Entities::encode($element->{'URL'})
                );
        }
```

And finally, serve the feed:

```
print header('application/xml+rss'), $rss->as_string;
```

The Entire Listing

```
#!/usr/bin/perl

use warnings;
use strict;
use XML::RSS;
use CGI qw(:standard);
use HTML::Entities ();
use SOAP::Lite;

my $query = param("q");
my $key   = param("k");

my $service = SOAP::Lite -> service('http://api.google.com/GoogleSearch.wsdl');

my $result = $service -> doGoogleSearch ($key, $query, 0, 10, "false", "", "false",
"", "latin1", "latin1");

my $rss = new XML::RSS (version => '2.00');

$rss->channel(  title  => "Google Search for $query",
                link => "http://www.google.com/search?q=$query",
                description => "Google search for $query",
                        language => "en",
                      );

foreach my $element (@{$result->{'resultElements'}}) {
        $rss->add_item(
                title    => HTML::Entities::encode($element->{'title'}),
                link     => HTML::Entities::encode($element->{'URL'})
                );
        }

print header('application/xml+rss'), $rss->as_string;
```

Last-Modified Files

There are lots of reasons to have an ever-updating list of recently modified files: security, for one. However, it's also a useful system for helping you group working files in your mind. I'm forever loosing track of files I'm working on—especially overnight—and this feed helps a great deal. For collaborative working, it's a godsend because you can see what other activity is going on automatically. I also have one of these pointed at a shared directory where friends drop music and silly MPEGs. Altogether, for something so simple, it's remarkably useful.

It's a CGI script that takes a single parameter `path`, which should be equal to the absolute path on your filesystem that you wish to look under—for example, `http://www.example.org/lastmodified.cgi?path=/users/ben`.

Walking Through the Code

Let's trek once again into the `warnings;`, `strict;`, `XML::RSS`, and `CGI`, plus `Date::Manip` for the dateline and `File::Find` for its directory traversing capabilities. Lovely. All set? Good.

```
use warnings;
use strict;
use XML::RSS;
use CGI qw(:standard);
use File::Find;
use Date::Manip;
```

By now you should be getting the hang of this. We're firing up the CGI module, snaffling the parameter we are passing to it, then setting up the feed. No great mystery here, in other words. Really, this is somewhat the point: feeds are very simple things. It's the ideas of how to use them that are valuable.

```
my $cgi             = CGI::new( );
my $start_directory = $cgi->param('path');

my $rss = new XML::RSS( version => '2.0' );
$rss->channel(
    title       => "Last modified from $start_directory",
    link        => "file:/$start_directory",
    description =>
"A list of all of the files in $start_directory, with their modification dates added
in"
);
```

Here's the real meat of the script. We're using the `find` function from the `File::Find` module, to traverse the directory we've given it and throw each individual file it finds into a small subroutine:

```
find( \&search_and_rss, $start_directory );

sub search_and_rss {
```

Here's an interesting thing. You can use `File::Find` and the standard `stat` function to grab the last-modified date of each file and then use `Date::Manip` to convert it from the standard epoch seconds to the required format. Note that, unlike most other date strings, `Date::Manip` requires the word "epoch" in front of the raw time value to help it along. This caused me to do a lot of shouting before I remembered it.

```
    my $last_modified_date = ( stat($File::Find::name) )[9];
    my $parsed_date        = &ParseDate("epoch $last_modified_date");
    my $pubDate            = &UnixDate( $parsed_date, "%g" );
```

It's then just a matter of creating each item, and, once the whole directory has been traversed, serving up the feed:

```
    $rss->add_item(
        title       => "$File::Find::name",
        link        => "file:\/\/$File::Find::name",
        description => "$File::Find::name",
        pubDate     => "$pubDate",
    );

}

print header('application/xml');
print $rss->as_string;
```

The Entire Listing

```
#!/usr/bin/perl

use warnings;
use strict;
use XML::RSS;
use CGI qw(:standard);
use File::Find;
use Date::Manip;

my $cgi             = CGI::new( );
my $start_directory = $cgi->param('path');

my $rss = new XML::RSS( version => '2.0' );
$rss->channel(
    title       => "Last modified from $start_directory",
    link        => "file:/$start_directory",
    description =>
"A list of all of the files in $start_directory, with their modification dates added
in"
);

find( \&search_and_rss, $start_directory );

sub search_and_rss {
```

```
    my $last_modified_date = ( stat($File::Find::name) )[9];
    my $parsed_date        = &ParseDate("epoch $last_modified_date");
    my $pubDate            = &UnixDate( $parsed_date, "%g" );

    $rss->add_item(
        title       => "$File::Find::name",
        link        => "file:\/\/$File::Find::name",
        description => "$File::Find::name",
        pubDate     => "$pubDate",
    );
}

print header('application/xml');
print $rss->as_string;
```

Installed Perl Modules

Another interesting way to use a Feed is to keep track of changing system configurations. The following is a simple example. I have two machines running my scripts; one is my laptop and the other a server in a rack somewhere in North America. I write mostly in Perl and use a lot of modules. It's useful to me to keep track of what's installed, and what's not, on each; this script produces a feed of the modules I have installed.

Walking Through the Code

We'll use the usual modules plus one more, `ExtUtils::Installed`. Written by Alan Burlison, this module really does all the work here. Again, this is somewhat the point of this chapter. Feeds aren't difficult things, and they are incredibly useful interfaces to list-like data.

```
use warnings;
use strict;
use CGI qw(:standard);
use XML::RSS;
use ExtUtils::Installed;
```

`ExtUtils::Installed` creates an array of all the installed modules; run the shell command `uname -n` to find the name of the machine we're running the script on:

```
my $installed    = ExtUtils::Installed->new();
my $machine_name = `uname -n`;
```

Now, set up the feed as usual, using the machine name to label it:

```
my $rss = new XML::RSS( version => '2.0' );
$rss->channel(
    title       => "Perl Modules on $machine_name",
    link        => "http://www.benhammersley.com/tools/",
    description => "A list of installed Perl modules on $machine_name"
);
```

Finally, go through the array, pulling out the name and version number of each module and creating the items. Then serve it up. Simple.

```
foreach my $module ( $installed->modules() ) {
    my $version = $installed->version($module) || "???";

    $rss->add_item(
        title       => "$module $version",
        description => "$module $version",
        link        => "http://search.cpan.org/search%3fmodule=$module",
    );
}

print header('application/rss+xml');
print $rss->as_string;
```

The Entire Listing

```
#!/usr/bin/perl

use warnings;
use strict;
use CGI qw(:standard);
use XML::RSS;
use ExtUtils::Installed;

my $installed    = ExtUtils::Installed->new();
my $machine_name = `uname -n`;

my $rss = new XML::RSS( version => '2.0' );
$rss->channel(
    title       => "Perl Modules on $machine_name",
    link        => "http://www.benhammersley.com/tools/",
    description => "A list of installed Perl modules on $machine_name"
);

foreach my $module ( $installed->modules() ) {
    my $version = $installed->version($module) || "???";

    $rss->add_item(
        title       => "$module $version",
        description => "$module $version",
        link        => "http://search.cpan.org/search%3fmodule=$module",
    );
}

print header('application/rss+xml');
print $rss->as_string;
```

The W3C Validator to RSS

Of all the tasks of Hercules, the one where he had to keep his web site's XHTML validated was the hardest. Without wanting to approach the whole Valid XHTML Controversy, we can still safely say that keeping a site validated is a pain. You have to validate your code, most commonly using the W3C validator service at *http://validator.w3.org*, and you have to keep going back there to make sure nothing has broken.

You have to do that unless, of course, you're subscribed to a feed of validation results. This script does just that, providing an RSS interface to the W3C validator.

You pass the URL you want to test as a query in the feed URL, like so: `http://www.example.org/validator.cgi?url=http://www.example.org/index.html`.

Walking Through the Code

We're using the traditional Perl start plus `LWP::Simple` and `XML::Simple`, which will parse the results coming back from the validator. Note that, in the classic gotcha, `LWP::Simple` and `CGI` clash, so we have to add those additional flags to prevent a type mismatch.

```
use warnings;
use strict;
use XML::RSS;
use CGI qw(:standard);
use LWP::Simple 'get';
use XML::Simple;
```

Now, grab the URL from the query string, and use `LWP::Simple` to retrieve the results. The W3C provides an XML output mode for the validator, and this is what we're using here. It is, however, classed as beta and flakey, and might not always work.

```
my $cgi = CGI::new( );
my $url = $cgi->param('url');

my $validator_results_in_xml =
  get("http://validator.w3.org/check?uri=$url;output=xml");
```

Curiously enough, the top of the XML that is returned causes `XML::Simple` to throw an error. Use a split function to trim off this broken section:

```
my ( $broken_xml_to_ignore, $trimmed_validator_results_in_xml ) =
  split ( /]>/, $validator_results_in_xml );
```

Now, place the valid XML into an `XML::Simple` object, and parse it:

```
my $parsed_validator_results = XMLin($trimmed_validator_results_in_xml);
```

Now is a good a time as any to set up the top of the feed:

```
my $rss = new XML::RSS( version => '2.0' );

$rss->channel( title => "XHTML Validation results for $url",
link  => "http://validator.w3.org/check?uri=$url",
description => "w3c validation results for $url" );
```

Then it's a simple matter of running through each error message the validator gives and turning it into a feed item:

```
foreach my $error ( @{ $parsed_validator_results->{'messages'}->{'msg'} } ) {
    $rss->add_item(
        title       => "Line $error->{'line'} $error->{'content'}",
        link        => "http://validator.w3.org/check?uri=$url",
        description => "Line $error->{'line'} $error->{'content'}",
    );
}
```

Finally, serve it up:

```
print header('application/xml+rss');
print $rss->as_string;
```

The Entire Listing

```
#!/usr/bin/perl

use warnings;
use strict;
use XML::RSS;
use CGI qw(:standard);
use LWP::Simple 'get';
use XML::Simple;

my $cgi = CGI::new( );
my $url = $cgi->param('url');

my $validator_results_in_xml =
  get("http://validator.w3.org/check?uri=$url;output=xml");

my ( $broken_xml_to_ignore, $trimmed_validator_results_in_xml ) =
  split ( /]>/, $validator_results_in_xml );

my $parsed_validator_results = XMLin($trimmed_validator_results_in_xml);

my $rss = new XML::RSS( version => '2.0' );

$rss->channel( title => "XHTML Validation results for $url",
link  => "http://validator.w3.org/check?uri=$url",
description => "w3c validation results for $url" );

foreach my $error ( @{ $parsed_validator_results->{'messages'}->{'msg'} } ) {
    $rss->add_item(
        title       => "Line $error->{'line'} $error->{'content'}",
        link        => "http://validator.w3.org/check?uri=$url",
```

```
        description => "Line $error->{'line'} $error->{'content'}",
    );
}

print header('application/xml+rss');
print $rss->as_string;
```

Game Statistics to Excel

Halo 2, a game for the XBox console, can be played as a multiplayer online game over the XBox-Live network. If you do this, your players statistics become available online as an RSS 2.0 feed. Example 10-1 shows an example of such a feed, courtesy of player "nedrichards."

Example 10-1. An RSS 2.0 feed from Halo 2

```
<?xml version="1.0" encoding="utf-8"?>
<rss version="2.0">
  <channel>
    <title>nedrichards's recent games</title>
    <link>http://www.bungie.net/stats</link>
    <description>Halo2 games played recently (courtesy of Bungie.Net)</description>
    <language>en-us</language>
    <pubDate>Tue, 21 Dec 2004 15:16:54 GMT</pubDate>
    <docs>http://blogs.law.harvard.edu/tech/rss</docs>
    <generator>BungieTest RSS Generator</generator>
    <webMaster>webmaster@bungie.net</webMaster>
    <item>
      <title>Arranged Game: Rockets on Headlong</title>
      <link>http://bungie.net/stats/gamestats.aspx?gameid=30084649&player=nedrichards</
link>

       <pubDate>Thu, 16 Dec 2004 22:49:33 GMT</pubDate>
       <guid>http://bungie.net/stats/gamestats.aspx?gameid=30084649&player=nedrichards</
guid>

       <description>Game played at Thu, 16 Dec 2004 22:49:33 GMT<br/><br/>Playlist:
Arranged
Game<br/>Rockets on Headlong<br/><br/><b>Gamertag (Team): Score, Kills, Deaths,
Assists</b><br/>Evil Ted Hed (4): 25, 25, 14, 1<br/>Cranium Oxide (0): 21, 21, 12,
2<br/>nedrichards (2): 15, 15, 25, 1<br/>smokingdrum (3): 12, 12, 18, 2<br/>Frizby
(1): 11, 11, 24, 1<br/></description>
         </item>
         <item>
            <title>Team Skirmish: 1 Flag CTF Fast on Burial Mounds</title>
            <link>http://bungie.net/stats/gamestats.
aspx?gameid=30068566&player=nedrichards</link>

            <pubDate>Thu, 16 Dec 2004 22:28:23 GMT</pubDate>
            <guid>http://bungie.net/stats/gamestats.
aspx?gameid=30068566&player=nedrichards</guid>
```

Example 10-1. An RSS 2.0 feed from Halo 2 (continued)

```
            <description>Team game played at Thu, 16 Dec 2004 22:28:23 GMT<br/><br/>
Playlist:
Team Skirmish<br/>1 Flag CTF Fast on Burial Mounds<br/><br/><b>Gamertag (Team):
Score, Kills, Deaths, Assists</b><br/>Frizby (1): 0, 3, 8, 1<br/>BoP Andy (0): 0, 4,
2, 1<br/>nedrichards (1): 0, 3, 7, 1<br/>smokingdrum (1): 0, 2, 8, 2<br/>Ninja Master
35 (0): 0, 10, 6, 1<br/>Snake9000 (1): 0, 11, 8, 2<br/>BEACONHILLGAMER (0): 0, 9, 5, 1<br/
>Spartan
736 (0): 0, 7, 6, 2<br/></description>
          </item>
          <item>
            <title>Team Slayer: Team Slayer on Foundation</title>
            <link>http://bungie.net/stats/gamestats.
aspx?gameid=30060296&player=nedrichards</link>

            <pubDate>Thu, 16 Dec 2004 22:17:44 GMT</pubDate>
            <guid>http://bungie.net/stats/gamestats.
aspx?gameid=30060296&player=nedrichards</guid>

            <description>Team game played at Thu, 16 Dec 2004 22:17:44 GMT<br/><br/>
Playlist:Team Slayer<br/>Team Slayer on Foundation<br/><br/><b>Gamertag (Team): Score,
Kills, Deaths, Assists</b><br/>AgelessPainter (0): 22, 22, 4, 3<br/>smokingdrum (1):
12, 12, 14, 0<br/>sfpipeman1 (0): 11, 11, 8, 2<br/>DARKNIGHT377 (0): 11, 11, 6, 1<br/>
nedrichards(1): 9, 9, 12, 5<br/>BlindJokerCard (0): 6, 6, 6, 6<br/>
Frizby (1): 4, 3, 15, 4<br/>Wang2 (1): 0, 0, 9, 4<br/></description>
            </item>
      </channel>
</rss>
```

Each `item` contains the statistics for a single game. I've removed most of the games from the example to save space.

Such statistics are perfect fodder for analysis, and so Samuel Radakovitz—a program manager for Excel within Microsoft—has built a workbook for Excel 2003 that can import Halo2 feeds and produce beautiful reports from them. It is getting ever more powerful, and the latest version can be downloaded from *http://www.isamrad.com/Halo2RSS/*.

Feeds by SMS

In most of the examples so far, we have written the parsed feed to the screen of a computer. This is just the start. You can use the same basic structure to output to just about anything that handles text. Example 10-2 is a script that sends the top headline of a feed to a mobile phone via the Short Message Service (SMS). It uses the `WWW::SMS` module, outputting to the first web-based free SMS service it can find that works.

Example 10-2. rsssms.pl sends the first headline title to a mobile phone via SMS

```
#!/usr/local/bin/perl
use strict;
use warnings;
use LWP::Simple;
use XML::Simple;
use WWW::SMS;

# Take the command line arguments, URL first, then complete number of mobile
my $url=$ARGV[0];
my $number=$ARGV[1];

# Retrieve the feed, or die disgracefully
my $feed_to_parse = get ($url) or die "I can't get the feed you want";

# Parse the XML
my $parser = XML::Simple->new( );
my $rss = $parser->XMLin("$feed_to_parse");

# Get the data we want
my $message = "NEWSFLASH:: $rss->{'channel'}->{'item'}->[0]->{'title'}";

# Send the message
my @gateway = WWW::SMS->gateways( );
my $sms = WWW::SMS->new($number, $message);
foreach my $gateway(@gateway) {if ($sms->send($gateway)) {
          print 'Message sent!';
            last;
     } else {
          print "Error: $WWW::SMS::Error\n";
     }}
```

You can use the script in Example 10-2 from the command line or crontab like so:

```
perl rsssms.pl http://full.urlof/feed.xml 123456789
```

You can see how to set this up on crontab to send the latest news at the desired interval. But how about using the system status module, `mod_systemstatus`, to automatically detect and inform you of system failures? Perhaps you can use something like Example 10-3.

Example 10-3. mod_systemstatusSMS.pl

```
#!/usr/local/bin/perl

use strict;
use warnings;
use LWP::Simple;
use XML::Simple;
use WWW::SMS;
```

Example 10-3. mod_systemstatusSMS.pl (continued)

```
# Take the command line arguments, URL first, then complete number
my $url=$ARGV[0];
my $number=$ARGV[1];

# Retrieve the feed, or die gracefully
my $feed_to_parse = get ($url) or die "I can't get the feed you want";

# Parse the XML
my $parser = XML::Simple->new( );
my $rss = $parser->XMLin("$feed_to_parse");

# initialise the $message
my $message;

# Look for downed servers
foreach my $item (@{$rss->{'item'}}) {
    next unless ($item->{'ss:responding'}) eq 'false';
    $message .= "Emergency! $item->{'title'} is down.";
           }

# Send the message
if ($message) {
my @gateway = WWW::SMS->gateways( );
my $sms = WWW::SMS->new($number, $message);
foreach my $gateway(@gateway) {if ($sms->send($gateway)) {
          print 'Message sent!';
     } else {
          print "Error: $WWW::SMS::Error\n";
     }}
     };
```

Again, run from cron, this little beasty will let you monitor hundreds of machines—as long as they are generating the correct RSS—and inform you of a server outage via your mobile phone.

This combination of selective parsing, interesting output methods, and cron allows you to do many things with RSS feeds that a more comprehensive system may well inhibit. Monitoring a list of feeds for mentions of keywords is simple, as is using RSS feeds of stock prices to alert you of falls in the market. Combining these techniques with Publish and Subscribe systems (discussed in Chapter 9) gives you an even greater ability to monitor the world. Want an IRC channel to be notified of any new weblog postings? No problem. Want an SMS whenever the phrase “Free Beer” appears in your local feeds? Again, no problem.

Podcasting Weather Forecasts

The podcasting technique described in Chapter 4 is a hotbed of development at the moment. One idea put forward was to use it to deliver weather forecasts via a web service and a text-to-speech application.

Jorge Velázquez put together a script to do just that. Released at *http://www.jorgev.com/archives/000115.html*, it requires an account with weather.com and an installation of `Lame` (from *http://lame.sourceforge.net/*) and `text2wave` on the server.

How to Use It

The URL accepts two parameters, `locid` and `unit`. The `locid` is the weather.com location identifier for the city you require. For U.S. cities, this can be a zip code, and for non-U.S. cities, it is a special weather.com code. (e.g., 92126 for San Diego, CA, or ITXX0067 for Rome, Italy). The unit parameter is optional and can be either `m` for metric or `s` for imperial measurements. It defaults to imperial.

The location code for Florence, Italy, is ITXX0028, so the URL for the feed would be *http://www.example.com/cgi-bin/weather.cgi?locid=ITXX0028*. Simple.

The Code Itself

Jorge's code is, in his own words, very simple. This is how he describes it:

> A brief explanation of how the script works, it's actually quite simple: I first call into weather.com's XML Data Feed. Then I use XPath to extract the data in which I am interested. I format this information into a text file, which I then pass onto the text2wave utility which performs the text-to-speech conversion. Finally, since wav files are so huge, I convert it to MP3 using the LAME encoder. Piece of cake, eh?

```
#!/usr/bin/perl -w
# 2004-12-13 Jorge Velázquez

use strict;
use CGI qw(:standard);
use XML::RSS;
use XML::XPath;
use LWP::Simple;
use File::Temp;
use File::Basename;

# partner and key information
my $par = 'partneridhere';
my $key = 'keyhere';

# get parameters
my $cgi   = CGI::new( );
my $locid = $cgi->param('locid');
my $unit  = $cgi->param('unit');
```

```
if ( not $unit ) {
    $unit = 's';
}
my $mp3dir = 'enter/mp3/path/here';

# query weather info, current conditions with 2 day forecast
my $xml =
  get(
"http://xoap.weather.com/weather/local/
$locid?cc=*&dayf=2&prod=xoap&par=$par&key=$key&unit=$unit"

  );

#load it into XPath object
my $xp = XML::XPath->new($xml);

# extract unit information from feed
my $ut = $xp->findvalue('/weather/head/ut');
my $ud = $xp->findvalue('/weather/head/ud');
my $us = $xp->findvalue('/weather/head/us');

# create rss 2.0 feed
my $rss = new XML::RSS( version => '2.0' );

# channel information
$rss->channel(
    title       => 'Weather Podcast',
    link        => 'http://www.weather.com/',
    description => 'Local weather podcasting feed',
    language    => 'en'
);

# get current weather conditions
my $dnam   = $xp->findvalue('/weather/loc/dnam');
my $ccobst = $xp->findvalue('/weather/cc/obst');
my $cclsup = $xp->findvalue('/weather/cc/lsup');
my $cctemp = $xp->findvalue('/weather/cc/tmp');
my $ccwind = $xp->findvalue('/weather/cc/wind/s');
my $cct    = $xp->findvalue('/weather/cc/t');
my $ccbarr = $xp->findvalue('/weather/cc/bar/r');
my $ccbard = $xp->findvalue('/weather/cc/bar/d');

# convert the units to words
my $utword = $ut eq 'F' ? 'fahrenheit' : 'celsius';

# build the text file for converting to speech
my $text =
  "Current conditions for $dnam. $cct. The temperature is $cctemp $utword.";

# write the file and get the stats
my $filename = &writefile($text);
my $basename = basename $filename;
my $filesize = ( stat $filename )[7];
```

```
# add rss item for current weather
$rss->add_item(
    title       => "Current weather conditions for $ccobst",
    link        => "http://www.weather.com/weather/local/$locid",
    description => $text,
    pubDate     => $cclsup,
    enclosure   => {
        url    => "$mp3dir$basename",
        length => $filesize,
        type   => 'audio/mpeg'
    }
);

# get forecast timestamp
my $lsup = $xp->findvalue('/weather/dayf/lsup');

# iterate through forecast days
my $nodeset = $xp->find('/weather/dayf/day');
foreach my $node ( $nodeset->get_nodelist ) {

    # get the items of interest to our script
    my $t   = $node->findvalue('@t');
    my $dt  = $node->findvalue('@dt');
    my $hi  = $node->findvalue('hi');
    my $low = $node->findvalue('low');
    my $d   = $node->findvalue('part[@p="d"]/t');
    my $n   = $node->findvalue('part[@p="n"]/t');

    # build the text file for converting to speech
    $text = "Weather forecast for $t, $dt in $dnam. ";
    if ( $d eq 'N/A' ) {
        $text .= "Daytime conditions not available. ";
    }
    else {
        $text .= "Daytime $d. ";
    }
    if ( $n eq 'N/A' ) {
        $text .= "Nighttime conditions not available. ";
    }
    else {
        $text .= "Nighttime $n. ";
    }
    if ( $hi eq 'N/A' ) {
        $text .= "The high is unavailable. ";
    }
    else {
        $text .= "The high is $hi $utword. ";
    }
    if ( $low eq 'N/A' ) {
        $text .= "The low is unavailable. ";
    }
    else {
        $text .= "The low is $low $utword. ";
    }
```

```
    # write the file and get the stats
    $filename = &writefile($text);
    $basename = basename $filename;
    $filesize = ( stat $filename )[7];

    # add this forecast
    $rss->add_item(
        title       => "Weather forecast for $t, $dt at $dnam",
        link        => "http://www.weather.com/weather/local/$locid",
        description => $text,
        pubDate     => $lsup,
        enclosure   => {
            url    => "$mp3dir$basename",
            length => $filesize,
            type   => 'audio/mpeg'
        }
    );
}

print header('application/rss+xml');
print $rss->as_string;

sub writefile {

    # write the text file
    my $fhtxt = new File::Temp( suffix => '.txt' );
    print $fhtxt $_[0];
    close $fhtxt;

    # write the wav file
    my $fhwav = new File::Temp( suffix => '.wav' );
    system "text2wave", "-o", $fhwav->filename, $fhtxt->filename;

    # convert it to mp3
    my $fhmp3 =
      new File::Temp( unlink => 0, dir => '../mp3', suffix => '.mp3' );
    system "lame", "-h", $fhwav->filename, $fhmp3->filename;

    # return the file name
    return $fhmp3->filename;
}
```

Having Amazon Produce Its Own RSS Feeds

Andrew Odewahn, an editor at O'Reilly, spotted how you can have Amazon.com produce RSS feeds from any search within its own site. So, he says:

> You could subscribe to a search for books on "software engineering," "Java," and "history of europe" to easily keep track with what's going on.

To do this, you only need play with a URL. The URL for an RSS 0.91 feed of a keyword search for "software engineering" is:

> *http://xml.amazon.com/onca/xml3?t=webservices-20&dev-t=amznRss&KeywordSearch=software%20engineering&mode=books&bcm=&type=lite&page=1&ct=text/xml&sort=+salesrank&f=http://xml.amazon.com/xsl/xml-rss091.xsl*

As you can see, this is actually calling the Amazon web services system and then formatting it by passing it through an XSLT stylesheet.

Andrew goes on to say,

> By default, the search results are sorted by Amazon rank. After hacking around a bit, I found that you can change this default to any of a variety of other orders. For example, you can modify the feed so that books are sorted by publication date to get an automatically updated list of new books published on a particular topic.

To do this, scroll over the URL until you see the "&sort=+salesrank" part. To change the sort order, replace "salesrank" with the option you'd prefer. Here's a list of possible options found on Amazon's Web Services page, *http://www.amazon.com/gp/aws/landing.html*:

- Publication Date → daterank
- Featured Items → pmrank
- Sales Rank → salesrank
- Customer reviews → reviewrank
- Price (Lo-Hi) → pricerank
- Price (Hi-Lo) → inverse-pricerank

So, to get a feed of all the new books published in Software Engineering, just replace "salesrank" with "daterank" and click update. From now on, you easily see all the new stuff coming out in one place. For example:

> *http://xml.amazon.com/onca/xml3?t=webservices-20&dev-t=amznRss&KeywordSearch=Ben%20Hammersley&mode=books&bcm=&type=lite&page=1&ct=text/xml&sort=+pricerank&f=http://xml.amazon.com/xsl/xml-rss091.xsl*

produces a feed of the books I have written, in order of price. This technique highlights a very good point: it is well worth looking at complex URLs quite carefully: they're invariably hackable.

Cross-Poster for Movable Type

By now, the traditional use of feeds as a form of content syndication is beginning to look somewhat old-fashioned. But fear not: here's a use that is as traditional as can be.

I needed a script to check all of the weblogs I write for and to cross-post everything I write onto my own weblog. Bear in mind that I'm not the only author on these other sites.

To do this, check their RSS feeds on a set schedule, grab the content within, build a big entry, and then post it. This code is for a Movable Type installation, but it isn't hard to modify it to fit another weblogging platform.

Walking Through the Code

You open the proceedings by defining all of the libraries and modules. This is the exact same code as I have running on my own server, so you need to modify the following paths to point to your own Movable Type libraries, blog IDs, and so on:

```
use lib "/web/script/ben/mediacooperative.com/lib";
use lib "/web/script/ben/mediacooperative.com/extlib";
use lib "/web/script/ben/lib/perl";
use MT;
use MT::Entry;
use Date::Manip;
use LWP::Simple 'get';
use XML::RSS;

my $MTauthor = "1";
my $MTblogID = "3";
my $MTconfig = "/home/ben/web/mediacooperative.com/mt.cfg";
my $guts     = "";
```

Now, let's set up a list of sites to check. For each site, you need to define only the feed URL and the `<dc:creator>` or `<author>` name under which I am posting. Everything else you can get from the feed itself. For example:

> *http://del.icio.us/rss/bhammersley "bhammersley" http://www.oreillynet.com/feeds/author/?x-au=909 "Ben Hammersley" http://monkeyfilter.com/rss.php "DangerIsMyMiddleName" http://www.benhammersley.com/expeditions/northpole2006/index.rdf "Ben Hammersley"*

You can do this with an array of arrays:

```
my @sites_to_check = (
    [ "http://del.icio.us/rss/bhammersley",                   "bhammersley" ],
    [ "http://www.oreillynet.com/feeds/author/?x-au=909", "Ben Hammersley" ],
    [ "http://monkeyfilter.com/rss.php", "DangerIsMyMiddleName" ],
    [
        "http://www.benhammersley.com/expeditions/northpole2006/index.rdf",
        "Ben Hammersley"
    ],
);
```

Now, the loop. You go through each feed, downloading, parsing, and so on. Let's start by taking the `site_feed_url` and the `site_author_nym` (the name under which I go on that site) out of the array. This step could be omitted, but for the sake of clarity, we'll leave it here.

```
for my $site_being_checked (@sites_to_check) {

    my $site_feed_url   = @$site_being_checked[0];
    my $site_author_nym = @$site_being_checked[1];
```

Now, retrieve the feed, or go to the next one if it fails:

```
    my $feed_xml = get("$site_feed_url") or next;
```

And now, to parse it. You do so by spawning a new instance of the `XML::RSS` parser and jamming the feed into it:

```
my $rss_parser = XML::RSS->new( );
$rss_parser->parse($feed_xml);
```

To set up for the strange occasion where there might be new content to post, let's query the newly created RSS parser object for its name:

```
 my $feed_name = $rss_parser->{channel}->{title};
 my $feed_link = $rss_parser->{channel}->{link};
```

Now, go through each of the items within the field, and grab all needed data out of them: the link, title, description, author, and date. Note that you have to include the fallbacks of the guid, content, and the various dc values to deal with different versions of RSS.

```
foreach my $item ( @{ $rss_parser->{items} } ) {

    my $item_link        = $$item{link} || $$item{guid};
    my $item_title       = $$item{title};
    my $item_description = $$item{description};
    my $item_author      = $$item{author} || $$item{dc}->{creator};
    my $item_date        = $$item{pubDate} || $$item{dc}->{date};
```

Now, check to see if any were written today by me. First, work out what time and date it is now. Then, compare the post's date with the date now, and, if it's less than 24 hours behind, *and* it was written by me, then all is good.

Note: to get this code to work with del.icio.us and any other sites that use date strings with z instead of +00:00 (which `Date::Manip` can't deal with), you have to use a nasty substitution. Sorry about that.

```
my $todays_date = &UnixDate( "now", "%Y-%m-%dT%H:%M:%S+00:00" );
$item_date =~ s/Z/+00:00/;
my $date_delta = DateCalc( "$item_date", "$todays_date", \$err, 1 );
my $parsed_delta = Delta_Format( "$date_delta", exact, '%dh' );

if ( ( $parsed_delta < 1 ) and ( $item_author eq $site_author_nym ) ) {
```

If all the tests turn out to be true, add a bunch of HTML to the `$guts` variable, within which you're building the new entry:

```
            $guts .=
qq|<div id="CrossPoster"><blockquote><a href="$item_link">$item_title</a><br/>posted
to <a href="$feed_link">$feed_name</a><br/></p><p>$item_description</p></blockquote>
</div>|;

        }
    }
}
```

Now, having worked our way through the feeds, if the $guts has anything in it, you need to post it and take care of that end:

```
if ( $guts ne "" ) {

    my $mt    = MT->new( Config => $MTconfig ) or die MT->errstr;
    my $entry = MT::Entry->new;

    $entry->blog_id($MTblogID);
    $entry->status( MT::Entry::RELEASE() );
    $entry->author_id($MTauthor);
    $entry->title("Posted elsewhere today");
    $entry->text($guts);
    $entry->convert_breaks(0);
    $entry->save
      or die $entry->errstr;

    # rebuild the site

    $mt->rebuild( BlogID => $MTblogID )
      or die "Rebuild error: " . $mt->errstr;

    # ping aggregators

    $mt->ping($MTblogID);

}
```

The Entire Listing

```
#!/usr/bin/perl

use lib "/web/script/ben/mediacooperative.com/lib";
use lib "/web/script/ben/mediacooperative.com/extlib";
use lib "/web/script/ben/lib/perl";
use MT;
use MT::Entry;
use Date::Manip;
use LWP::Simple 'get';
use XML::RSS;

my $MTauthor = "1";
my $MTblogID = "3";
my $MTconfig = "/home/ben/web/mediacooperative.com/mt.cfg";
my $guts     = "";
```

```
my @sites_to_check = (
    [ "http://del.icio.us/rss/bhammersley",                "bhammersley" ],
    [ "http://www.oreillynet.com/feeds/author/?x-au=909", "Ben Hammersley" ],
    [ "http://monkeyfilter.com/rss.php", "DangerIsMyMiddleName" ],
    [
        "http://www.benhammersley.com/expeditions/northpole2006/index.rdf",
        "Ben Hammersley"
    ],
);

for my $site_being_checked (@sites_to_check) {

    my $site_feed_url   = @$site_being_checked[0];
    my $site_author_nym = @$site_being_checked[1];

    my $feed_xml = get("$site_feed_url") or next;

    my $rss_parser = XML::RSS->new( );
    $rss_parser->parse($feed_xml);

    my $feed_name = $rss_parser->{channel}->{title};
    my $feed_link = $rss_parser->{channel}->{link};

    foreach my $item ( @{ $rss_parser->{items} } ) {

        my $item_link        = $$item{link} || $$item{guid};
        my $item_title       = $$item{title};
        my $item_description = $$item{description};
        my $item_author      = $$item{author} || $$item{dc}->{creator};
        my $item_date        = $$item{pubDate} || $$item{dc}->{date};

        my $todays_date = &UnixDate( "now", "%Y-%m-%dT%H:%M:%S+00:00" );
        $item_date =~ s/Z/+00:00/;
        my $date_delta = DateCalc( "$item_date", "$todays_date", \$err, 1 );
        my $parsed_delta = Delta_Format( "$date_delta", exact, '%dh' );

        if ( ( $parsed_delta < 1 ) and ( $item_author eq $site_author_nym ) ) {

            $guts .=
qq|<div id="CrossPoster"><blockquote><a href="$item_link">$item_title</a><br/>posted
to <a href="$feed_link">$feed_name</a><br/></p><p>$item_description</p></blockquote>
</div>|;

        }
    }
}

if ( $guts ne "" ) {

    my $mt    = MT->new( Config => $MTconfig ) or die MT->errstr;
    my $entry = MT::Entry->new;

    $entry->blog_id($MTblogID);
    $entry->status( MT::Entry::RELEASE( ) );
```

```
    $entry->author_id($MTauthor);
    $entry->title("Posted elsewhere today");
    $entry->text($guts);
    $entry->convert_breaks(0);
    $entry->save
      or die $entry->errstr;

    # rebuild the site

    $mt->rebuild( BlogID => $MTblogID )
      or die "Rebuild error: " . $mt->errstr;

    # ping aggregators

    $mt->ping($MTblogID);
}
```

CHAPTER 11

Developing New Modules

Inventions reached their limit long ago, and I see no hope for further development.
—Sextus Julius Frontinus

In this chapter, we will create a new module and extend a desktop reader (AmphetaDesk) to understand it. We will also discuss the differences between the RSS 1.0, RSS 2.0, and Atom data models and the effect of these differences on module design.

Namespaces and Modules Within RSS 2.0 and Atom

As mentioned earlier, RSS 2.0 introduced namespaced modules to the simple strand of RSS. RSS 1.0 was designed with namespace support from the very beginning. The specification document states:

> A RSS feed may contain elements not described on this page, only if those elements are defined in a namespace. The elements defined in this document aren't themselves members of a namespace, so that RSS 2.0 can remain compatible with previous versions in the following sense—a version 0.91 or 0.92 file is also a valid 2.0 file. If the elements of RSS 2.0 were in a namespace, this constraint would break, a version 0.9x file would not be a valid 2.0 file.

Other than not defining a namespace for the core elements of RSS 2.0, the modules work the same way as the modules for RSS 1.0: declare the module's namespace in the root element (which in the case of RSS 2.0 is, of course, `rss`) and then use the module elements as directed by their specification. Parsers that don't recognize the namespace just ignore the new elements.

Differences from RSS 1.0

RSS 1.0 modules can't be reused within RSS 2.0. To do so requires the feed author to declare two additional namespaces within the root element: the namespace of the module and the namespace of RDF. This isn't explicitly forbidden but is heavily frowned upon.

Because of this, you need to recall the simplest ways to convert between the default module styles. RSS 1.0 modules, you will remember, declare everything in terms of RDF resources. This is done with the `rdf:resource` attribute. For example, a fictional element `pet:image`, used to denote an image of the feed author's pet, is written:

```
<pet:image rdf:resource="
URI of image"/>
```

whereas in RSS 2.0, the default lack of RDF means you must just declare the URI of the image as a literal string:

```
<pet:image>
URI of image</pet:image>
```

However, the differences go deeper than this, which you'll see when we design a new module: `mod_Book`.

Modules in Atom

If you go to the version of the Atom specification I have based this book on, at *http://www.ietf.org/internet-drafts/draft-ietf-atompub-format 05.txt,* you will see that Section 9, the section designated to explain the expansion of the Atom format, is entirely empty.

This presents a problem. I can't with any authority tell you what to do with an Atom feed. I can, however, make some suggestions. I don't think you will have any trouble if you use modules in Atom in exactly the same way as in RSS 2.0. The syntax can probably remain the same, although preferably, you should design the Atom module following the same pattern of constructs for people, links, and so on as the core Atom specification itself. It just makes coding easier. With that in mind, it is probably more sensible to design the module for Atom and move it to RSS 2.0, than the other way around. But again, I can't make any definitive statements on modules within Atom in this edition. For now, therefore, we'll talk only about RSS.

Case Study: mod_Book

My wife and I recently moved from London, England, to Florence, Italy, via Sweden. In the first edition of this book, we were just about to leave, and to that effect, much of the contents of our home was already in storage: most of it being books. In the end, it turned out we sent 86 tea chests full of books across Europe.

So now we're unpacking. Many people really like our books and would like to borrow them, and so, for many reasons, it would be quite cool to list details of our books into a feed. As we unpack the books, we will most likely try to scan their barcodes and arrange our library (we're geeky like that), so we will have all sorts of data available.

The challenge is then to design a module for both 1.0 and 2.0 (and Atom, eventually) that can deal with books.

What Do We Know?

The first thing to think about is precisely what knowledge you already have about what you're trying to describe. With books, you know a great deal:

- The title
- The author
- The publisher
- The ISBN
- The subject
- The date of publication
- The content itself

There are also, alas, things that you might think you know, but which, in fact, you don't. In the case of books, unless you are dealing with a specific edition in a specific place at a specific time, you don't know the number of pages, the price, the printer, the paper quality, or how critics received it. For the sake of sharable data, these aren't universally useful values. They will change with time and aren't internationally sharable. Remember that once it has left your machine, the data you create—in this case, each `item`—is lost to you. As the first author, it is your responsibility to create it in such a way that it retains its value for as long as possible with as wide an audience as possible.

So, Rule 1 of module design is: *decide what data you know, and what data you do not know.*

Can We Express This Data Already?

Rule 2 of module design is: *if possible, use another module's element to deliver the same information.*

This is another key point. It is much less work to leverage the efforts of others, and when many people have spent time introducing Dublin Core support to desktop readers, for example, you should reward them by using Dublin Core as much as possible. Module elements need to be created only if there is no suitable alternative already in the wild.

So, to reexamine the data:

The title

Titles can be written within the core `title` element of either 1.0 or 2.0, or within the `dc:title` element of the Dublin Core module. You should always strive to use the core namespace first, so `title` it is.

The author

Here, you have the first core split between 1.0 and 2.0. In 2.0, you can use the core `author` element. There is no such thing in 1.0, so you must use the `dc:creator` element of Dublin Core. Because you should always strive to use the core namespace first, RSS 2.0 users should use `author`. However, because it's best to have as simple a module specification as possible, use the same element in both module versions. You might want to import the RSS 2.0 namespace into the 1.0 feed and use `author` in both; however, this can't be done. RSS 2.0's root namespace is `""`, which can't be imported because there isn't a namespace URI to point to. You can possibly use the URL of the 2.0 specification document as the URI, declare `xmlns:rss2="http://backend.userland.com/rss"`, and then use `rss2:author`, but because the URI is different, technically this doesn't refer to the same vocabulary as that used in RSS 2.0. As you'll see, using the same element—even if it is in a slightly different syntax—is very useful if you wish to develop RSS applications. So, for the sake of simplicity, let's opt for `dc:creator`. You can also use `dc:contributor` to denote a contributor.

The publisher

Publishers are lovely people and happily have their very own Dublin Core element, `dc:publisher`.

The ISBN

ISBNs are fantastically useful here. Because the ISBN governing body ensures that each ISBN is unique to its book, this can serve as a globally unique identifier. What's more, you can even turn an ISBN into a URI using the format *urn:isbn:0123456789*. For RSS 1.0, this will prove remarkably useful, as we will discuss in a moment. Meanwhile, denoting the ISBN is a good idea. Let's invent a new element. Choosing `book` as the namespace prefix, let's call it `book:isbn`.

The subject

A book's subject can be a matter of debate—especially with fiction—so it may not be entirely sane to make this element mandatory or to trust it. Nevertheless, there are ways to write it. RSS 2.0's core element `category` may help here, as will `dc:subject`, especially when used with RSS 1.0's `mod_taxonomy`.

All these schemes, however, rely on being able to place the subject within a greater hierarchy. Fortunately, library scientists are hard at work on this, and there are many to choose from. For our purposes, let's use the Open Directory hierarchy—just to provide continuity throughout this book.

The date of publication

Again, you can see a clash between the extended core of RSS 2.0 and RSS 1.0's use of Dublin Core. Within RSS 2.0 `pubDate` is available, and within RSS 1.0, we rely on `dc:date`. Given that Dublin Core is more widely recognized within the RDF world and perfectly valid within the RSS 2.0 world, it saves time and effort to standardize on it. This is a good example of Rule 3: *because you can't tell people what they can't do with your data, you must make it easy for them to do what they want.*

The content itself

Now to the content itself. The core `description` doesn't work here: we're talking about the content, not a précis of it, and we certainly don't want to include all the content, so `content:encoded` is out too. We really need an element to contain an excerpt of the book: the opening paragraph, for example.

Hurrah! We can invent a new element! Let's call it `book:openingPara`.

So, out of all the information we want to include, we need to invent only two new elements: `book:isbn` and `book:openingPara`. This isn't a bad thing: modules do not just consist of masses of new elements slung out into the public. They should also include guidance as to the proper usage of existing modules in the new context. Reuse and recycle as much as possible.

To summarize, we now have:

```
<title/>
<dc:author/>
<dc:publisher/>
<book:isbn/>
<dc:subject/>
<dc:date/>
<book:openingPara/>
```

Putting the New Elements to Work with RSS 2.0

Before creating the feed `item`, let's decide on what the `link` will point to. Given that my book collection isn't web-addressable in that way, I'm going to point people to the relevant page on *http://isbn.nu*, Glenn Fleishman's book-price comparison site.

For an RSS 2.0 item, you can therefore use Example 11-1.

Example 11-1. mod_Book for RSS 2.0

```
<item>
  <title>Down and Out in the Magic Kingdom</title>
  <link>http://isbn.nu/0765304368/</link>
  <dc:author>Cory Doctorow</dc:author>
  <dc:publisher>Tor Books</dc:publisher>
  <book:isbn>0765304368</book:isbn>
  <dc:subject>Fiction</dc:subject>
  <dc:date>2003-02-01T00:01+00:00</dc:date>
```

Example 11-1. mod_Book for RSS 2.0 (continued)

```
  <book:openingPara> I lived long enough to see the cure for death; to see the rise of the
Bitchun Society, to learn ten languages; to compose three symphonies; to realize my
boyhood dream of taking up residence in Disney World; to see the death of the workplace
and of work.</book:openingPara>
</item>
```

As you can see in this simple strand of RSS 2.0, the inclusion of book metadata is easy. You know all about the book, and a mod_Book-compatible reader allows you to read the first paragraph and, if it's appealing, to click on the link and buy it. All is good.

Putting the New Elements to Work with RSS 1.0

With RSS 1.0, let's make a few changes. First, the book needs a URI for the rdf:about attribute of item. This isn't as straightforward as you might think. You need to think about precisely what you're describing. In this case, the choice is between a specific book—the one that is sitting on my desk right now—and the concept of that book, of which my specific book is one example.

The URI determines this. If I make the URI *http://www.benhammersley.com/myLibrary/catalogue/0765304368*, the item refers to my own copy: one discreet object.

If, however, I make the URI *urn:isbn:0765304368*, the item refers to the general concept of Cory Doctorow's book. For our purposes here, this is the one to go for. If I were producing an RSS feed for a lending library, it might be different. Example 11-2 makes these changes to mod_Book in RSS 1.0.

Example 11-2. mod_Book in RSS 1.0

```
<item rdf:about="urn:isbn:0765304368">
  <title>Down and Out in the Magic Kingdom</title>
  <link>http://isbn.nu/0765304368/</link>
  <dc:author>Cory Doctorow</dc:author>
  <dc:publisher>Tor Books</dc:publisher>
  <book:isbn>0765304368</book:isbn>
  <dc:subject>Fiction</dc:subject>
  <dc:date>2003-02-01T00:01+00:00</dc:date>
 <book:openingPara> I lived long enough to see the cure for death; to see the rise of the
Bitchun Society, to learn ten languages; to compose three symphonies; to realize my
boyhood dream of taking up residence in Disney World; to see the death of the workplace
and of work.</book:openingPara>
</item>
```

The second thing to think about is the preference for all the element values within RSS 1.0 to be rdf:resources and not literal strings. To this end, you need to assign URIs to each possible value. Within RSS 1.0, you can keep extending all the information you have to greater and greater detail. At this point, you must think about your audience. If you foresee people using the feed for only the simplest of tasks—such as displaying the list in a reader or on a site—you can stop now. If you see people using the data in deeper, more interesting applications, then you need to give guidance as to how far each element should be extended.

For the purposes of this chapter, we need to go no further, but for an example, let's go anyway. Example 11-3 expands the dc:author element via RDF and the use of a new RDF vocabulary: FOAF, or Friend of a Friend (see *http://www.rdfweb.org*).

Example 11-3. Expanding the module even further

```
<?xml version="1.0"?>
<rdf:RDF
xmlns:rdf="http://www.w3.org/1999/02/22-rdf-syntax-ns#"
xmlns:dc="http://purl.org/dc/elements/1.1/"
xmlns:foaf="http://xmlns.com/foaf/0.1/"
xmlns:book="http://www.exampleurl.com/namespaces"
xmlns="http://purl.org/rss/1.0/"
>

<item rdf:about="urn:isbn:0765304368">
  <title>Down and Out in the Magic Kingdom</title>
  <link>http://isbn.nu/0765304368/</link>
  <dc:author rdf:resource="mailto:doctorow@craphound.com" />
  <dc:publisher>Tor Books</dc:publisher>
  <book:isbn>0765304368</book:isbn>
  <dc:subject>Fiction</dc:subject>
  <dc:date>2003-02-01T00:01+00:00</dc:date>
  <book:openingPara> I lived long enough to see the cure for death; to see the rise of the
Bitchun Society, to learn ten languages; to compose three symphonies; to realize my
boyhood dream of taking up residence in Disney World; to see the death of the workplace
and of work.</book:openingPara>
</item>

<dc:author rdf:about="mailto:doctorow@craphound.com">
 <foaf:Person>
   <foaf:name>Cory Doctorow</foaf:name>
   <foaf:title>Mr</foaf:title>
   <foaf:firstName>Cory</foaf:firstName>
   <foaf:surname>Doctorow</foaf:surname>
   <foaf:homepage rdf:resource="http://www.craphound.com"/>
   <foaf:workPlaceHomepage rdf:resource="http://www.eff.org/" />
 </foaf:Person>
</dc:author>

</rdf:RDF>
```

Because only you, as the module designer, know the scope of the data you want to put across, you must document your module accordingly. Speaking of which...

Documentation

You *must* document your module. It is obligatory. The place to do so is at the address you use as the namespace URI. Without documentation, no one will know precisely what you mean, and no one will be able to support your module. Without support, the module is worthless on the wider stage.

Extending Your Desktop Reader

Of the 30 or so desktop viewers to appear, most are closed source and either shareware or try-then-buy packages. For our pedagogic purposes, therefore, they aren't much good. (As products in their own right, of course, things may be a different. I am not making any comment as to the value of commercial packages, apart from the fact that I can't show you their code and explain how it works. For commercial success, this is irrelevant, but for this book it is quite key.)

For our purposes, therefore, one relative newcomer gives plenty of scope. So, for the rest of this chapter, we'll study the brainchild of Morbus Iff (or Kevin Hemenway to the uncool): AmphetaDesk.

Introducing AmphetaDesk

AmphetaDesk was started by Morbus Iff in January 2001 and continues to be developed; this book uses Version 0.93. Apart from being a very popular tool for reading RSS feeds, AmphetaDesk's internal architecture makes it eminently hackable and a great way to learn how to use RSS feeds in your own programs. It also runs on Windows, Linux, and Mac OS, so most readers will be able to try it out.

The system works like this: the innards are written in Perl and HTML templates and come accompanied by an operating system–specific program that acts as the Perl interpreter. Because of this, you can access and change the source code even while the program is running, and you will see the changes happen immediately. Plus, you can add any feature you like by just dropping the correct Perl module into the right directory and writing a template file to call it.

In this section, we will download AmphetaDesk, install it, examine how it works, and then move on to customizing it.

Installing AmphetaDesk

Installing AmphetaDesk is simplicity itself: download the latest version from *http://www.disobey.com/amphetadesk/*, unpack the archive, and save the resulting directory structure and files to wherever you want to keep it. You are then presented with the following files and directories.

/AmphetaDesk.exe
: The AmphetaDesk runtime file. This is the file you run to use the program. It contains all the necessary aspects of Perl needed by your machine to go about its RSS-reading business.

/AmphetaDesk.pl
: The Perl version of the AmphetaDesk runtime file.

/data/myChannels.opml
: An OPML file containing the details of the feeds to which you are subscribed.

/data/mySettings.xml
: An XML file containing the user's settings.

/data/channels/
: A directory to contain local copies of the subscribed-to feeds.

/data/internal/
: This directory contains files created and used as the program is running, namely:

  /data/internal/version.txt
  : This file contains the version number of the AmphetaDesk installation you are using. It is compared at startup with a version on the AmphetaDesk server, and appropriate messages are displayed.

  /data/internal/AmphetaDesk.log
  : This file, recreated every time you run AmphetaDesk, contains the logged messages from the program—very useful for debugging.

/data/lists/
: This directory stores lists of RSS feeds (called *channels* in this context) that you can add to your AmphetaDesk display. It consists of:

  /data/lists/services-channels-complete.xml
  : This lists all the channel services that are still publishing something. The feed isn't checked for anything at all, except that it's actually there to read.

  /data/lists/services-channels-failure.xml
  : This lists all the feeds that have failed to be retrieved correctly three times in a row.

  /data/lists/services-channels-recent.xml
  : This is a cut-down version of the complete list, removing only those feeds known definitively to have not updated within a month.

/docs
: This directory contains the system documentation and one subdirectory:

  /docs/images
  : The directory that contains images for use within the documentation.

/lib

This directory contains the Perl modules used by the program. It contains:

AmphetaDesk.pm

This directory controls the data traffic between the different modules and the templates.

/lib/AmphetaDesk/

This directory contains all the original modules used within the workings of AmphetaDesk. They include:

- */lib/AmphetaDesk/Channels.pm:* `AmphetaDesk::Channels` handles the parsing of the feed. It takes the feed and returns it in a common data structure, regardless of which version of RSS you are using.
- */lib/AmphetaDesk/ChannelsList.pm:* `AmphetaDesk::ChannelsList` handles the channel listing in the "Add a Channel" section of the program. It takes an OPML file and converts it to something more useful for displaying on the screen.
- */lib/AmphetaDesk/MyChannels.pm:* `AmphetaDesk::MyChannels` handles all the functions that deal with the user's subscription list.
- */lib/AmphetaDesk/Settings.pm:* `AmphetaDesk::Settings` controls the program settings: loading, saving, and providing an API for changing every tweakable configuration.
- */lib/AmphetaDesk/Utilities.pm:* `AmphetaDesk::Utilities` provides all the little functions that make RSS readers run nicely—`strip_newlines_and_tabs`, for example.
- */lib/AmphetaDesk/Versioning.pm*: `AmphetaDesk::Versioning` handles the versioning of the package. By comparing */data/internal/version.txt* with the AmphetaDesk server's mirror, it checks to see if the installation you use is the latest.
- */lib/AmphetaDesk/WebServer.pm*: `AmphetaDesk::WebServer` provides a subclass of the `HTTP::Daemon` module used to serve the pages the system creates. As the author says in the comments, "This package is here merely to provide a subclass for `HTTP::Daemon` so that we can override the `product_tokens` routine and set our own Server name."
- */lib/AmphetaDesk/WWW.pm*: `AmphetaDesk::WWW` provides functions that retrieve data from the Net.

/lib/Text/Template.pm

The classic `Text::Template` module, written by Mark-Jason Dominus, deals with replacing text in templates. As the user interface to AmphetaDesk is written in templates, this module is required to make it work.

/lib/XML/Simple.pm

Our old friend from Chapter 8, `XML::Simple` is a simple XML parser. AmphetaDesk uses it to make sense of the feeds it retrieves.

/templates/default

The *templates* directory and its subdirectories hold the template files that AmphetaDesk parses through `Text::Template`. It is here that you'll find *index.html*—the page that displays the feeds' content—which we will now customize.

index.html

AmphetaDesk works by first downloading the feed and then using *Channels.pm* to convert it to a common data structure. This lessens the load on the next section, the templates, because they need to give the address of the data they want within only one structure, and not two different versions for 1.0 and 2.0.

If you open *index.html* in a text editor, you'll find this code about halfway down:

```
foreach my $item (@{$data->{item}}) {

# check to see if mod_content is used, which is a module to RSS 1.0
# allowing more data in a feed as well as embedded HTML. this is NOT
# a full implementation, as it'll only support CDATA's. if it does
# exist, then we stick the data into our $item->{description}.

my $rdf_value = $item->{"content:items"}{"rdf:Bag"}{"rdf:li"}{"content:item"}{"rdf:
value"}
if defined($item->{"content:items"}{"rdf:Bag"}{"rdf:li"}{"content:item"}{"rdf:
value"});
        $item->{description} = $rdf_value if defined($rdf_value);

# display the actual item.
$OUT .= qq{        };

$OUT .= qq{<tr><td width="15" bgcolor="#ffffff"> </td><td bgcolor=
"#ffffff" align="left">};

$OUT .= qq{<a href="$item->{link}" target="$link_target">} if $item->{link};
$OUT .= qq{$item->{title}} if $item->{title};
$OUT .= qq{</a>} if $item->{link};

$OUT .= qq{ $item->{description} } if $item->{description};

$OUT .= qq{</td></tr>\n};

       }
```

As you can see, this steps through each `item` in the feed; takes the contents of the `link`, `title`, and `description` elements; and outputs some HTML with the form:

```
<a href="LINK" target="_blank">TITLE</a> DESCRIPTION
```

Those links are surrounded by some table markup to make them look pretty, as shown in Figure 11-1.

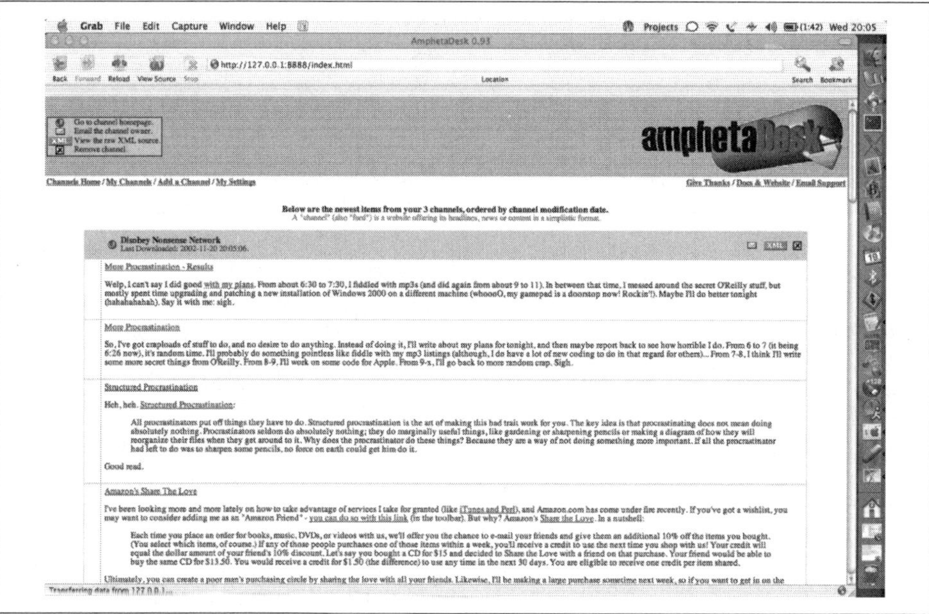

Figure 11-1. A screenshot of AmphetaDesk displaying a feed

Adding code to this template to allow it to display your module is therefore quite straightforward. Note the section of the code that does the work:

```
$OUT .= qq{<a href="$item->{link}" target="$link_target">} if $item->{link};

$OUT .= qq{$item->{title}} if $item->{title};
$OUT .= qq{</a>} if $item->{link};

$OUT .= qq{$item->{description} } if $item->{description};

$OUT .= qq{</td></tr>\n};
```

By slipping in your own code, you can take the value you want from the module. In this case, I'd like to allow people to buy one of the books in my feed from the popular online store Amazon.com.

By experimentation, I know that the URL *http://www.amazon.com/exec/obidos/ASIN/* followed by the ISBN number will lead to the correct page. This seems to be a good use for the `book:isbn` element.

I also know that people using my module might not have included a `description` element. So, I will want to get `book:openingPara` in there somewhere.

Here's how to do it:

```
$OUT .= qq{<a href="$item->{link}" target="$link_target">} if $item->{link};

$OUT .= qq{$item->{title}} if $item->{title};
$OUT .= qq{</a>} if $item->{link};

$OUT .= qq{<a href="http://www.amazon.com/exec.obidos/ASIN/$item->{"book:isdn"}">
Buy At Amazon</a>} if $item->{"book:isdn"};

$OUT .= qq{$item->{description} } if $item->{description};
$OUT .= qq{<blockquote>$item->{"book:openingPara"}</blockquote> } if $item->{"book:
openingPara"};

$OUT .= qq{</td></tr>\n};
```

Note that whereas `$item->{title}` produces the value of the `title` element, if you want to bring in a namespaced element, you need to wrap it in quotes:

```
$item->{"book:openingPara"}
```

If you save *index.html* and refresh it in your browser, you will find that the template now displays `mod_Book` information. Cool, huh?

You can now add support for your own modules in the same way. Be sure to pass any changes you make back to Morbus Iff at *http://www.disobey.com/amphetadesk*. He will likely include it in the next release, and you will have made the RSS world a better place for it.

APPENDIX A

The XML You Need for RSS

The purpose of this appendix is to introduce you to XML. A knowledge of XML is essential if you want to write RSS documents directly, rather than having them generated by some utility. If you're already acquainted with XML, you don't need to read this appendix. If not, read on.

The general overview of XML given in this appendix should be more than sufficient to enable you to work with the RSS documents. For further information about XML, the O'Reilly books *Learning XML* and *XML in a Nutshell* are invaluable guides, as is the weekly online magazine *XML.com*.

Note that this appendix makes frequent reference to the formal XML 1.0 specification, which can be used for further investigation of topics that fall outside the scope of RSS. Readers are also directed to the "Annotated XML Specification," written by Tim Bray and published online at *http://XML.com*, which provides an illuminating explanation of the XML 1.0 specification, and "What is XML?" by Norm Walsh, also published on *XML.com*.

What Is XML?

XML (Extensible Markup Language) is an Internet-friendly format for data and documents, invented by the World Wide Web Consortium (W3C). *Markup* denotes a way of expressing the structure of a document within the document itself. XML has its roots in a markup language called SGML (Standard Generalized Markup Language), which is used in publishing and shares this heritage with HTML. XML was created to do for machine-readable documents on the Web what HTML did for human-readable documents—that is, provide a commonly agreed-upon syntax, so that processing the underlying format becomes a commodity and documents are made accessible to all users.

Unlike HTML, though, XML comes with very little predefined. HTML developers are accustomed to both the notion of using angle brackets (<>) for denoting elements (that is, syntax) and also the set of element names themselves (such as head, body, etc.). XML shares only the former feature (i.e., the notion of using angle brackets for denoting elements). Unlike HTML, XML has no predefined elements but is merely a set of rules that lets you write other languages like HTML. (To clarify XML's relationship with SGML: XML is an SGML subset. In contrast, HTML is an SGML application. RSS uses XML to express its operations and thus is an XML application.)

Because XML defines so little, it is easy for everyone to agree to use the XML syntax and then build applications on top of it. It's like agreeing to use a particular alphabet and set of punctuation symbols, but not saying which language to use. However, if you come to XML from an HTML background (and have an interest in extending RSS), you may need to prepare yourself for the shock of having to choose what to call your tags!

Knowing that XML's roots lie with SGML should help you understand some of XML's features and design decisions. Note that although SGML is essentially a document-centric technology, XML's functionality also extends to data-centric applications, including RSS. Commonly, data-centric applications don't need all the flexibility and expressiveness that XML provides and limit themselves to employing only a subset of XML's functionality.

Anatomy of an XML Document

The best way to explain how an XML document is composed is to present one. The following example shows an XML document you might use to describe two authors:

```
<?xml version="1.0" encoding="us-ascii"?>
<authors>
    <person id="lear">
        <name>Edward Lear</name>
        <nationality>British</nationality>
    </person>
    <person id="asimov">
        <name>Isaac Asimov</name>
        <nationality>American</nationality>
    </person>
    <person id="mysteryperson"/>
</authors>
```

The first line of the document is known as the *XML declaration*. This tells a processing application which version of XML you are using (the version indicator is mandatory) and which character encoding you have used for the document. In this example, the document is encoded in ASCII. (The significance of character encoding is covered later in this appendix.)

If the XML declaration is omitted, a processor makes certain assumptions about your document. In particular, it expects it to be encoded in UTF-8, an encoding of the Unicode character set. However, it is best to use the XML declaration wherever possible, both to avoid confusion over the character encoding and to indicate to processors which version of XML you're using.

Elements and Attributes

The second line of the example begins an element, which has been named `authors`. The contents of that element include everything between the right angle bracket (>) in `<authors>` and the left angle bracket (<) in `</authors>`. The actual syntactic constructs `<authors>` and `</authors>` are often referred to as the element *start tag* and *end tag*, respectively. Don't confuse tags with elements! Note that elements may include other elements, as well as text. An XML document must contain exactly one root element, which contains all other content within the document. The name of the root element defines the type of the XML document.

Elements that contain both text and other elements simultaneously are classified as *mixed content*. RSS doesn't generally use mixed content.

The sample `authors` document uses elements named `person` to describe the authors themselves. Each `person` element has an attribute named `id`. Unlike elements, attributes can contain only textual content. Their values must be surrounded by quotes. Either single quotes (') or double quotes (") may be used, as long as you use the same kind of closing quote as the opening one.

Within XML documents, attributes are frequently used for metadata (i.e., "data about data"), describing properties of the element's contents. This is the case in our example, where `id` contains a unique identifier for the `person` being described.

As far as XML is concerned, the order in which attributes are presented in the element start tag doesn't matter. For example, these two elements contain the same information, as far as an XML 1.0–conformant processing application is concerned:

```
<animal name="dog" legs="4"/>
<animal legs="4" name="dog"/>
```

On the other hand, the information presented to an application by an XML processor after reading the following two lines is different for each `animal` element, because the ordering of elements is significant:

```
<animal><name>dog</name><legs>4</legs></animal>
<animal><legs>4</legs><name>dog</name></animal>
```

XML treats a set of attributes like a bunch of stuff in a bag—there is no implicit ordering—while elements are treated like items on a list, where ordering matters.

New XML developers frequently ask when it is best to use attributes to represent information and when it is best to use elements. As you can see from the `authors` example, if order is important to you, then elements are a good choice. In general, there is no hard-and-fast "best practice" for choosing whether to use attributes or elements.

The final author described in our document has no information available. All that's known about this person is his or her id, mysteryperson. The document uses the XML shortcut syntax for an empty element. The following is a reasonable alternative:

```
<person id="mysteryperson"></person>
```

Name Syntax

XML 1.0 has certain rules about element and attribute names. In particular:

- Names are case-sensitive: e.g., <person/> isn't the same as <Person/>.
- Names beginning with xml (in any permutation of uppercase or lowercase) are reserved for use by XML 1.0 and its companion specifications.
- A name must start with a letter or an underscore, not a digit, and may continue with any letter, digit, underscore, or period. (Actually, a name may also contain a colon, but the colon is used to delimit a namespace prefix and isn't available for arbitrary use as of the second edition of XML 1.0. Knowledge of namespaces isn't required for understanding RSS, but for more information, see Tim Bray's "XML Namespaces by Example," published at *http://www.xml.com/pub/a/1999/01/namespaces.html*.)

A precise description of names can be found in Section 2.3 of the XML 1.0 specification at *http://www.w3.org/TR/REC-xml#sec-common-syn*.

Well-Formedness

An XML document that conforms to the rules of XML syntax is said to be *well-formed*. At its most basic level, well-formedness means that elements should be properly matched, and all opened elements should be closed. A formal definition of well-formedness can be found in Section 2.1 of the XML 1.0 specification at *http://www.w3.org/TR/REC-xml#sec-well-formed*. Table A-1 shows some XML documents that aren't well-formed.

Table A-1. Examples of poorly formed XML documents

Document	Reason it's not well-formed

`<foo>`
`  <bar>`
`  </foo>`
`</bar>`
	The elements aren't properly nested, because foo is closed while inside its child element bar.

`<foo>`
`  <bar>`
`</foo>`
	The bar element was not closed before its parent, foo, was closed.

`<foo baz>` `</foo>`	The baz attribute has no value. While this is permissible in HTML (e.g., <table border>), it is forbidden in XML.
`<foo baz=23>` `</foo>`	The baz attribute value, 23, has no surrounding quotes. Unlike HTML, all attribute values must be quoted in XML.

Comments

As in HTML, it is possible to include comments within XML documents. XML comments are intended to be read only by people. With HTML, developers have occasionally employed comments to add application-specific functionality. For example, the server-side include functionality of most web servers uses instructions embedded in HTML comments. XML provides other ways to indicate application-processing instructions. A discussion of processing instructions (PIs) is outside the scope of this book. For more information on PIs, see Section 2.6 of the XML 1.0 specification at *http://www.w3.org/TR/REC-xml#sec-pi*. Comments should not be used for any purpose other than those for which they were intended.

The start of a comment is indicated with <!--, and the end of the comment is indicated with -->. Any sequence of characters, aside from the string --, may appear within a comment. Comments tend to be used more in XML documents intended for human consumption than those intended for machine consumption. Comments aren't widely used in RSS.

Entity References

Another feature of XML that is occasionally useful when writing RSS documents is the mechanism for escaping characters.

Because some characters have special significance in XML, there needs to be a way to represent them. For example, in some cases the < symbol might really be intended to mean "less than" rather than to signal the start of an element name. Clearly, just inserting the character without any escaping mechanism will result in a poorly formed document, because a processing application assumes you are starting another element. Another instance of this problem is the need to include both double quotes and single quotes simultaneously in an attribute's value. Here's an example that illustrates both difficulties:

```
<badDoc>
  <para>
    I'd really like to use the < character
  </para>
  <note title="On the proper 'use' of the " character"/>
</badDoc>
```

XML avoids this problem by using the predefined entity reference. The word *entity* in the context of XML simply means a unit of content. The term *entity reference* means just that: a symbolic way of referring to a certain unit of content. XML predefines entities for the following symbols: left angle bracket (<), right angle bracket (>), apostrophe ('), double quote ("), and ampersand (&).

An entity reference is introduced with an ampersand (&), which is followed by a name (using the word "name" in its formal sense, as defined by the XML 1.0

specification) and terminated with a semicolon (;). Table A-2 shows how the five predefined entities can be used within an XML document.

Table A-2. Predefined entity references in XML 1.0

Literal character	Entity reference
<	<
>	>
'	'
"	"
&	&

Here's the problematic document, revised to use entity references:

```
<badDoc>
  <para>
    I'd really like to use the &lt; character
  </para>
  <note title="On the proper &apos; use &apos;  of the &quot;character"/>
</badDoc>
```

XML 1.0 allows you to define your own entities and use entity references as shortcuts in your document, but the predefined entities are often all you need for RSS or Atom; in general, entities are provided as a convenience for human-created XML. Section 4 of the XML 1.0 specification, available at *http://www.w3.org/TR/REC-xml#sec-physical-struct*, describes the use of entities.

Character References

You may find *character references* in the context of RSS documents. Character references allow you to denote a character by its numeric position in the Unicode character set (this position is known as its *code point*). Table A-3 contains a few examples that illustrate the syntax.

Table A-3. Example character references

Actual character	Character reference
1	0
A	A
~	Ñ
®	®

Note that the code point can be expressed in decimal or, with the use of x as a prefix, in hexadecimal.

Character Encodings

The subject of *character encodings* is frequently a mysterious one for developers. Most code tends to be written for one computing platform and, normally, to run within one organization. Although the Internet is changing things quickly, most of us have never had cause to think too deeply about internationalization.

XML, designed to be an Internet-friendly syntax for information exchange, has internationalization at its very core. One of the basic requirements for XML processors is that they support the Unicode standard character encoding. Unicode attempts to include the requirements of all the world's languages within one character set. Consequently, it is very large!

Unicode encoding schemes

Unicode 3.0 has more than 57,700 code points, each of which corresponds to a character. (You can obtain charts of all these characters online by visiting *http://www.unicode.org/charts/*.) If you were to express a Unicode string using the position of each character in the character set as its encoding (in the same way as ASCII does), expressing the whole range of characters would require four *octets* for each character. (An octet is a string of eight binary digits, or bits. A byte is commonly, but not always, considered the same thing as an octet.) Clearly, if a document is written in 100% American English, it would be four times larger than required—all the characters in ASCII fitting into a 7-bit representation. This places a strain on both storage space and on memory requirements for processing applications.

Fortunately, two encoding schemes for Unicode alleviate this problem: UTF-8 and UTF-16. As you might guess from their names, applications can process documents in these encodings in 8- or 16-bit segments at a time. When code points are required in a document that can't be represented by one chunk, a bit-pattern indicates that the following chunk is required to calculate the desired code point. In UTF-8, this is denoted by the most significant bit of the first octet being set to `1`.

This scheme means that UTF-8 is a highly efficient encoding for representing languages using Latin alphabets, such as English. All of the ASCII character set is represented natively in UTF-8; an ASCII-only document and its equivalent in UTF-8 are identical byte for byte.

This knowledge will also help you debug encoding errors. One frequent error arises because of the fact that ASCII is a proper subset of UTF-8; programmers get used to this fact and produce UTF-8 documents but use them as if they were ASCII. Things start to go awry when the XML parser processes a document containing, for example, characters such as `Á`. Because this character can't be represented using only one octet in UTF-8, a two-octet sequence is produced in the output document; in a non-Unicode viewer or text editor, it looks like a couple of characters of garbage.

Other character encodings

Unicode, in the context of computing history, is a relatively new invention. Native operating system support for Unicode is by no means widespread. For instance, although Windows NT offers Unicode support, Windows 95 and 98 don't.

XML 1.0 allows a document to be encoded in any character set registered with the Internet Assigned Numbers Authority (IANA). European documents are commonly encoded in one of the ISO Latin character sets, such as ISO-8859-1. Japanese documents normally use Shift-JIS, and Chinese documents use GB2312 and Big 5.

A full list of registered character sets can be found at *http://www.iana.org/assignments/character-sets*.

XML processors aren't required by the XML 1.0 specification to support any more than UTF-8 and UTF-16, but most commonly support other encodings, such as US-ASCII and ISO-8859-1. Although most RSS transactions are currently conducted in ASCII (or the ASCII subset of UTF-8), there is nothing to stop RSS documents from containing, say, Korean text. However, you will probably have to dig into the encoding support of your computing platform to find out if it is possible for you to use alternate encodings.

Validity

In addition to well-formedness, XML 1.0 offers another level of verification called *validity*. To explain why validity is important, let's take a simple example. Imagine you invented a simple XML format for your friends' telephone numbers:

```
<phonebook>
  <person>
    <name>Albert Smith</name>
    <number>123-456-7890</number>
  </person>
  <person>
    <name>Bertrand Jones</name>
    <number>456-123-9876</number>
  </person>
</phonebook>
```

Based on your format, you also construct a program to display and search your phone numbers. This program turns out to be so useful, you share it with your friends. However, your friends aren't so hot on detail as you are, and they try to feed your program this phone book file:

```
<phonebook>
  <person>
    <name>Melanie Green</name>
    <phone>123-456-7893</phone>
  </person>
</phonebook>
```

Note that, although this file is perfectly well-formed, it doesn't fit the format you prescribed for the phone book, and you find you need to change your program to cope with this situation. If your friends had used `number` as you did to denote the phone number, and not `phone`, there wouldn't have been a problem. However, as it is, this second file isn't a valid `phonebook` document.

Document type definitions (DTDs)

For validity to be a useful general concept, we need a machine-readable way of saying what a valid document is—that is, which elements and attributes must be present and in what order. XML 1.0 achieves this by introducing *document type definitions* (DTDs). For the purposes of RSS, you don't need to know much about DTDs. Rest assured that RSS does have a DTD, and it spells out in detail exactly which combinations of elements and attributes make up a valid document.

The purpose of a DTD is to express the allowed elements and attributes in a certain document type and to constrain the order in which they must appear within that document type. A DTD is generally composed of one file, which contains declarations defining the element types and attribute lists. (In theory, a DTD may span more than one file; however, the mechanism for including one file inside another—*parameter entities*—is outside the scope of this book.) It is common to mistakenly conflate element and element types. The distinction is that an element is the actual instance of the structure as found in an XML document, whereas the instance's kind of element is the element type.

Putting It Together

If you want to validate RSS against a DTD, you need to know how to link a document to its defining DTD. This is done with a document type declaration, `<!DOCTYPE ...>`, inserted at the beginning of the XML document, after the XML declaration in our fictitious example:

```
<?xml version="1.0" encoding="us-ascii"?>
<!DOCTYPE authors SYSTEM "http://example.com/authors.dtd">
<authors>
    <person id="lear">
        <name>Edward Lear</name>
        <nationality>British</nationality>
    </person>
    <person id="asimov">
        <name>Isaac Asimov</name>
        <nationality>American</nationality>
    </person>
    <person id="mysteryperson"/>
</authors>
```

This example assumes the DTD file has been placed on a web server at *example.com*. Note that the document type declaration specifies the root element of the document, not the DTD itself. You can use the same DTD to define `person`, `name`, or `nationality` as the root element of a valid document. Certain DTDs, such as the DocBook DTD for technical documentation (see *http://www.docbook.org*), use this feature to good effect, allowing you to provide the same DTD for multiple document types.

A validating XML processor is obligated to check the input document against its DTD. If it doesn't validate, the document is rejected. To return to the phone book example, if your application validated its input files against a phone book DTD, you would have been spared the problems of debugging your program and correcting your friend's XML, because your application would have rejected the document as being invalid. While some of the programs that read RSS files do worry about validation, most don't.

XML Namespaces

XML 1.0 lets developers create their own elements and attributes, but it leaves open the potential for overlapping names. "Title" in one context may mean something entirely different than "Title" in a different context. The "Namespaces in XML" specification (which can be found at *http://www.w3.org/TR/REC-xml-names*) provides a mechanism developers can use to identify particular vocabularies using URIs.

RSS 1.0 uses the URI *http://purl.org/rss/1.0/* for its base namespace. The URI is just an identifier; opening that page in a web browser reveals some links to the RSS, XML 1.0, and Namespaces in XML specifications. Programs processing documents with multiple vocabularies can use the namespaces to figure out which vocabulary they are handling at any given point in a document.

Namespaces are very simple on the surface but are a well-known field of combat in XML arcana. For more information on namespaces, see O'Reilly's *XML in a Nutshell* or *Learning XML*. The use of namespaces in RSS is discussed in much greater detail in Chapters 6 and 7.

Tools for Processing XML

While RSS can be parsed directly using text-processing tools, XML parsers are often more convenient. Many parsers exist for using XML with many different programming languages. Most are freely available, and the majority are open source.

Selecting a Parser

An XML parser typically takes the form of a library of code that you interface with your own program. The RSS program hands the XML over to the parser, and the parser hands back information about the contents of the XML document. Typically, parsers do this either via events or via a document object model.

With event-based parsing, the parser calls a function in your program whenever a *parse event* is encountered. Parse events include things like finding the start of an element, the end of an element, or a comment. Most Java event-based parsers follow a standard API called SAX, which is also implemented for other languages such as Python and Perl. You can find more about SAX at *http://www.saxproject.org*.

Document object model (DOM)-based parsers work in a markedly different way. They consume the entire XML input document and hand back a tree-like data structure that the RSS software can interrogate and alter. The DOM is a W3C standard; documentation is available at *http://www.w3.org/DOM*.

Choosing whether to use an event- or DOM–based model depends on the application. If you have a large or unpredictable document size, it is better to use event-based parsing for reasons of speed and memory consumption (DOM trees can get very large). If you have small, simple XML documents, using the DOM leaves you less programming work to do. Many programming languages have both event-based and DOM support.

As XML matures, hybrid techniques that give the best of both worlds are emerging. If you're interested in finding out what's available and what's new for your favorite programming language, keep an eye on the following online sources:

- XML.com Resource Guide (*http://xml.com/pub/resourceguide*)
- XMLhack XML Developer News *(http://xmlhack.com)*
- Free XML Tools Guide *(http://www.garshol.priv.no/download/xmltools)*

XSLT Processors

Many XML applications can transform one XML document into another or into HTML. The W3C has defined a special language, called XSLT, for doing transformations. XSLT processors are becoming available for all major programming platforms.

XSLT works using a stylesheet, which contains templates that describe how to transform elements from an XML document. These templates typically specify what XML to output in response to a particular element or attribute. Using a W3C technology called XPath gives you the flexibility not only to say "do this for every `person` element," but also to give instructions as complex as "do this for the third `person` element, whose `name` attribute is `Fred`."

Because of this flexibility, some applications have sprung up for XSLT that aren't really transformation applications at all but take advantage of the ability to trigger actions on certain element patterns and sequences. Combined with XSLT's ability to execute custom code via extension functions, the XPath language has enabled applications such as document indexing to be driven by an XSLT processor.

The W3C specifications for XSLT and XPath can be found at *http://w3.org/TR/xslt* and *http://w3.org/TR/xpath*, respectively. For more information on XSLT, see *XSLT* (O'Reilly); for more on XPath, see *XPath and XPointer* (O'Reilly).

APPENDIX B

Useful Sites and Software

Since feeds are technologies born of the Web, it isn't a surprise that a great deal of good information can be gleaned with your browser. This appendix will give you links to some excellent resources, including client software.

Uber Resources

Because of the rapidly changing RSS and Atom landscape, it's hard to provide links that will remain useful over the lifetime of the rest of the book. For the very latest, you should look at (and subscribe to) the following categories within Del.icio.us. I regularly update these categories myself, and they're always on the cutting edge notwithstanding.

http://del.icio.us/tag/rss
: Del.icio.us RSS

http://del.icio.us/tag/atom
: Del.icio.us Atom

http://del.icio.us/tag/atom
: Del.icio.us Syndication

Specification Documents

http://web.resource.org/rss/1.0
: The RSS 1.0 specification

http://backend.userland.com/rss
: The RSS 2.0 specification

http://www.intertwingly.net/wiki/pie/FrontPage
: The Atom development wiki

http://www.ietf.org/internet-drafts/draft-ietf-atompub-format-03.txt
: The Atom 0.3 specification

http://purl.org/rss/1.0/modules
: The RSS 1.0 modules known to the working group

Mailing Lists

http://groups.yahoo.com/group/rss-dev
: rss-dev: the RSS 1.0 Interest Group list

http://groups.yahoo.com/group/syndication
: Syndication: a general list for RSS matters

http://www.imc.org/atom-syntax/
: The Atom syntax mailing list

http://groups.yahoo.com/group/syndic8
: Syndic8: a list for Syndic8 support matters

http://groups.yahoo.com/group/RSS2-Support
: RSS2 Support: support for RSS 2.0 matters

http://groups.yahoo.com/group/aggregators/
: Aggregators: a list for discussion of aggregator software

Validators

Online validators can check to ensure your feeds are correctly formed:

http://feedvalidator.org/
: The most up-to-date validator, for both Atom and RSS

http://www.ldodds.com/rss_validator/1.0/validator.html
: Leigh Dodd's experimental RSS 1.0 validator

http://aggregator.userland.com/validator
: Userland Software's RSS validator

http://www.w3.org/RDF/Validator
: The W3C's RDF validator

Desktop Readers

http://bitworking.org/Aggie.html
: Aggie: a .NET-based application for reading RSS files. Open source, for Windows and Linux-with-Mono.

http://www.disobey.com/amphetadesk
: AmphetaDesk: a Perl-based desktop reader that runs in the browser. Windows, Linux, and Mac OS versions available.

http://www.cincomsmalltalk.com/BottomFeeder

BottomFeeder: a Smalltalk desktop RSS Reader. Open source, runs on Windows, Mac, and various Unix flavors.

http://www.headlineviewer.com

Carmen's Headline Viewer: a shareware news reader client for Windows.

http://www.feedreader.com

FeedReader: a freeware application for Windows.

http://www.fetchserver.com

Fetch: an "Enterprise RSS" client and server system, for internal corporate messaging and information flow.

http://members.bellatlantic.net/~vze3szvh/friday

Friday: a Java frontend for viewing news aggregation sites and site syndication feeds on mobile devices.

http://fyuze.com

fyuze: acts as a personal news portal for searching, sorting, and sifting daily news from RSS feeds.

http://www.johnmunsch.com/projects/HotSheet

Hotsheet: a Java-based desktop news reader. Works on Windows, Mac, Linux, and anything else with a Java Virtual Machine.

http://www.blueelephantsoftware.com

InfoSnorkel News Aggregator: a Windows application that aggregates RSS feeds, plus content from sites without feeds.

http://www.jayeckles.com/news

JERSS: allows seamless integration of RSS news feeds into web sites. It is a Java servlet generating JavaScript objects the web author can manipulate.

http://www.serence.com/site.php?page=prod_klipfolio

Klipfolio: a Windows-based desktop news reader. Reads simple XML files that point to RSS feeds.

http://www.mulle-kybernetik.com/software/MulleNewz

MulleNewz: a Mac OS X docking RSS reader.

http://www.jmagar.com

MyHeadlines: a content syndication search engine and news reader that can be integrated into a web site running PHP and MySQL.

http://radio.weblogs.com/0100875/outlines/myRadio

myRadio: an extension to Radio Userland aggregation from RSS to any data source, including XML, HTML, and SOAP.

http://ranchero.com/software/netnewswire

NetNewsWire: an OS X desktop RSS reader. My personal favorite.

http://www.newsisfree.com

NewsIsFree: a directory of feeds that also allows for personalized news pages.

http://www.proggle.com/novobot
: Novobot: a heavily featured desktop news reader that can also scrape non-RSS'd sites.

http://www.postal-code.com/pineapple.php
: Pineapple: a web site news aggregator for Mac OS X.

http://www.furrygoat.com/Misc/Software.html
: PocketFeed: an RSS/RDF news aggregator that runs on Pocket PC 2002 PDAs.

http://radio.userland.com
: Radio Userland: a news aggregator included with a weblog software application for Mac and Windows platforms.

http://40hz.org/Raissa
: Raissa: a headline and news reader for Newton MessagePad.

http://reptile.openprivacy.org
: Reptile: a P2P project, with RSS reading.

http://sourceforge.net/projects/rssview
: RSS Viewer: a Java-based, open source RSS reader.

http://homepage.mac.com/stas/slashdock.html
: Slashdock: a simple Mac OS X application that fetches and updates headlines for the latest postings on Slashdot-compatible sites and RSS-compatible sites.

http://www.nongnu.org/straw
: Straw: a desktop news aggregator for the GNOME environment, with project information, news, and downloads.

http://www.eastgate.com/Tinderbox
: Tinderbox: a Mac OS feed reader.

Index

Symbols

A

B

We'd like to hear your suggestions for improving our indexes. Send email to *index@oreilly.com*.

C

D

E

F

G

H

I

O

P

R

S

T

U

V

W

X

Y

About the Author

Ben Hammersley is an English emigré living in Florence, Italy, with his wife, three greyhounds, and Galileo's little finger in a jar only 400 yards from his desk. For a day job, he writes for the British national press, appearing in *The Times*, *The Guardian,* and *The Observer*, and develops new media technology for old media companies. In his free time, he blogs excessively at *http://www.benhammersley.com*. As a member of the RSS 1.0 Working Group, he survived the Great Fork Summer, and as a journalist, he has been accosted by the secret police of two countries. To this day, he doesn't know which was worse.

Colophon

Our look is the result of reader comments, our own experimentation, and feedback from distribution channels. Distinctive covers complement our distinctive approach to technical topics, breathing personality and life into potentially dry subjects.

The animal on the cover of *Developing Feeds with RSS and Atom* is an American kestrel (*Falco sparverius*). Though it is also commonly known as a "sparrow hawk," because it occasionally eats sparrows and other small birds, this name does not accurately reflect the American kestrel's much more diverse diet. American kestrels also eat small mammals, insects, reptiles, and amphibians. In the summer, or in warmer climates, their diet consists primarily of insects.

American kestrels are the smallest, most colorful, and most common falcons in North America. On average, they are 8.5 to 11 inches long, with a wingspan of 19 to 22 inches, and they weigh between 3.5 and 6 ounces. Though males and females are similar in size, they differ in their markings and coloration. Both sexes have reddish-brown backs and tails and two black stripes on their faces. Adult males have slate-blue wings and are redder than females. Females are browner, with reddish wings and black bands on their tails.

Kestrels nest throughout North America in small cavities, such as tree holes, building eaves, or human-provided nesting boxes. The female lays between three and seven eggs, about half of which usually develop into healthy young. The off-white or pinkish eggs hatch after incubating for 28 to 30 days, and the young fledglings leave the nest 28 to 30 days later. While the female and young hatchlings nest, the male hunts and brings them food. Kestrels are quite noisy; their high-pitched call of excitement or alarm is a sharp "klee, klee, klee."

Mary Anne Weeks Mayo was the production editor and copyeditor for *Developing Feeds with RSS and Atom*. Matt Hutchinson proofread the book. Genevieve d'Entremont and Claire Cloutier provided quality control. Peter Ryan, Keith Fahlgren, and Lydia Onofrei provided production assistance. John Bickelhaupt wrote the index.

Ellie Volckhausen designed the cover of this book, based on a series design by Edie Freedman. The cover image is a 19th-century engraving from the Dover Pictorial Archive. Karen Montgomery produced the cover layout with Adobe InDesign CS using Adobe's ITC Garamond font.

David Futato designed the interior layout. This book was converted by Joe Wizda to FrameMaker 5.5.6 with a format conversion tool created by Erik Ray, Jason McIntosh, Neil Walls, and Mike Sierra that uses Perl and XML technologies. The text font is Linotype Birka; the heading font is Adobe Myriad Condensed; and the code font is LucasFont's TheSans Mono Condensed. The illustrations that appear in the book were produced by Robert Romano, Jessamyn Read, and Lesley Borash using Macromedia FreeHand MX and Adobe Photoshop CS. The tip and warning icons were drawn by Christopher Bing. This colophon was written by Brian Sawyer.

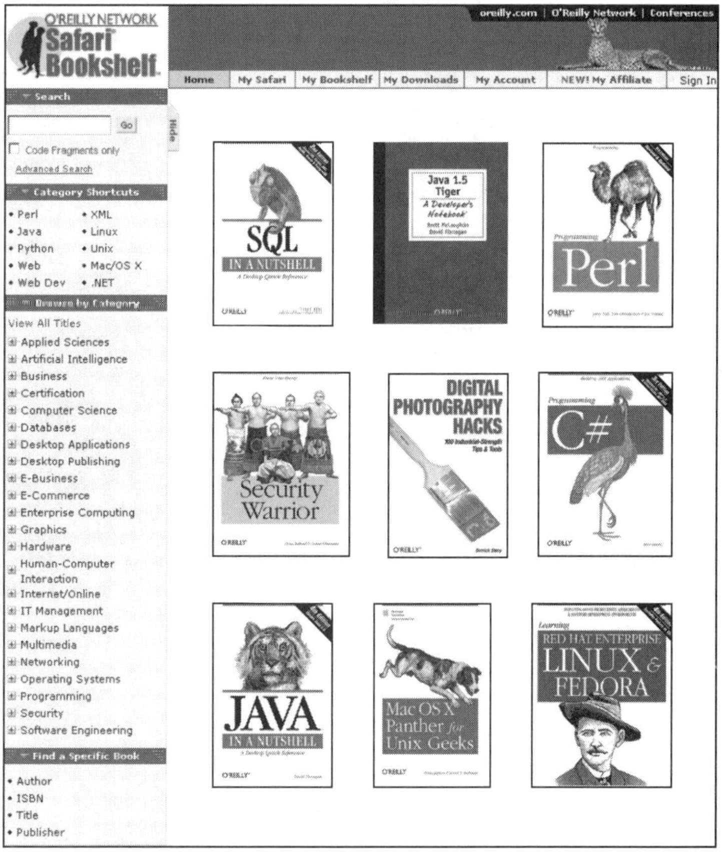

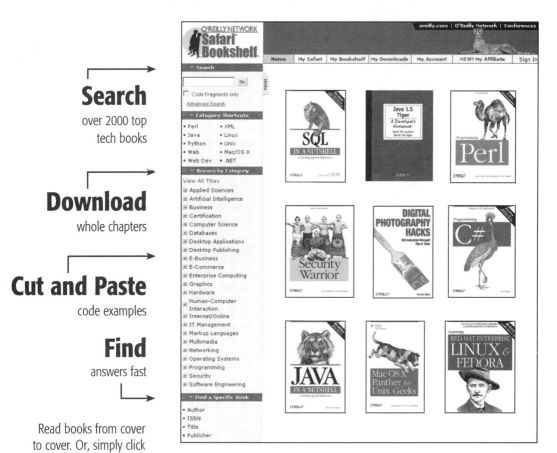

Keep in touch with O'Reilly

1. Download examples from our books

To find example files for a book, go to:

www.oreilly.com/catalog

select the book, and follow the "Examples" link.

2. Register your O'Reilly books

Register your book at *register.oreilly.com*

Why register your books?
Once you've registered your O'Reilly books you can:

- Win O'Reilly books, T-shirts or discount coupons in our monthly drawing.
- Get special offers available only to registered O'Reilly customers.
- Get catalogs announcing new books (US and UK only).
- Get email notification of new editions of the O'Reilly books you own.

3. Join our email lists

Sign up to get topic-specific email announcements of new books and conferences, special offers, and O'Reilly Network technology newsletters at:

elists.oreilly.com

It's easy to customize your free elists subscription so you'll get exactly the O'Reilly news you want.

4. Get the latest news, tips, and tools

www.oreilly.com

- "Top 100 Sites on the Web"—PC Magazine
- CIO Magazine's Web Business 50 Awards

Our web site contains a library of comprehensive product information (including book excerpts and tables of contents), downloadable software, background articles, interviews with technology leaders, links to relevant sites, book cover art, and more.

5. Work for O'Reilly

Check out our web site for current employment opportunities:

jobs.oreilly.com

6. Contact us

O'Reilly Media
1005 Gravenstein Hwy North
Sebastopol, CA 95472 USA

TEL: 707-827-7000 or 800-998-9938
(6am to 5pm PST)

FAX: 707-829-0104

order@oreilly.com
For answers to problems regarding your order or our products. To place a book order online, visit:

www.oreilly.com/order_new

catalog@oreilly.com
To request a copy of our latest catalog.

booktech@oreilly.com
For book content technical questions or corrections.

corporate@oreilly.com
For educational, library, government, and corporate sales.

proposals@oreilly.com
To submit new book proposals to our editors and product managers.

international@oreilly.com
For information about our international distributors or translation queries. For a list of our distributors outside of North America check out:

international.oreilly.com/distributors.html

adoption@oreilly.com
For information about academic use of O'Reilly books, visit:

academic.oreilly.com